Home to Roost

Also available by Tessa Hainsworth

Up with the Larks
Seagulls in the Attic

Home to Roost

TESSA HAINSWORTH

arrow books

Published by Arrow Books 2014

2 4 6 8 10 9 7 5 3 1

Copyright © Tessa Hainsworth 2012

Tessa Hainsworth has asserted her right under the Copyright, Designs
and Patents Act 1988 to be identified as the author of this work

This book is substantially a work of non-fiction based on the life,
experiences and recollections of the author. In some cases details
have been changed. The author has stated to the publishers that,
except in such respects the contents of this book are true.

First published in Great Britain in 2012 by
Preface Publishing

Random House, 20 Vauxhall Bridge Road,
London SW1V 2SA

www.randomhouse.co.uk

Addresses for companies within The Random House Group Limited can be found at:
www.randomhouse.co.uk/offices.htm

The Random House Group Limited Reg. No. 954009

A CIP catalogue record for this book
is available from the British Library

ISBN 9780099573944

The Random House Group Limited supports the Forest
Stewardship Council® (FSC®), the leading international forest-
certification organisation. Our books carrying the FSC label are
printed on FSC®-certified paper. FSC is the only forest-certification
scheme supported by the leading environmental organisations,
including Greenpeace. Our paper procurement policy can be found at:
www.randomhouse.co.uk/environment

Printed and bound by CPI Group (UK) Ltd, Croydon, CR0 4YY

The best journeys are filled with inner smiles!

Richard, Tom, Georgie, my wonderful family
and friends – you constantly enrich my life! Thank you.
Extra special thanks to the incredible Karen Hayes,
Jane Turnbull and the Preface team.

This is also for Chris and Gabrielle, with love.

Prologue

Mid-January, and it seems as if the exceptional frost, the ice and snow usually so foreign to Cornwall, has gone for good. Today is a perfect winter's day, cold but still, so still that even here at the edge of the sea there isn't a breath of wind. The water is like a smooth carpet, the grey and black of the last weeks transformed to a deep blue-green.

It is late morning, and I'm still working, walking from the tiny post office in the seaside town of Morranport to deliver my last batch of post. My Royal Mail winter uniform seems heavy in this gift of a day, as I watch the oystercatchers scurrying along the shoreline. With their black feathers on top and the white plumage underneath, they remind me of commuters in London, hurrying to work with hasty, stressful steps. Their shadows, running along beside them, add to this image and I laugh out loud, once again not believing my luck that I'm no longer part of that scene. Even though I, too, am working, I'm certainly not scurrying but walking slowly, savouring the sea air, pausing to look at an interesting rock formation, or a flock of seabirds.

This is my third year in Cornwall, and I can't imagine ever living anywhere else. I knew from the day we arrived that this was home now, and every day, every month, and every year, this feeling intensifies.

It's so warm I open the jacket of my uniform. This beautiful day, this sudden winter's prize, gives me a surge of energy and I jump over the low wall to walk along the pebbles and damp sand. The oystercatchers are ahead of me now, their skinny red legs flashing as they paddle in and out of the sea. I should be tired; I was up at four as usual to get ready for my round and it's been an especially long morning, not over yet, either. My customers, who have been locked inside their houses during the last icy winter weeks, have come out with the sun, delighted, like me, with the spring-like day. Of course, they all want to talk, even more so than usual, which is fine with me. I've grown fond of many of them, and some have even become good friends. Mostly I just listen, my head bobbing up and down, nodding as they talk, just like the oystercatchers pecking on the wet shore.

Above me, the herring gulls are shrieking as they fly over the sea and sand. The sound is wonderfully familiar, somehow rooting me to this amazing coastal area I now call home. I take deep breaths, enjoying the relative warmth of the air after the bitter cold of the past weeks. I feel so full of energy that I start doing some Jumping Jacks right there and then, feeling my winter muscles stretch, my lungs fill with clean sea air.

Suddenly I stop. Ahead of me, a cormorant dives into the sea with such grace it nearly takes my breath away. There is hardly a ripple in the water. I stare, wondering where and when it will come up. Finally, after what seems ages, it surfaces, far from where it dived. The bird stays floating serenely on the water for some time, while I stand serenely watching. London, my old life there as a high-flying career woman, seems a million years away.

Then I turn, hop over the wall onto the footpath, and get on with my round. As I walk, the sun glitters on the sea with such promise that I know the New Year is going to be fantastic. My first two in Cornwall have been magical, so why not the third?

I take a few deep breaths, hoist my bag over my shoulder, and set off to finish delivering the day's post.

CHAPTER ONE

New Year, New Beginnings

As I leave our house with Jake, the family spaniel, preparing to walk to our tiny village shop, my eyes widen in surprise. There, on the narrow road between our house and the front lawn of the church, is a traffic jam. Hardly any cars drive along that road, for Treverny isn't on a main road to anywhere big or touristy. Yet right there in front of me is a whole line of cars, trying to get up the road but not moving an inch. I can tell by the grim looks on the faces of the drivers that they've been there for some time.

Jake barks madly at this unexpected phenomenon. He's not used to traffic either, though he should be as we brought him with us when we moved from London. But like all of us – Ben my husband, our two children Will and Amy, now nine and seven, and me, of course – Jake has become countrified. Not for him the city pavements, the roar of cars and motorbikes, lorries and ambulances, day and night. Not for him the neon brightness and high rises and not enough trees to wee on. The adaptation from town dog to rural hound has been swift and complete, as it has for all of us.

I walk up to a cluster of villagers perched on the grass verge of the green next to the church. I notice that it really is green, too, the snow finally nearly all gone. This creeping of colour back into the landscape after the unseasonal snow and ice makes me heady, feeling as if spring is here when it's only January. The trees on the green, by the pond, are still nothing but trunks and branches but you can almost feel them getting ready to burst into bud and leaf. I keep telling myself it's too early, but after all, spring does come early here in Cornwall.

I see Daphne standing with the other villagers, watching the cars. She and her husband Joe have a farm outside the village. Their children and ours have become firm friends, just as we have. 'What's up?' I say, indicating the cars.

Daphne rolls her eyes. 'It's that thing. Look.' She points up the road. There, blocking traffic from both ways, is the biggest removal van I've ever seen.

'Goodness, that's crazy, bringing such a huge vehicle down through the village. It's almost wider than the road. And look how long it is!'

The other locals standing around join in our conversation. 'It's been there for half an hour.'

''Tis daft. The thing can't go forward, can't go backward. It be stuck now, I do believe.'

'Fancy sending a great van like that down here.'

'Must be one of them lunatics from Up Country.'

Everyone is nodding his or her head sagely as these words are bandied about, especially the remark about coming from 'Up Country'. To the Cornish, anyone from the other side of the Tamar River is Up Country, and suspect.

One of the locals is up ahead chatting to the driver of the removal van. When he finishes, he heads towards our little group. 'Doug,' several people call to him, 'what's going on? Where's that thing heading for, d'ya know?'

Doug's face is smugly smiley, delighted to be the bearer of a bit of gossip. He's a middle-aged bachelor, still living with his mother who must be a good cook as he's got a belly as plump and round as his face. Doug works here and there doing gardening jobs as well as being a part-time farm worker on Daphne and Joe's farm.

'Oh, 'tis very interesting, very in-ter-est-ing,' Doug says, dragging out each syllable to keep up the suspense. 'Especially for this maid here.' He gives me a nudge. My heart sinks. Doug is harmless, a decent sort, but he does like to wind me up, and has done so since I first arrived. He thinks, quite rightly I'm sure, that I'm a naïve city girl who hasn't a clue about the countryside, and he gets a buzz out of trying to prove it sometimes.

Everyone looks at me. 'OK, Doug, I'll bite. Why would I be especially interested in that removal van?'

Doug grins widely. His face would be like a full moon, especially now that he's starting to lose his hair, if it weren't so ruddy. 'Now wouldn't you like to know, my handsome.' He winks and nudges me again. He's thoroughly enjoying this.

Though I'm dying of curiosity – this is rural life after all, and we tend to get excited about little things like huge removal vans blocking our narrow, windy roads – I know Doug, know that the more I want to know, the more he'll hold back. So I pretend disinterest and say, 'I'd better be on my way; it's getting quite cold standing here.' This part is true. In one of those sudden temperature shifts that happen in Cornwall, the mild weather I'd been wallowing in just a few minutes ago seems to have disappeared. Clouds have obscured the sun and it feels several degrees colder. The branches on the skeletal trees alongside the road and on the green no longer look as if they are ready to bud but seem to be drawing in against this new onslaught of winter. I'm so lost in staring at the beech tree next to me, admiring its shape and the pattern of its branches, that I jump when Doug shouts in my ear, 'Tessa, maid, didya hear what I said? Lordie, you do be a dozy maid sometimes!'

I shift my focus from the trees to Doug. When he's got my attention he goes on. 'That van, 'tis sent by your new neighbours. The ones moving here from London. Mebbe you know each other, eh? Being as how you're from the same place.'

This isn't the first time that Doug has assumed I know everyone who lives in London. I guess it's because he knows absolutely everyone who lives not only in Treverny, but in half of Cornwall, or so he makes out. I say, 'I've met them once, when they bought the house. Kate and Leon Winterson.'

Doug puts on his best sombre look, purses his lips, nods knowingly. 'Nice is as nice does,' he announces enigmatically. Since he's always making enigmatic pronouncements, no one takes much notice of this.

Daphne, who is stamping her feet with the cold by now, says, 'Are you saying, Doug, that the van is going to Treetops?'

'Exactly that, my lover,' Doug replies. 'Treetops, that empty house right next door to Tessa here. That's why he be havin' such trouble; 'tis such a narrow road, and the drive to the house is near impossible to get up, it be that rutted and slidey. It be stuck right where it is now. Ain't making them car drivers happy, let me tell you.'

That fact is pretty obvious. Several of the car drivers are out and talking with the driver. They're mostly locals on their way home from picking up children from school, or from shopping, or work. They're used to country ways, waiting around patiently for a tractor to go up a hill, or sheep and cattle to be moved from field to field, but this monster of a removal van is a bit much, you can tell by the looks on their faces.

From further up the road behind the van, behind the six or seven cars stuck there waiting to get by, I see a sleek black Land Rover pull up. That's not a local farmer, I know; the vehicle is too new, too trendy. This Land Rover looks far too posh to get Cornish mud or dung or straw all over it. The doors open and two people get out. I recognise them as our new neighbours, Kate and Leon Winterson.

While Leon goes to talk to the driver of the van, his wife Kate comes running up to me. 'Oh, you're our new neighbour, uh, Teresa isn't it?'

'Tessa. Welcome to Treverny.'

'Yes, welcome,' Daphne says. The others standing around nod once or twice. They are a wonderful lot, the villagers, but it takes them time to get to know and trust the people who move into their village from Up Country. You can't blame them; in the past, they've seen so many people come and go as Cornwall has become more and more desirable over the years, as a summer holiday destination, as a place for a second home, and for some, a dream, an idyllic paradise in which to start a new life. The locals have been witnessing this for years, so they will wait, watch, bide their time, and judge the new couple, as they do all the incomers, by their actions over the months or even years, until they make up their minds. I know from experience: the first year we were here, I didn't feel accepted for months and months. It wasn't until Ben got ill and the villagers all rallied around that I realised we were at last welcomed wholeheartedly into the life and soul of the community.

And so it will take the Wintersons some time, but I hope it will turn out well for them. I'm sure it will; when Ben and I met them, they both seemed delighted to be here, and eager to start settling in. Right now, though, they are not off to a good start.

'Oh Tessa, I'm so relieved to see you,' Kate says. 'We just got here; we were following the van but had to stop for petrol, said we'd meet the removal men at the house. It seems a terrible muddle! What's the matter with the driver? Can't he drive properly?'

Doug, who is enjoying all this immensely, says, 'Well now, maid, I reckon the problem be not with the driver, but the fact of that big vehicle you got there. Far too big for these roads. You should of thought of that before you hired 'im, my handsome.'

Poor Kate is so flustered by these words that she doesn't know what to say. By now a cold wind has come up and with it, an icy rain, so the villagers reluctantly start to disperse, back to their warm homes. Daphne says goodbye and goes off as well, leaving me, Doug, and Kate standing there shivering. Kate looks lost and frozen. She's an attractive woman but right now her face is twisted with anxiety. She's so wound up she can hardly stand still, but keeps tapping one foot then the other. I can't help noticing her gorgeous knee high boots which look elegant but not snow and rain proof. Her thin wool trousers, tucked inside the boots, are far too fine to withstand the wind now whipping around the village. 'C'mon, Kate,' I say. 'Come on into my house, have a warm drink. Let the men sort it out.'

Doug snorts. 'Hah, there be only that lot from Up Country, they be no use.' He points to Leon Winterson talking heatedly to the two removal men. 'I'd best go give'em a bit of advice.' He swaggers up to them. Oh dear, I think, well-intentioned as he is, he'll only make it worse. Doug always does, somehow.

Luckily, at that point Ben comes out of the house where he'd been at the computer, juggling our finances, trying to make ends meet as we've done ever since coming to Cornwall – it's been a constant struggle, but a small price to pay for living the life we've chosen. 'What's going on?' Ben asks while Jake leaps about in excitement, hoping Ben's arrival signals another walk today. He's already had one, straight after I got home from my morning postie round. We went to Penwarren Beach, not far from the village. The breeze was getting up and the sea choppy, but it was still fantastic. We had the beach to ourselves so we ran together as if we were trying to outrun the wind. Well, OK, I exaggerate; I'm not exactly a runner, but all that ozone gave me so much energy I ran for a few minutes anyway.

After Ben and Kate greet each other briefly, Ben takes over. He orders us into the house to warm up – Kate is turning blue with cold in her flimsy winter coat, long and sylish, but with only two large buttons to keep out the cold. That's no good for a Cornish winter, not even the short kind of mild ones we usually have in this part of Cornwall. She says, 'I can't go in and leave poor Leon.' She looks along the road at the van. Leon and Doug, the removal men, and several of the car drivers are all talking and pointing and getting hot under the collar, or so it seems from here.

Ben says, 'I'll see what I can do to help. I'm sure we can manoeuvre the cars around to get them past, and somehow get the van at least a bit closer to the house.'

Kate looks so relieved that for a mad minute I think she's going to throw her arms around Ben and give him a big hug and kiss. But he's run up to the other men and I take her into the house to put the kettle on. Jake, following me, gives me his hangdog look, designed to pull on my heartstrings. But I stare him down. 'You had an extra long walk on the beach this morning,' I tell him sternly as I bring out mugs and milk for the tea. 'So don't try giving me a guilt trip.'

Kate is looking at me strangely. 'D'you always talk to your dog?' she asks.

The question surprises me; I hadn't thought about it before. 'I guess I do. Why, don't you?'

'We've never had a dog. Oh, but we can have one now. Since I was a child, living in the city, I've always wanted pets. A rabbit, and a guinea pig, and maybe a hen, or even a goat . . .' She looks rapturous and I don't have the heart to tell her it's not as easy as all that, having tried some of these things. But she'll learn, just like I did.

Much later, Ben comes in with Leon. It's dark by then and I've got a chicken casserole in the oven. Will and Amy are home from school and lounging about watching a favourite half hour of television. I ask Kate and Leon to stay for a meal, and they accept gratefully. Luckily there is plenty there for everyone after I've thrown in some more veg and taken some homemade bread rolls out of the freezer and popped them into the oven as well. Ben and some of the locals have managed to clear the traffic jam, get the van driver to steer down a helpful neighbour's wider drive to get closer to

Treetops, and all the furniture has at last been unloaded. Though the removal men did the bulk of the work, of course, Ben and some of the other villagers helped with the smaller items until finally it was all done. 'I can't believe they did that,' Leon says as he settles down at our kitchen table. 'It would never happen in London. All those men, who don't know me at all, have never seen me before, pitching in and giving a hand.'

He and Kate shake their heads in amazement. Ben says, 'That's one of the best things about village life in Cornwall. People always seem to give a hand if you're in trouble.'

Leon nods. 'Well, we were certainly in a mess. No one seemed to know what to do until you came along, Ben. Thanks for that. Now how about sharing this with us?' He holds up the bottle of champagne he brought in from his car. I nearly yelp. It's a very fine champagne, and extraordinarily expensive. Kate says, 'We were going to have a romantic evening in our new Cornish home, but this is much better, meeting our new neighbours properly.'

Though we protest, they insist on sharing not only that bottle but a second one, and we end up having a very merry evening. Luckily I've got a day off tomorrow so don't need to set my alarm for four in the morning. We talk for ages, have some good laughs, and Ben and I listen as Kate and Leon talk of their dream of living in Cornwall coming true. 'We're sick of the city, of the rat race. Always work, trying to get ahead, or someone else will get your job. No time for each other, or for more children. But that will all change now. We want the good life, the simple life.'

They sound so much like Ben and me talking when we were discussing our move to Cornwall that we smile at each other.

Leon sees our fleeting smiles and says, 'You two look so happy here. You're living the dream we want to live now.'

He looks so hopeful, and so full of confidence, that Ben and I raise our glasses to him and wish him luck. He nods in acknowledgement. He's a nice-looking man, dark-haired, dark-eyed. Like Kate, he's obviously straight from the city with his expensive new casual clothes, his haircut which certainly wasn't styled by a rural barber. His ankle boots are more suited for city streets than our lanes and footpaths, that's for sure, but the couple have only just arrived; no doubt we looked quite citified when we got here, too. It'll be fun watching them change, become countrified, just as we did.

When we go to the front door to see them off, I give Kate an impulsive hug, saying, 'It's so good to have you next door. Treetops has been a rental cottage for so long that it's a real joy to know you're here permanently.'

Outside, to our surprise, a light snow has fallen; the ground is white, sparkling in the moonlight for the clouds have cleared. The trees in front of the house creak as their bare branches rub together in the wind. Their silhouettes are starkly beautiful. Across the road the old stone church keeps vigil over this village as it has done for centuries. On its sloping porch roof, glistening snowflakes settle and ice over. The bell tower gleams in the moonlight. I decide I love Cornwall just as much in winter as I do in the other seasons.

Kate and Leon, arms around each other, thank us again for dinner. Kate says, 'And now to our new home to face the cold. Luckily we've brought some electric radiators down with us for tonight. I can't wait to get our central heating in.'

I nearly said that they wouldn't need central heating, with that huge new wood burner they had installed when they bought the house. It'll heat the water and at least a couple of other rooms with the back boiler, so what else do they need? But I've learned not to give advice unless it's asked for. When I first came here I sometimes tried to organise people and events too much, for that was my job in London, and I prided myself on doing it well. But I learned that in the country, people quite rightly like to do things their own way, and changes have to come slowly, grow organically.

Ben and I, arms wrapped around each other, watch them walk down our path and along the road towards their own house, slipping and sliding on the ice in their city boots. But they're giggling and clutching each other. 'Goodness, they seem so young,' I say.

'Younger than us by about ten years, maybe a bit more. But not so young that they don't know what they're doing.'

'I'm not so sure.' We close the door and go back into the warmth of the house. 'We didn't know what we were doing did we, looking back. When we first came here.'

'Maybe not. But we learned quickly enough, like they will, too. C'mon, let's go to bed, it's late. You might not have to get up early but I do; I've got an early call.' Ben is an actor, and though it's been a struggle for him to find acting jobs in Cornwall, he's managed to get some voice-over work here and there, which is what he's doing tomorrow. He's just been offered another small part in a *Doc Martin* series that's filming in Port Isaac, but that won't start till spring. It's great when he gets acting jobs for, like me, he's had to turn his hand to all sorts of work since moving down here. Most of us do. We struggle with several part-time jobs as full-time employment is hard to find, with too many qualified people for each job.

I'm still thinking of the Wintersons as I get ready for bed.

'You know,' I say to Ben, 'I think we're still learning. About Cornwall. About this life. I think we'll be learning new things about the countryside for ever.'

But Ben's asleep. Before I join him, I'm wondering what other new and wonderful things I'll learn as this year develops. Whatever they'll be, I know for sure they will be interesting. Life here has certainly always been that.

CHAPTER TWO

A Slippery Slope

Ice and snow has returned with a vengeance to Cornwall, and none of us can stop talking about it. It's just so unusual, to have so much for such a long period. Those few fine days in mid-January fooled us into believing that the wayward weather had finished once and for all, but we were wrong.

It is now the first week of February and the temperature hasn't been above freezing for days. We haven't had any more snow since the couple of inches that fell that night the Wintersons moved in, but neither has it melted. A thin coating of ice still covers many ponds and puddles, and some of the roads are treacherously slippery.

So I've been extra careful, delivering the post. Extra careful, too, in dressing properly, snug jumpers underneath my thick outerwear, thermal gloves, woolly hat. I even bought a pair of those funny ice grips that fit over boots or shoes to keep you from slipping on the ice. My round takes extra time, not only because I walk and drive much more slowly than normal, but also because I, and the other postmen and -women, are concerned about the folk who might be stuck in their homes because of the weather, especially the elderly and the isolated. I've delivered steaming hot pots of soup from one customer to another a mile or so away, and medicine prescriptions from the pharmacy to those kept inside because of the snow.

Despite the icy mornings, the extreme cold, the precarious roads, I feel exhilarated. In the past week the wind has dropped and at least during the day, it feels warmer than the temperature says, for the sun has come out and although it's not strong enough to even begin to melt the ice, the blue of the sky belies the freezing air. But there's no sign of dawn yet this early morning as I pick up the Royal Mail van and prepare for my round. The sky is rampant with stars, and there's not a sound but the soft lapping of waves on the sandy shore near the boat yard. All the little shops and cafés that line the long main street are dark, except for a few low-key security lights. The street runs parallel to the sea, and at this early hour, the water seems to reflect the town, totally dark except for a lone light on the horizon from some faraway freighter. I stand still for a few moments, watching my breath steam out into the icy air. When I look up, I see a falling star shoot down into the sea.

The main roads are fine now but many of the narrow country lanes remain icy. I go dead slow up a long, steep hill and it's a good thing I do, for a tractor carrying a load of hay is chuntering down. I back up carefully to the nearest layby. When the tractor passes, the driver, a farmer I deliver to, stops. 'Still not gritted this bit yet,' he mutters. 'Good job you be going slow, maid.'

'It's the only way to go on these roads,' I reply.

'Hah, tell that to some of the second homers who were

here holiday time. 'Twas ice and snow then, but did that stop some of them zooming around as if they'd be late for the New Year if they'd slowed a bit? No way.'

I commiserate, saying I noticed it, too, on my rounds. There were too many drivers who assumed that just because the main roads were cleared and gritted, every road in Cornwall would be the same. They had no idea that there are far too many for the snow ploughs and gritters to get to every single tiny lane. 'But at least the holiday homers are gone now,' I say. 'We'll have the roads mostly to ourselves till half term.'

'A good thing, too. Look, maid, I'll take the post seeing as I'll be on my way home soon as I take this hay to the sheep. Save you going down our long drive.'

As I thank him he adds, 'I'll take the post up to me old matey at the farm above as well, if you like.'

Seeing me hesitate, he says, 'Don't worry, I won't just put it somewhere without checking that he's all right. The missus has been keeping an eye on him, too. I know you do as well, all this ice and snow about.'

I'm relieved at this, for it'll save me some time and a drive up two pot-holed farm lanes, part of which are still covered in snow. I'm glad that the neighbours are keeping an eye on each other in this weather.

Later, I'm in the village of Poldowe, where I leave the van by the church and walk up and down the main street to deliver this part of the post on foot. Though the footpath there is mostly cleared of snow, and sand has been put on the worst icy bits, it's very patchy and I walk carefully. I pass several of my customers walking to the local shop, a farmer called Jim who tells me his bad hip is better now, and a young woman, Mary, who has just split up from her boyfriend but has already

found another. Men and women of all ages have armed themselves with walking sticks after a flurry of falls and broken
bones when the ice and snow first came. Many are clutching
on to each other to keep from slipping. Everyone seems cheery
enough, though, because the storms and gales have stopped
and the sky is a clear blue panorama. In the distance beyond
the town, the sea glitters. Everything is doubly bright with the
sun reflecting the snow, and I've dug out my old sunglasses
from the glove compartment of the van where I left them last
summer. No matter what van I'm in, I always manage to leave
a pair of sunglasses behind. It's a good thing I can only afford
the cheap kind so I don't worry about it; I know they'll turn
up eventually.

I stop at the shop for some provisions for my next lot of
customers who live slightly further out. Although for a long
time now I've delivered odds and ends for some of them,
especially the old and isolated ones, this winter has seen my
errands double and even triple. This is fine with me; I learned
very early on that in Cornwall, a postie is not just a deliverer
of mail but a social worker, therapist, errand woman/man,
newspaper deliverer, and an array of other things. I like this
part of the job enormously for not only do I feel I'm doing
a bit of good, I've also met some interesting people whose
conversation and company I've enjoyed.

Today the tiny shop is crowded. The fact that the fierce east
wind, which brought much of the snow and blizzard-like condi-
tions, has gone, and the sun is actually out, have brought droves
of people venturing out for the first time in several days. I
greet Melanie, the shopkeeper, and listen to the talk around
me as I pick up supplies. 'I do believe you can't beat the hard-
woods, oak especially, for burning. Gives more heat than

anything, lasts longer, too. Mind, it must be dry.' Three locals, two men and a woman, are standing around having a lively discussion about wood. This is a conversation that's been repeated in every village shop I've been in, as well as amongst friends and neighbours whenever a couple of us get together. Everyone is obsessed with keeping warm this winter. It's understandable, as in this part of the world we've been lucky to live in a pocket of relatively mild weather, so trying to cope with this new phenomenon of extended below-freezing temperatures is on everyone's mind.

'To be sure the oak needs be dry and seasoned. All summer, outdoors.' The first man who spoke is still musing about firewood.

'All summer?' the woman snorts. 'You must be joking. A year, is what I reckon. Oak needs a year of drying to be right.'

As they start arguing this fine point, the second says. 'Me. Well, I got a load of softwood. Pine, larch. Burns like nobody's business. Good heat, too.'

The other two pounce on this. 'Might be as you say, but pine fouls up your chimney sure enough. All that resin.'

He nods, acknowledging this. 'I just ordered a load of ash. Freshly chopped, but that don't matter. Burns all right, just cut.'

The faces of the other two light up. 'Ah, ash! Like my dad used to say, Ash green, fit for a queen! 'Tis the only wood I know you can burn green. Beech, oak, larch – they all be needing seasoning.'

Melanie, handing me my change, gives me a wink. 'They go on about wood every time they come in. Mind you, I'm all ears. It's not been easy, keeping warm this winter. And I wouldn't be surprised if there be more to come.'

'You're not the only one thinking like that,' I say, looking around the shop. 'Looks like people are stocking up for the next batch of snow.'

'So they are. Folk don't like leaving their homes in this, and not just the old ones either. A couple of the younger ones have broken a wrist and an ankle on the ice.'

'So I heard.'

'And Clara.' Melanie rolls her eyes. She's a motherly woman of indeterminate age, with salt and pepper hair pinned back helter skelter with several hairgrips. She and her husband Tufty – his real name is Bill but no one calls him that – both wear colourful fingerless gloves when serving in the shop, winter and summer. Tufty, who is serving someone while Melanie chats with me, is wearing a deep blue pair with a bright neon green stripe around the knuckles and thumb, while his wife's gloves are crimson with a fluorescent yellow stripe in the same place. They have quite a collection of these gloves, all knitted with wonderfully vivid yarns with the same two edgings of a bright neon colour on each pair. Tufty's mother knits them for the couple. She's a quiet, placid woman living on her own in a tiny, tumbledown cottage behind the village at St Geraint, a cottage that despite its state of disrepair will be worth a fortune when she finally has to sell. Unfortunately none of her children will be able to afford to buy it, so that will be another house gone to second homers.

We go back to talk of Clara. 'Is she still refusing to go out?' I ask. 'She's not ill, is she? I only saw her the other day.'

'No, she's not physically ill. But she won't go out. Hasn't been outside since this freezing weather began.'

This is not the first time we've discussed Clara, as the villagers are getting concerned about her. Tufty comes over and joins us, saying, 'I just don't understand that woman. She's not old, not frail, but she won't even take a peep out of her house.'

Melanie nods. 'She doesn't even call in on Delia, but that's no problem, she knows the rest of us look in on her every day, and I've told Clara she's done enough anyway. She always takes over seeing to Delia during holiday times, when the shop is extra busy.'

Delia is an elderly woman living in the village, who has hardly left her little terraced house since her husband died nearly a decade ago. As she has no family, the locals have taken over her care, bringing her meals, keeping an eye on her. Melanie goes on, 'It's Clara I'm worried about. I hope she's not going to get like Delia, not wanting to go out. Let's face it, Delia was seventy when she became housebound, and Clara's thirty-odd years younger.'

'I've got some post for Clara. I'll see how she's doing.'

'Well, try to get her out of that house. It's not healthy, stopping in the way she's been doing.'

I promise Melanie I'll do my best and leave the shop. Clara's house is at the edge of the village, a small bungalow next to a field. When I arrive she's waiting at the door, looking out over the footpath in front of the house with dismay. 'Tessa, oh, look it's not melting at all. It's still icy. Another day gone.'

Clara, from what I've gathered from the others, is pathologically terrified of snow and ice. Many years ago, on a trip to Canada to visit her husband's relatives, she was involved in a bad car crash. Her husband, a reckless driver anyway (so the villagers say), skidded on a patch of ice and careered off the road down a sharp incline, hitting a tree. Miraculously, the two survived, though Clara came home badly bruised and shaken from the accident. The terror of hurtling off the road in a snowstorm has never left her, and she still has nightmares about it. Now, she not only refuses to drive on ice but to walk on it as well, for unfortunately that same holiday, she slipped on a patch of wet snow and ended up with a broken elbow and numerous stitches on her face. She still has the scar on her cheek, though it's very faint.

Her obsessive avoidance of frozen weather was manageable when she moved back to her native Cornwall after her husband left and they divorced. Here on the south coast the winters are unusually mild, but this year has been traumatic for Clara and I worry that if she doesn't get out soon she'll have a breakdown, for her anxieties are definitely getting worse.

I hand Clara the newspaper from the shop she's asked me to bring daily since the temperatures dropped below freezing, along with a carton of milk, a loaf of bread, and some cat food. 'Thanks so much, Tessa.' She takes the supplies gratefully. I look at her carefully, noting how pale she is. As she takes the groceries from me I see that her nails are bitten down to the quick. The poor woman really is a mess.

'Can you come on in for a minute?' she says. 'I've got a big favour to ask.'

She shuts the door behind us and I follow her into the kitchen, where three sleek black and white cats mill around our ankles. They set up a yowl as Clara pours dry cat food into their bowls. I know there are at least another three cats, probably more, somewhere around the house: half-grown kittens, elderly toms, strays of all sizes and shapes that Clara has rescued from homelessness. She runs the Cats Protection Service in our area, something she started from nothing when she moved back here and discovered there was a need for a cat rescue organisation in the community.

She's cooing over the eating cats, which ignore her as they munch away. 'Oh, little pusskins, how hungry you were! You must thank the nice postie for bringing us food while the weather is so bad. Tessa, a cup of tea? Do say yes; it's so lonely these days when I can't get out.'

I refuse tea but sit down for a few minutes, watching her with the cats. Her whole body language has changed and she seems far less uptight. Even her face has softened, the grim frightened look gone. I say gently, 'Clara, actually you can get out. It's a beautiful day today, look out of the window.'

'I have, I know, but the temperature hasn't gone above freezing. There's still ice everywhere.'

'Yes, but there's sand on the footpath, over the ice. Why don't you give it a try? I'll go with you if you like.'

She looks as if I've thrown boiling water over her head. Her face is a picture of shock and dismay, as if her best friend has just betrayed her. But I know I'm not the first person who has tried to get her out during the last few weeks, especially on days like today when it's actually stopped snowing and the wind has dropped. Working from home as a freelance bookkeeper to supplement the small income she gets from her ex-husband, theoretically she never has to go out, especially as customers come to her. She has a friend who runs the Cat Protection Service with her who drives a van to collect the stray cats and take them to volunteers who keep them until they're found new homes, but he's getting concerned. 'You've got to get her out of that house, Tessa,' Guy said to me recently when I met him in St Geraint. 'She's always tended towards agoraphobia, and now with the snow and ice, she's got an excuse to stay in. If she doesn't get out soon, I'm worried she never will.'

I told him I'd try. I like Clara, and get on well with her.

We've had a coffee together a few times when we've run into each other in St Geraint, and I always stop for a chat when I deliver the post. She always seemed to have her anxieties under control, seemed quite together and independent, until this crazy weather began.

The cats are yowling, despite having consumed their food. Clara says, 'I can't believe it, I'm out of tinned food.' She's rummaging around the cupboard under the kitchen sink as she talks. 'Tessa, the cats will be frantic. And it's not good for them to eat only dried food. Look, it's a huge favour I know, but d'you mind popping to the shop to get some tins? I'm so sorry to ask, I really am.'

She does look crestfallen. She's never asked me any favours before this winter. 'I wouldn't ask if it were for myself, but for the cats . . .' She trails off. I look at her woebegone face, creased with nerves. She's always been a bit nervous and hesitant, but basically a pleasant, ordinary woman seemingly in control of her life. Now, she seems a total mess, physically as well as mentally. Her curly brown hair, usually cut short and frisky, has grown long and straggly over the last two months; she looks years older, too, probably because she's lost weight, become scrawny and ill at ease in her body.

I feel so sorry for her that I'm about to say yes, when I remember Guy's words, remember Melanie's worry. Ginger, another woman living in the village and a friend of Clara's as well, had also told me that she'd tried several times to get her out of the house, even for a few moments, but Clara wouldn't budge. Guy is right, she might never, if this keeps up.

So to be kind, I force myself be cruel. 'Clara, I can't. I'm late already delivering this last lot of post.' I feel like a heel. She looks like I've slapped her across the face. Her cheeks redden and tears begin to roll down her cheeks. I'm about to go to her, to give her a hug, tell her I've changed my mind, when one of the black and white cats starts to mew in a most pathetic tone. It's the largest of the three in the kitchen, and it looks up at Clara with wide, unblinking eyes. I'm a bit suspicious of this. A moment ago the cats were all yowling with fury as they weren't getting their favourite food, but now they're turning piteous. The other two cats take up the mewing sound, and before I can say a word, a couple of ginger kittens and a fluffy white cat come in to join the din. It's a cats' chorus of piteous whines and deep tragic yowls, the whole range of catty catcalls. If I didn't know better, I'd think it a conspiracy. I'm half expecting Clara to start whining, too, but instead she says, accusingly, 'You see? They're starving.'

I stare at the cats. They ignore me as they wind around Clara's ankles, still keeping up their vocal offensive. They are without a doubt the healthiest cats I've ever seen. Their fur is sleek and glossy, their eyes clear, and they're certainly well fed.

By now Clara is on the floor, soothing them, telling them they'll soon be getting some proper food. 'Our nice postie will be bringing it in just a moment, don't you worry.' I surprise myself by standing firm. 'No, Clara, I'm not doing it. If they, or you, were really starving, I would. But none of you are.'

Now two more cats come into the kitchen. How many does she have? I know they are supposed to be here temporarily, but like everything else, the Cat Protection Service is feeling the effects of the economic downturn. It runs as a charity, and donations are not as huge as they used to be, though they still do all right. Apparently more people leave money in their wills to cat charities than to anything else. But there's another knock-on effect of the recession – people are getting rid of their pets because of the high cost of feeding them. Although it's not as bad as it is for dogs, cats are also a problem. I'm sure Clara never used to keep so many for so long before they found a home.

I say a determined goodbye and start walking to the door. But I can't leave. Clara is crying, the cats are yowling. What to do? Both Ginger's and Guy's pleas to do what I could to get her out are ringing in my ears. 'She'll listen to you, Tessa,' both of them had said at different times. 'She's too stubborn with us; we've known her too long.'

One of the cats, the oldest I think, for he's been with Clara longer than the others, is cradled in her arms. It's a fluffy black cat with blobs of white all over his face. He's called Splodge, and she obviously adores him. As she buries her tearful face in his fur, I have an idea. I say softly, 'Poor Splodge, he'll be missing his tin of sardines tonight. But you've got other food.'

'You don't understand! He can't eat the other stuff. It upsets his tummy.' She looks hopefully at me again, thinking I'm changing my mind.

'Poor Splodge.' I tickle the cat under his chin, making him purr madly. He doesn't know that he can't get round me, not now. Gently I take him from Clara's arms and put him down on the floor. 'C'mon, Clara, get your jacket on. You can't let Splodge starve. If you're keeping the cats, you've got to look after them, not rely on others to do it for ever. This winter could go on a long time.'

Before she can react I've got her quilted jacket down from its peg in the hallway. Clara stares at me. 'It's up to you,' I say. 'I'll go with you to the shop, you can hold onto my arm, and we can get the cat food together.'

She's already shaking her head, refusing to come near the door. 'Fine,' I say, 'I'm off, then.'

There's a moment when I think she's going to call my bluff. The cats have followed us into the hallway and are mewing pathetically. I stare at them defiantly and hold firm. At last Clara takes her jacket, slowly putting it on. I open the door and pull her outside, shutting the door firmly behind us. 'Don't want the cats to get out,' I murmur, but my main concern is her bolting back inside.

A kind neighbour has cleaned the lingering snow from her steps and path, and the ice here is gone. 'Take my arm,' I say. 'I'll walk with you to the shop, like I promised.'

'And back?' She's clinging to me like a drowning woman in deep water.

I pretend not to hear. Slowly we go down her steps and path. The day is still splendid, and I start raving about it, hoping to distract her from the wide patches of ice on both the footpath and road on the way to the shop. 'Look how blue the sky is! It could be summer, the light is so bright. I love the sheep in that field behind the church, don't you? Their black faces and feet look so stark against the frozen snow. They seem happy enough though, munching through that load of hay the farmer's brought.'

But Clara won't look; she keeps staring at the ground as if it is about to swallow her up. 'I can't,' she stammers. Her face is chalk white. She won't take another step, and now says she can't go back either. What have I done? She's truly frightened. She needs a therapist, a doctor, some kind of professional help, not a friendly postie trying to do a good deed.

We're halfway to the shop by now and I don't know what to do. Clara seems pathologically unable to move. Should I ring 999, get help? We've been standing here at least five minutes. I start fumbling in my jacket pocket for my mobile phone.

But then a cheery voice greets us. It's her neighbour and friend, Ginger. 'Clara, how great to see you out, and what a good day for it, too. Have you noticed there's not a breath of wind? Are you off to the shop? C'mon then, I'll go with you.'

She takes Clara's other hand, links it through her arm as mine is linked on the other side. Over Clara's head she winks at me encouragingly. A moment passes when time seems suspended. No one moves. Ginger and I seem to have silently agreed it would be counter-productive to force Clara to move. She's now starting to shiver, and I know it's fear, not cold.

And then, just as I think, well, now it's three of us stuck here for ever instead of two, there's a screech of brakes as a rough old red van stops slightly in front of us. A man in his forties with hair like a brush and a smile as big as a dustbin, bounces out. 'Guy,' Clara calls to him. But she doesn't move. With horror I see her eyes filling with tears, and her shaking is getting worse. Ginger glances at me with a worried look.

'Good to see you out, Clara.' Guy starts walking towards us but suddenly, seeing the three of us standing there like frozen statues, he gets the gist of what's going on. Staying by the van, which is about three metres away from us, he calls out, 'Look here, Clara. Got another stray for you. Poor kitten, nearly feral from sleeping rough, though he's been at least partly domes-ticated. I caught him easily enough but he's scared out of his wits.'

Guy opens the van door and takes out a large travelling cat basket. Inside the basket, a terrified kitten is huddled in the corner. Guy goes on, 'He's shivering, too. Desperate for some food and warmth, poor thing.'

There is a moment when time seems to stop, nothing seems to happen. No one speaks, and even the birds, which had been chirping happily on this sunny, windless day, are quiet. Then, from inside the basket, comes a plaintive, heart-breaking mewling sound. Within seconds Clara is there, opening the basket, fussing over the cat, cradling it in her arms, and crying her eyes out.

Ginger whispers to me, 'She just walked right over the iciest part of the path. Didn't even notice it.'

'Didn't slip either. I'm glad she did it, but if she's going to start getting out and about, she'd better look where she's going.'

'What a relief!' Ginger grins at me. She's another one of my long-standing customers, a middle-aged woman with a warm smile. I grin back and she gives me a high-five. We're pleased with our little victory. Guy, too, is delighted; he gives us a thumbs up behind Clara's back. But as we celebrate our little victory over Clara, I slip on the ice and fall flat on my bottom.

Guy and Clara rush up to me, Clara clutching the kitten, her fear of walking on ice totally forgotten. Ginger is crouching beside me asking if I'm hurt. Luckily I fell on the soft snow at the sloping verge of the footpath, and within moments I'm up and laughing at my mishap. Clara says, 'You really ought to be more careful on the ice, Tessa.' We all stare at her but she doesn't notice, she's too preoccupied with the kitten. She gives it to Guy, asking him to take it to her house to settle it in. 'I'll be back in a minute, just going to the shop to get some cat food. D'you want a pasty? I'm starving,' she says to him.

Guy smiles his wide, toothy, endearing smile. 'Me, too. Yeah, a pasty would be great. Should I put the kettle on?'

Clara is already at the shop's door. She hollers back at him, 'Yes please. I want to hear all about the kitten, where you found it – everything.'

As Guy jumps back into his van, Ginger and I follow Clara into the shop where she is being greeted warmly by the villagers who are there. All the locals know about her ice phobia and are pleased she's out and about at last. I say goodbye and tell her I'm off; she's got Ginger there if she needs help going home, but somehow I doubt if she will. It's like so many of our fears – if they're not faced they loom larger and larger until they become monsters in our mind.

Brushing off her effusive thanks, happy and flushed with the successful end to this story, I go down the shop steps with a merry little spring in my step and nearly slip again on the patch of ice at the bottom. Luckily, with some not very graceful swinging of arms and twisting of body to regain my balance, I manage not to fall a second time. A little cheer ripples through the people gathered at the open door of the shop who saw my near-fall, and my ungainly, though successful, attempt to stay upright.

Mickey, the young man who works at the boat yard, says, 'You be lookin' dreamy, maid. What's up?'

'Oh nothing much. I was just thinking how that trite old saying might be true after all. You know, about feeling the fear and doing it anyway.'

Mickey snorts, shakes his head at me. 'That's the daftest thing I ever did hear of. Sharks frighten the hell out'a me and let me tell you, if I hear there's one about and the fear hits me, facing it 'tis the last thing I'd do. I'd run the hell out'a there, or swim I mean, like any sensible person. Anyone tell you anything different, maid, is a bigger fool than any of us.'

I laugh, tell him he's got a good point. I love his typical Cornish pragmatism; it keeps me grounded, keeps me from getting too carried away with some of my crazier ideas. 'You're right, Mickey, you're absolutely right,' I say, leaving him to his repair work in the boat shed.

'So I am, maid, so I am. Time you started to listen to old Mickey here, you'll learn a thing or two about this place.'

Now I laugh out loud. He's young enough to be my son, and we both know it. 'I'll remember that,' I say as a gull, flying above us, plops his guano on my forehead as I look up to watch it swoop over us.

When he's stopped guffawing, Mickey says, 'And there's another lesson for you, maid. Don't look up at seagulls.'

'Lesson learned,' I say ruefully, wiping my forehead with a hankie. Ah well, at least I've made Mickey's day. He's got another story about the daft postie from Up Country to tell his mates.

Later that afternoon, I walk slowly and carefully along icy lanes to visit Edna and Hector Humphrey, a couple I'm fond of who are well into their nineties. I sit in their kitchen, drinking some kind of herbal brew Edna has concocted. It's never the same, and sometimes the taste is disastrous, but mostly it's delicious. This one is a winner and I say so. 'Do you think so, Tessa? I'm glad you like it. I found the dried leaves only last week, hidden in one of those books over there.' I look over to the piles of books stacked all over the room, on shelves, in open cupboards, on the floor in neat piles – as they are in every room. Edna and Hector live alone in this hugely eccentric house. Hector's father used to farm here, decades ago, but no one's touched the land for years, except for me. The couple very kindly offered me a piece of ground near the tumbledown orchard, where I keep my hens, so that I could have an allotment. I tried growing vegetables last year but this year I'm giving it up. I've realised I just haven't got green fingers, and there's no use going on with it. Though the idea of growing all our own food sounded wonderful, I've finally accepted that I can't do it. Besides, where we live, I can get amazing fresh produce without producing it myself. Plenty of my customers grow more than they can eat, and they're always offering their surplus to me. This year I'll take it gratefully, and in return, I'll give them eggs from my hens, or my homemade chutneys and jams. People are always exchanging things in this way. I love the bartering system that seems to have sprung up spontaneously in this rural area.

I'm explaining my decision not to carry on with the allotment to Edna and Hector. Their house is at the edge of the village, and it's a wonderful mixture of styles, some parts are medieval with other bits and pieces added on throughout the centuries. Well, maybe not recently. I don't think it's been redecorated for the last fifty years; it's like stepping back in time when you go inside, with the oak-beamed ceiling smoky from the fires of decades, and what was probably the world's first wood stove that Edna still uses for cooking.

Edna says, nodding. 'Well, my dear, you have to do what you think best. But we'll miss seeing you pottering around the vegetables.'

'Oh, I'll still be around, feeding the hens, popping in to see that you're all right.'

Whoops! The look on both their faces – distant, a sudden closing off – reminds me what I learned the hard way last year: that these two, old as they are, are fiercely independent.

They want to be treated as normal neighbours, not as two fragile ancients. And in truth they do seem to be very good at looking after themselves, and very fit. Underneath their somewhat fragile appearance – both are quite thin, Edna short and Hector long, but each has bird-like bones – there is a surprising toughness.

Despite 'the look' I plough on stubbornly. During this frozen weather I ask everyone how they are, old or young, so I'm not being condescending when I enquire about their provisions, how they're managing with all the snow and ice clinging so long and so tenaciously to the ground. I know the supermarket van that usually delivers to them once a week has not been able to get around the back lanes which remain treacherously icy.

They accept my query gracefully. Hector says, 'We have more than enough food, thank you, Tessa. We stocked up in September and October. Dried pulses, a fifty-pound sack of potatoes, plenty of rice and pasta, dried milk powder, tinned goods. We've even got enough cat food in for the Venerable Bede, here.'

The scruffy cat sitting on an old tartan blanket on the slate floor of the kitchen swishes his tail as we turn to look at him. Goodness knows how old the cat is, or where he got that name. Hector and Edna tried to explain it to me once – something to do with a long dead monk – but I ended up knowing as little about their cat as I, or any of the villagers, know about them. All anyone knows is that although they are both Cornish, they have travelled extensively, and lived for long periods of time in faraway places.

I'm impressed by their foresight, and tell them so. 'You're streaks ahead of the rest of us. No one predicted such a hard winter.'

Edna nods sagely, her huge specs bobbing up and down on her tiny nose, making her look uncannily like a wise owl. She, like her husband, is wearing a furry hat that appears to be a cross between a Cossack's hat and an extinct animal. They've not taken their hats off, inside or outside, since the snows began, not that I've seen anyway. When I commented on their headgear, saying how warm and perfect for this weather they looked, Hector had replied, 'In Russia, we needed to know how to survive the cold. Tibet, too. It was there we learned how to tell when a winter would be hard, learned to recognise the signs.'

I keep quiet, hoping they'll say more, for questions never work; they clam up. Silence isn't working either, now, for Edna is asking if I'd like more tea. I resign myself to unfulfilled curiosity yet again. I just hope they've left diaries and journals somewhere, telling of their travels. I for one would love to know their history, but I'm afraid I never will.

As I finally get up to go, Edna says, 'There is something worrying us terribly, though. And this hard winter has made it worse . . .' She trails off. Hector puts his arms around her. They look so stricken that my mind starts running all over the place, imagining all sorts of dreadful things. Is one of them seriously ill? A heart condition? One that can be aggravated by severe cold? I've heard of old people falling down dead while taking out their rubbish on a freezing morning.

Perhaps it's severe arthritis? They're standing up as I start to leave and seem as upright as always, but they're wearing so many layers of clothing it's hard to tell – woollies and capes, and about three or four scarves wound around each neck, all a riot of different patterns and colours. Hector has on some kind of thick corduroy trousers, tucked into bright red, heavy knee socks sewn onto worn leather soles, and Edna has an ankle-length skirt made from fuzzy material that sends fluff balls scattering like confetti as she moves around the kitchen. Together the pair looks like a couple of whacky snow sculptures dressed by a party of mischievous children.

'What is it?' I ask. 'What can I do to help?'

Edna, reading my thoughts, says with a warm smile, 'My dear, don't look so concerned. We're both in amazing health, considering it is winter and we are indoors more than out.'

I don't comment on this. All the villagers have been concerned about these two this winter. They still do their slow, up-and-down, meditative walk along the bumpy stone path in front of the house, nearly every day. I've seen them walking sedately as snow fell all around them, looking like yetis from some alien Arctic land. The ice that had formed on the naked branches of the trees and bushes in their haphazard front garden added to the bizarre impression as Edna and Hector, arm and arm, propping each other up, walked back and forth, back and forth. They'd told me once, when I suggested they went inside as the falling snow was very wet and they were getting soaked, that this walk was necessary not just for their physical health but for their 'mental, spiritual, and emotional well-being'. That put me in my place – what could I say? I wanted to add that a fat lot of good mental, spiritual, and emotional well-being would be if they were gasping with pneumonia after their soaking, but they gave me the look again so I had to keep quiet.

Hector suddenly makes a weird movement with his right leg and left arm. I'm sure he's about to fall over onto the slate floor and rush to him, grabbing him around the waist. He wrests himself from my grasp and says, with dignity, 'I was perfectly all right, dear girl. I was merely trying to show you one of the Qigong exercises Edna and I do inside in the winter, to keep mobile, and also to retain our balance.'

Edna adds, 'Would you like us to teach you the little sequence we've concocted? A mixture of Qigong and Tai Chi and Tibetan yoga, and one or two other movements we've picked up here and there.' As she speaks she lifts one foot slowly off the floor and at the same time, lifts a hand gracefully, as if the hand is pulling the leg on an invisible string. She looks so old, so frail, so wobbly, that I am completely terrified, yet I don't dare go to her. I stay close by, though, just in case. I do notice that she's being very careful, performing her movements very slowly. These two might be totally eccentric and odd, but they're not bonkers.

Now Hector is joining her. They look like arthritic storks, all unnatural angles and skinny bones. Not that I can see their bones, with all the layers of clothes they're wearing. But I've seen them in summer. I can't take any more. I'm so worried that one of them is going to fall that I can't watch another minute. I say, 'It looks a marvellous exercise, and perhaps you can teach it to me another time, in summer when it's warmer.' I rub my hands together and put on the gloves I'd taken off to drink my tea. At least it is reasonably warm in here. They have the wood burner here in the large kitchen where they live in the winter months, and Doug takes care of their wood supply. There are plenty of fallen or rotting trees on their property. The kitchen is homey, too, with a faded brown sofa in front of the wood burner, piled with plenty of multi-coloured cushions. An old radio sits on a small table nearby, with Radio 4 on seemingly day and night. Once the villagers got together to buy them a digital television, as they'd once had a black and white set years ago that had packed up and never been replaced. But Edna and Hector politely refused. Instead, they suggested the set be raffled to raise funds for repairs to the church. This turned out to be a huge success, with everyone participating. The irony was, Hector's ticket was pulled first, so the television went to them. They declined, of course, and the draw went ahead a second time.

I remember now that something is troubling them. It's so rare for either of them to admit problems that I ask again, though I'm relieved it's not their health that is the worry.

The serene look on their faces changes immediately to one of chagrin. 'It's the rooks,' Hector says. 'I fear all is not well with the rooks.'

I must have looked blank, for Edna says patiently, 'You know we've had rooks here for years. Generations.'

Hector nods. 'I remember the rookery being here when I was growing up. And my father said it was there when he was a boy, too.'

I nod. 'I've heard that rooks like to stay in the same place for ages.'

Hector looks grave. 'Yes, and that's why we're worried. I think our rooks are getting restless.'

'What? How can you tell?'

He taps the end of his nose enigmatically. 'We just can, maid. When you live with rooks long enough, you get to know what they're thinking.'

I can go along with this. My dog knows exactly when the idea of a walk crosses my mind, and I swear I can read his mind when he's deciding whether or not to chase a squirrel at the top of our garden. But rooks? 'So what are they thinking?' I ask.

A hint of scepticism must have sounded in my voice for he says, 'It's not exactly thinking, you mustn't take me literally, Tessa. It's more an instinct thing. When they get agitated, we can feel it somehow.'

Edna looks at him with a little smile as if to say, don't even try to explain our ways, Hector. Turning back to me she says, 'Come on outside with us, dear, and we'll show you.'

There is a wooden coat stand in the wide, drafty hallway and they each take what look like ancient horse blankets from the stand and wrap themselves up. Hector opens the heavy oak door, worn and splintered in places, and a blast of icy wind nearly knocks him over. Neither he nor Edna take any notice but totter and teeter down the glazed white steps sprinkled liberally with salt, clinging to each other. I dare not insult them by helping, but I stick close enough by to grab them if they fall.

Somehow they manage and we walk down the path to the far end of their front garden. Here, the couple stop in front of an immense evergreen tree. It's a magnificent specimen, with broad leaves that appear more black against the grey sky than the dark green they usually are in winter. This isn't a conifer, though, but a holm oak, a broadleaf tree. We've got some wonderful trees around here and I'm still amazed at the lushness and variety of them in our area. Most people think of the coastline, the sea, when they think of Cornwall, but there are magical places inland, too, where mysterious wooded valleys and stunning forests run alongside hidden creeks and streams.

Edna and Hector have told me about the holm oak on other occasions. I've learned that it is a Mediterranean tree brought over to England in the 1500s. Looking up at this one at Poet's

Tenement (the house name, which also dates back centuries), I can almost believe it was one of the original imports. The bark is so old that it is cracked into small squares, and it too has blackened with the years. With the dark leaves turning almost inside out in the strong wind, stark against the smoky sky, the tree looks wild and formidable, yet solid and somehow comforting at the same time. I suppose it's the feeling of permanence, of something that's been there for hundreds of years and will probably still be there long after we're all gone.

But Edna shakes this illusion by saying, 'The rooks are restless because they know the tree is ill. Perhaps very ill.'

I tear my eyes from the tree to look at her. 'No, really? How can you tell?'

I can't hear her entire answer as a loud gust drowns her voice. I catch words such as leaves dying, even some branches, but the rest is lost in the noise. The tree seems to be roaring, and on top of that, the entire tribe of rooks have finished their feeding in a nearby field and are flying home to roost for the night. It's late afternoon now and in this weather, it will be dark soon.

The sky is alive with dozens of the birds, their outstretched wings blackening the coming twilight. The noise is fantastic. The kaar-kaar sounds the birds make vie with the rushing wind. They seem to be amicably arguing as they settle down in the branches; they are such sociable birds.

The rookery in this holm oak is not as visibly stark as those in leafless trees, but you can still see the immensity of it, at least a couple of feet high, all blackened twigs and sticks. As Edna and Hector said, the birds have been coming back for decades to nest in this tree, adding to the rookery each year, making the rough nest comfortable for the new eggs and chicks with more foliage. As we watch the birds settle with a flurry of wings, listening to the cacophony of sounds, I can feel how the rooks belong here, with their glistening black feathers mirroring the tree leaves. But is the tree really sickening? Could it be dying? After all these years? So much for the feeling of permanence it gave me, but of course things end, so others can begin.

These are all questions to be asked another time. The rooks have settled in the tree, and their cries have stopped, with only the odd caw competing with the wind's eerie howl. It's freezing now; despite the cloud cover, the frost will continue tonight.

I part from the Humphreys with gestures and nods, for it's hard to talk in this wind. I tell them I'm off to shut in my hens, but I surreptitiously make sure that the couple are safely up their few steps and into the house before I go.

Soon the hens are all inside, tucked up in their house, all snug against the wind. No eggs today; there haven't been many for the last few weeks – it's what I like to think of as the hens' resting period, during these weeks when they are off their laying. After all, they worked hard for months, keeping our family, and many of our friends, supplied with fresh free-range eggs, so they deserve a rest. The cockerel, Pavarotti, greets me with an especially loud cock-a-doodle-do that makes me glad we live in an easy-going village. There was a piece in the local paper a year or so ago about a group of villagers making a fuss over the cries of a bunch of cockerels a woman kept in pens in her back garden. I don't remember the story exactly but I think she was selling them for breeding. The trouble was, they crowed day and night, and there were quite a lot of them. 'At least you're only one single bird, even though you're loud,' I tell Pavarotti. 'So you can keep singing.'

Before I go, I also look in on the peafowl. The cock and the hen are new to Poet's Tenement, having arrived just before Christmas. The Humphreys have revamped the shed behind the house into cosy quarters for them, to overwinter, so they haven't been out and about yet. I open the door a tiny crack, to check on them, as Edna and Hector asked me to. Doug has shovelled a path and covered the short distance from the house to the shed with a thick layer of sand, so that the couple can come out and feed their new pets every day. But I always take a peek whenever I visit my hens.

They're asleep and barely open their eyes when I look round the door. It's warm in the shed, there is plenty of food and water for them, so I don't go inside to disturb them. I leave the peafowl to their winter's rest, looking forward to seeing them shortly, when spring is finally here and the Humphreys decide it's warm enough for the peafowl to live in their garden.

The short walk home through the churchyard is magic. It is more sheltered here so the wind is not so fierce. The coating of snow on the grass, the tombstones, and the shrubs and bushes, gives a serene feel to the scene, a kind of blanket of peace. I'm filled with a sense of well-being broken only by thoughts of Edna and Hector. If the old holm oak is really sickening, even dying, then it could be dangerous. A gale like this one today could blow it right over, on top of their house, crushing it and the couple inside.

They need an expert opinion on this and I know just who to ask. There's a young man on my postal round who has recently qualified as a tree surgeon. With a bit of luck, Edna and Hector will agree to let him visit to look at the oak. Feeling better now that I've thought of this, I walk quickly towards home, the wind again fierce and blowing me into the house with a whoosh. Jake, who had to stay behind as he and the Humphrey's cat do not get on, barks with glee, and from the sitting room and kitchen the various members of my family call out greetings. The warmth of the house wraps around me like a cashmere glove, feeling cosy and safe as the sound of the wind intensifies outside.

CHAPTER THREE

Chivalry Lives On

The frost stays for the next week. Another light snowfall fills the lanes. Work gets even busier as the winter starts taking its toll, with more people than usual on sick leave. By now many more customers are also housebound by the weather or seasonal illness and we bring them supplies, news, and gossip.

There are still many farms and houses I can't reach by road because the lanes are blocked either by snow or a sheet of ice. I park the van as close as I can and walk the rest of the way. I don't mind except when the only post is junk mail, the unsolicited mailings that most people loathe. I've had customers get quite cross with me and either give it straight back, or tear it up in front of me. I don't blame them. I decided once to simply stop delivering it, as there wasn't one of my customers who wanted it. But then Susie, another postie and a mate of mine at the Royal Mail, told me that what I was doing was a big no-no; that we were legally obliged to deliver the wretched stuff.

Today it's a small package from New Zealand that I'm delivering, and I know who it's from. Going on to the next village, where the roads are clearer than most, I park the van in front of the small bungalow where Annie lives with her husband, Pete. 'A letter from your mum, City Mouse,' I holler as I poke my head in at the door.

Annie is there at once, giving me a quick kiss, taking the letter, pulling me into her warm kitchen, and at the same time saying, 'You can't call me that any more, Country Mouse. I won't allow it. I'm as rural and bovine as you are now.'

'How can you say that? You've not been here a year yet!' I plop myself down at the kitchen table, enjoying the smell of something baking, the sound of the kettle hissing, the warmth pumping out from the Aga. But especially I'm enjoying the special warmth of being here with my dearest and oldest friend. When we moved from London, leaving so many people behind was hard, but parting from Annie was particularly sad. I'm still pinching myself that she's actually here, living in a village only a few miles away from Treverny.

'How're your parents, by the way?' I ask, indicating the small package from New Zealand. 'Do open it, I don't mind.'

'I know what it is. I left my favourite earrings behind when we were staying there – they were a present from Pete – and Mum said she'd send them on. They're both fine. Missing us, I think. It was so good being with them after the wedding, since they couldn't come.'

She pours us tea and sits down opposite me. Her once perfectly cut hair hangs messily on her shoulders in a random manner, her lips are chapped with cold, and her nose, like everyone's nose these freezing days, is red. And she looks terrific, which I tell her. 'Better than you ever looked in London, Annie. Not as sophisticated maybe, but healthier. Glowing.'

'That's what Pete says.' She pauses, looking dreamily into space, as she always does when she thinks of her husband. Well, they are newlyweds after all. They married less than a year ago, here in Cornwall, where Pete, an agricultural merchant, was born and raised. Annie, a city girl through and through, and a researcher for the BBC, met him on one of her visits to us, and it really was love at first sight.

I pull her back to earth. 'Well, your nose is glowing anyway. Like Rudolph's.' I give her a mischievous grin.

'Oh, don't get me started!' She's already starting to giggle. 'What a fiasco that was!'

We were chuckling about the Christmas pantomime in Annie's village last month. Annie, only recently settled into the village after her wedding, her extended honeymoon, and visit to her parents in New Zealand, volunteered to help. 'Pete's been here for ever,' she told me, 'and I'm the newcomer, so it's a great way for me to start fitting in, to become part of the community.'

Not only did the villagers accept her help, they roped her into taking a role: Rudolph the Red-Nosed Reindeer. This entailed her wearing huge fake antlers and a contraption on her nose that lit up when she pressed a hidden button.

The week before the performance in the village hall was funnier than the pantomime itself. Annie, determined to be a good sport, and knowing she was going to be on show as the local boy's Up Country new wife, threw herself into her role. I spent hours with her, getting her costume just right, helping her learn lines – the script called for talking, singing, and dancing reindeers – and laughing helplessly as she tried to balance the antlers on her head. These were immense. 'God knows where the villagers got hold of them,' Annie said. 'No one knows. Apparently they get dragged out every Christmas; they've been in a cupboard in the village hall for ever.'

They looked it, too. They were attached to a sort of cap which fitted precariously on Annie's head; luckily there were straps she could secure under her chin. They were heavy, too, made of wood and actually exquisitely carved. She and Pete brought the antlers to my house when she was first given her costume. With Pete's help, she tied them onto her head and we all ceremoniously drank a toast with a glass of mulled wine to the new Rudolph. Annie started to take a sip and then began sneezing ferociously. The antlers bobbed about totally out of control, knocking down some DVDs from a shelf and nearly poking Pete's eye out. Somehow he managed to get them off Annie while she continued to shake helplessly with the sneezes.

When she finally stopped, had blown her nose, mopped up her watery eyes, and taken an antihistamine, she said mournfully, 'I thought I was over all my allergies. I haven't taken a pill for them for ages. Oh, they can't be coming back, surely!' She looked so forlorn that we all rushed to reassure her. Before she moved here, she suffered from all sorts of allergies, living practically permanently on antihistamines, especially when she visited us in Cornwall. But for months she'd not been plagued by them at all, until this evening.

Pete looked at her fondly and put his arm around her. He'd been looking closely at the antler headpiece and now said, 'This cap is made of some kind of burlap, quite old, too, and dusty. Smells terribly musty. It's the kind of thing that would make anyone sneeze.'

Annie looked horrified. 'Oh no! What do I do?'

'You'll get used to it, I'm sure you will.'

'Air it out a bit. And give it a good clean.'

'And don't forget to take an antihistamine before you go on stage.'

The next few days were hilarious. Every time I popped in to see Annie, she was wearing her antlers. Once as I drove up to the village I saw her actually leave the house with them on her head. She went down a few steps before she realised and ran back inside. 'I can't believe I did that,' she said when I called in. 'But I need to practise wearing the thing; it's so heavy and awkward. And get used to its smell so it stops making me sneeze.'

The night of the performance saw the village hall packed. Ben and I were there, with Will and Amy. We arrived early to get a good seat so I went backstage to wish Annie luck, and take a quick photo of her in full reindeer regalia. 'Annie, you look magnificent,' I cried, and she really did. She was holding her head high and steady, not an antler wobble in sight and the red light on her nose glowed beautifully. Over her shoulders and covering her body was a kind of furry brown cape or blanket that also covered Rudolph's back end. This undistinguished role was played by a sweet young village boy who came up to Annie's shoulders, so that the blanket costume worked perfectly.

They were both in place, the front and back end of Rudolph, and I was filming a video of them performing some dance steps when there was a sharp cry from the lad at the back and he slumped to the floor, writhing in agony.

In the pandemonium of the next ten minutes, a doctor was summoned from the growing audience to take a look at the boy's ankle. It appeared he had sprained it somehow while he was gyrating around, perhaps showing off a bit too ambitiously for the video. It was pronounced not a bad sprain but in no way could he go onstage. The director, who was one of my customers, was stamping his feet in despair, throwing a truly theatrical hissy fit when he spotted me. 'Tessa! Thank the Good Lord you're here. You'll have to fill in.'

I looked at him in horror. He rolled his eyes impatiently. 'Oh don't worry, I'll make sure your ticket money is refunded,' he cried, as if that might be the reason I was shaking my head in protest.

Everyone, including Annie, ignored me while I objected that I didn't know what to do, didn't know the play, and they'd have to find someone else familiar with it. But apparently there was simply no spare person who could fill in; everyone had a job to do. 'Anyway you know lots of the script,' Annie said. 'All those times you helped me with my lines, or with the dance steps.'

So there I was, unceremoniously pushed behind Annie, the furry brown blanket cape over my head. The director cried, 'Tessa, you'll have to stoop. Rudolph looks like he has a hump in his back.'

'Is that all the stage direction he's giving me?' I muttered to Annie, or rather to Annie's back.

'Shush, we're on. Just follow me.'

'Do I have a choice?'

There was a blare of music and song and suddenly we were onstage. There was a wild round of applause, for the set, the costumes, and the twelve reindeer prancing about, though none as large and splendid as Rudolph as they were only one-person creatures, mostly village children with a small set of plastic antlers on their sweet heads.

I don't know how I got through the next hour and a half. There were certainly some dicey moments, like when Amy and Will suddenly recognised my shoes under the blanket and shouted to Ben, 'Oh no, that's Mum up there!' I nearly stuck my head out to shout back, 'So you've only just noticed I'm not sitting beside you?' I must have spoken aloud because Annie made a strangling noise that I knew, from years of being together in London, was the beginning of a laugh. What made it worse was that it was a particularly silent, sombre moment, when an angel or some such was about to float down, and all us reindeers were supposed to be watching in awe.

The muffled giggle coming from in front of me started me off, too. Within moments, we were both shaking as we struggled to control our about to become uncontrollable laughter. The furry blanket holding us together trembled and though I couldn't see them, I knew Annie's antlers were wobbling with the effort of holding in her giggles.

Finally I exploded. A huge guffaw escaped from my throat like water from a broken dam. Annie lost control at the same moment, but luckily for us both, the angel had descended and the choir roared out a riotously joyful song, drowning out our hysterical laughter, and saving us from shameful humiliation, not to mention the wrath of the director.

'Do you realise?' Annie said to Pete later when the four of us were alone together. 'I could have blown it. All my work to fit into your village, ruined in one mad, giggling moment.'

'But you didn't,' he said, hugging her affectionately. 'No one but Ben and I noticed that Rudolph had the shakes. Everyone was looking at the angel. Anyway, they love you, for taking part.'

'And I love you,' Annie said, eyes glistening, while Ben and

I gave a mock moan and told them to stop being such soppy newlyweds.

More snow has fallen during the night but only lightly, and the day is clear. However, my round is treacherous, and there are many places where I have to leave the van and walk a half mile or so to a farmhouse or isolated cottage. I actually don't mind this. Today is another of those clear, frosty, windless winter days, and I'm getting fitter and fitter with all this exercise.

And it's stunning. The frozen trees with their black trunks, the night's snow still clinging to their bare branches, stand out vividly against the blue sky. On the coast, the sea is a deep blue-black, still but tremulous, as if preparing for the onslaught of the next wintry gale. I pause in one of my seaside villages, stopping to watch a cormorant poised on some rocks leading up to a high cliff. The big black bird with its peculiar hooked beak and large ungainly feet, gazes out to sea like some old-fashioned prophet, majestic and formidable-looking.

Once again I leave my van at the top of a lane, to deliver to my next customers, a young couple who live down a rutted lane in an old farm cottage they're renovating. When I first began delivering here, it belonged to an elderly farm worker called Mr Hawker, a shy and reclusive man of whom I grew quite fond during my first year as his postie. When he died, the son of the farmers at nearby Trelak Farm took it over, along with his partner Marilyn. The cottage was almost derelict, but they're slowly making it into a home.

Marilyn and Dave were both born and grew up in Cornwall but had to leave after they qualified as physiotherapists as they couldn't afford a place to live in the county. With all the second homers and tourists, prices to either rent or buy are sky high. But now they've got a chance to make a go of it back in Cornwall, and they know how lucky they are.

Both are at home, stripping off some ancient wallpaper from a back bedroom that looks as if it hasn't been used in fifty years. They ask me in and I accept their offer of a coffee; I've not talked to them for a while. But first I go around to the back where their pet billy goat, named Gruff, of course, has his quarters. I give him the carrot I always bring along for a morning treat and he rewards me with a few joyful leaps in the air after he has nuzzled my hand for his carrot. I play with him for a while, enjoying the stillness of the air, the blue sky. Despite the cold, you can feel the stirring of spring underground. It can't be far away now.

As I head back through the garden into the house, I see some bottles poking out through a snowdrift behind the house. Dave, opening the door, says, 'It's a great way to chill white wine, especially if you only have a tiny fridge like ours. It's Marilyn's birthday tomorrow and we're having some friends over. Come along as well, Tessa.'

I decline, with thanks. Marilyn can only be in her mid- to late twenties; it's another generation and I wouldn't barge in on their party, but it's nice of him to ask. I must remember to bring her a card and some kind of little gift tomorrow with the post.

A sudden burst of laughter and merriment comes from the front of the house, along with squeals from Marilyn. Dave grins. 'That must be her birthday present just arrived. Let's go see.'

I follow him through to the sitting room, marvelling along the way at how much work they've done in the short time since they've been here. More laughter, squeals, and voices greet us as we go into the room. Marilyn is there with two people I know, Clara the cat woman and Guy the cat man.

Marilyn sees me and rushes across, holding up a small fluffy kitten. It looks like the stray one Guy brought when Clara took her walk outside on the ice. 'Isn't he sweet?' Marilyn cries. 'I didn't know a thing about it until now. Dave has been in touch with the Cat Protection, asking about a kitten. This stray was found not long ago and needs a home. Oh, I've been wanting a cat since we moved here! Isn't he gorgeous? Here, Tessa, you can hold him for a minute if you like.' She thrusts the kitten at me while she runs to Dave, hugging and thanking him for the surprise. Clara and Guy are beaming with pride, as if I were cuddling their own baby. The 'baby' though is not so cuddly. He's starting to struggle, digging his sharp little claws into my Royal Mail jacket. 'He's frightened,' Clara exclaims, looking at me as if I'm murdering the thing.

The cat claws my hand. 'Oh you poor thing,' Guy cries. He means the kitten, not me.

Marilyn, Dave, Guy, and Clara all rush to me to take the kitten away from the horrid postie who obviously doesn't know how to handle cats. I try to tell them that it's still a feral thing and to be careful, but no one listens. Somehow in the handover, Guy gets a scratched cheek, Clara a claw mark on her neck, and the kitten gets his freedom. Out the door it goes, into the snow and ice. 'Who left the door open?' Marilyn cries as we all rush out after it. But no one bothers to answer. No good asking who left the stable door open after the horse bolts, is it?

There is now a frantic half hour while we search for the kitten. I can't help marvelling at how Clara seems to have totally overcome her fear of slipping on ice. She's sliding around some of the worst patches on the lane leading to the house, waving her arms frantically for balance, calling the kitten, making strange meowing noises which I suppose is her cat talk.

But the kitten is nowhere to be found. Finally we give up, or rather pause to warm up in the house before starting to search again. I say, 'Look, I hate leaving before your kitten is found, but I really need to get going on my round. The customers will be wondering what's happened to me.'

Clara is too distracted and panicked about the kitten to even hear me. 'The poor creature will freeze to death if we can't find him.'

Guy goes to her and puts his arm around her shoulders. 'There, there. We will, I promise you. Even if it takes all night. You're not to worry.'

Clara looks up to him as Guinevere must have done to Lancelot. Her face beams, her eyes shine. Guy's stoop vanishes, he stands straight and tall, ready to do battle. I watch, fascinated, as he presses his hand on her shoulder. She says, breathless, 'Oh Guy, thank you. If anyone can find the kitten, you can, I know.'

Well, well, well, I think. So that's how it is. Or rather, that's how it's beginning, for certainly there were no such vibes between them the other times I've seen them together. It's been all business, finding strays, finding homes for them, raising money for their charity by jumble sales, begging for donations. I watch with amused delight as their eyes meet, lock. Has Clara actually forgotten a cat in the romance of the moment?

I can't stop to find out. I've got customers waiting for bread, for newspapers, and for bags of kindling for their fires and wood burners. I say my goodbyes to them all and open the door to my van, shouting out that I hope they find the kitten soon.

And then I squash it. There is a horrific yowl as I sit on the kitten. I leap up, cracking my head on the windscreen, and turn to see the fluffy grey fur ball flattened on the cushion on the driver's seat. I'd left the window open; he must have jumped on the bonnet for warmth and then climbed into the van. Omigod is he dead? I reach for him with a beating heart but he suddenly leaps up and starts scrambling around the back of the van. I lunge about, trying to catch him before he finds the open window again. At least there's certainly nothing wrong with the creature; the kitten is meowing madly and running about all over the place.

I finally catch him just as he is about to leap from the window. Luckily I'd put my gloves on for he's clawing my hands like crazy, no doubt terrified of the hulking postie who not only nearly crushed him to death but also gave him a merry chase around the van.

Cheers of relief greet me as I walk in with the kitten. Clara takes him and he immediately starts to calm down. She really does have a way with cats for the little mite is actually looking around now, fear abating. Everyone thanks me and then Dave says, 'Tessa, what did you do to your forehead? You have a huge lump there!'

I toy with confessing, but the kitten looks fine; it was probably tucked into the back of the seat and I couldn't have squashed it as hard as I thought. 'Oh, bumped my head in the van,' I say, vaguely.

'Oh, you must be more careful!' Clara cries, not taking her eyes from the cat she's still cradling. 'Mustn't she, little pussy?'

The kitten looks at me coolly. I look back. *Don't you say a word*, I think, before I remember that it's a cat to which I'm sending telepathic messages. That bump on the head must be making me tizzy.

'Now I really do have to go,' I say. Marilyn has taken the kitten from Clara; she's in love with the little creature already and thanks me again for finding it. As I leave I look back at Clara, who is now holding hands with Guy. Well, holding a couple of fingers, because both of their hands are covered with the knitted fingerless gloves that I recognise as having been made by Tufty's mum. I hadn't noticed them before in the flurry of the kitten drama. Clara's are deep turquoise and the fluorescent stripe is lime green, and Guy's are an ocean blue with a pink neon stripe. They really are great gloves.

Clara and Guy notice me staring at their hands and furtively unlock their entwined fingers, obviously not yet willing to share this moment with any witnesses. How sweet, I think. I'm such a romantic. As I look away, I see their fingers inching towards each other again.

I hate to disturb their moment, but I have to know. 'Clara,' I say, 'I can't believe you're out in this weather. Did you really drive over here in Guy's van, and walk down that icy lane carrying a cat?'

Clara actually blushes. She looks pretty with colour in her cheeks. 'Oh, I'm so much better now. Guy's been helping me get out. And he's such a good driver, and held onto me down the lane, and held the cat basket . . .' she trails off, flustered.

'That's great, it really is.' I'm relieved. That's one less customer to worry about this winter. I wish the problems of some of the rest of them could be solved that easily.

* * *

One problem that troubles not just me but the other locals living in Poldowe is that of Delia, the widow that Melanie mentioned in the shop the other day. Delia is in her eighties but seems to be going on a hundred. She's frail, fragile, walks slowly, fearfully, even though there's not much wrong with her, not physically that is. She's been that way as long as I've known her, relying on Meals on Wheels for her food, and on her neighbours and the postie for other odds and ends. None of us mind, for she's a sweet lady, always with a smile of appreciation for the things we do for her. Her husband died many years ago, out at sea in a lifeboat accident, and Delia shrank from life after that. The villagers rallied around her, and still do, for she has no one else, no family anywhere.

Lately, though, I've noticed a huge change in her. She seems to be not only forgetting things, but also misplacing objects, some of them important, like her house keys, bills that need to be paid, and her glasses. Some days I come in to find her staring into space, a look of panic on her face because of something she's mislaid. Sometimes I find it for her, only to realise she's lost it again before I even leave the house.

Today I go in and start to light her tiny coal fire as I've done for over a year, after she asked me one morning if I wouldn't mind doing it. Now, winter or summer, I come in and do it automatically, but this time when I go in she looks at me oddly, almost as if she doesn't know who I am. 'Delia, it's me, Tessa,' I say, when she doesn't respond to my cheery good morning.

Finally she murmurs, gives me a small, uncertain smile. 'Oh, hello. How nice to see you.' She speaks politely but seems surprised, as if I'm an unusual visitor, not one she sees most days of the week.

I take the small coal bucket outside to the coal shed, fill it as I've done most days for over a year, and light her small fire. Usually she is effusive with thanks and gratitude, but today she is silent, watching me but with vacant eyes, as if she were somewhere else entirely. She doesn't even respond when I show her the scones Ginger has baked for her. I tell her I'm putting them in the kitchen and when I do, I get a shock. Kitty, the sweet tabby cat that Clara gave Delia nearly a year ago, is mewing weakly, and I can tell, even before I pick her up, that the creature is starving.

I open the cupboard, find a dozen tins of unopened cat food and four packs of dry food. The fridge is empty, except for a carton of milk. I know I'm being nosy, but I feel this is an emergency. I start scrounging around in the rubbish bin. To my relief, there are the remains of the Meals on Wheels Delia gets every day, so I assume she's been eating herself, even if she's forgotten to feed Kitty.

I cuddle the poor thing, giving her some food which she devours gratefully. I'm annoyed at myself for not checking on the cat before, but when I asked Delia, she always said Kitty was sleeping soundly upstairs on her bed. Knowing that the Venerable Bede, the Humphreys' cat, spends most of the winter months snuggled on their bed, this didn't surprise me. I assume that's what she told Clara and Ginger when they check up on her, as they do every day.

I go back to Delia and say gently, 'You know, I think Kitty was hungry. I hope you don't mind, but I gave her some food.'

Delia smiles, 'That's fine, dear. I did feed her this morning, though.'

I know there were no empty cat food tins or packets in the rubbish, and no opened ones anywhere. And Kitty wouldn't have devoured her food so savagely if she hadn't been ravenous.

I make a cup of weak tea for Delia, the way she likes it, and sit down to talk. I know she adores that cat. When Clara asked her if she'd take in a friendly stray that desperately needed a home, Delia was ecstatic. So was Clara, and I, along with Ginger, and other neighbours in Poldowe, for everyone hated to see Delia so lethargic, giving up on life and using the telly as a substitute, though she doesn't even do that now. The cat did cheer her up and though she still didn't go out, she at least went into her small garden in the summer months to watch Kitty play or sleep in the sun. Often when I came in, the cat would be sitting purring on her lap. I should have been suspicious the last few weeks when it wasn't around, but this was such an unlikely winter that I could easily believe Kitty was hibernating somewhere out of the cold. The poor thing was probably prowling about outside trying to catch mice or scrounge food from the neighbours.

Luckily Clara was in when I arrived at her house, a few doors down. I told her about Kitty, and how strange Delia had been. Clara promised to call that evening and see what she could do. 'I've been worried about Delia anyway,' she said. 'She's been acting a bit odd. Forgetting things, repeating things she told you five minutes ago. The other villagers who call in on her have noticed, too.'

Oh dear. It doesn't sound good. But thank goodness Delia lives in a village and has caring neighbours she's known for much of her life. I leave, relieved that I've been able to pass over some of the responsibility. I finish delivering in this part of the village and go back to my van, which I've parked on the High Street. To my chagrin I see that I'm blocked in. Parked right in front, leaving me about an inch of space, is a swish new Peugeot which I'm sure must belong to one of the second homers, obviously down for the weekend since the forecast is a brilliant one. Finally, a thaw is on its way, along with sunny skies and only a little cloud. It's Friday and already there's a steady stream of cars arriving as the second homers, mostly vanished since the Christmas and New Year holidays, come down to check out their houses after the snow and frost, and get them ready for the spring influx.

Behind me is Guy's old van. I'd parked fairly tight, to make room for other cars, but there was absolutely no need for the Peugeot to come in that ridiculously close, as there is nothing on the other side of it. Luckily, I see Guy coming out of the shop and I call out, 'Guy, I'm stuck, can you move your van?'

He lopes over to me in that gawky but endearing way he has. 'Right'o, Tessa, will do it now. Hold these, will ya?' He hands me a bouquet of carnations, not exactly at their best. He adds, anxiously, 'They're, uh, for Clara.' He stops, blushes, looks at his feet. 'Now I've bought them, I don't know if she likes flowers. What'd'ya think?'

'I think she'd love them.'

He looks even more doubtful. 'I dunno. I'm not sure she's the flower type.'

'Most women love getting flowers,' I say patiently. 'And now, please can you move the van?'

But he's not budging. He takes the flowers out of my hands with sudden determination. 'She might hate carnations. I'm taking them back, I'll change them for chocolates or something.'

'Guy!' I holler as he's heading off back to the shop. 'I really need to get on. Clara might be on a diet or something; flowers are really much better.'

Back he comes. 'Clara can't be on a diet. She's not fat. She's perfect.'

'I didn't imply she was. Maybe she doesn't eat chocolates to keep herself perfect. Give her the flowers but please let me out of here first.'

He doesn't move but stands forlornly, indecisively looking at the carnations. 'Maybe it's too early,' he says, finally.

'What is?' I'm trying to be patient. I'm trying to remember that this slow easy life is why we moved here. No hurry, no rush, no stress. I try to go with what is happening at the moment without worrying about being even more late finishing my round. I take a deep breath. 'What's too early, Guy?' I ask when he doesn't answer.

'Our relationship. Giving her flowers. So early on.'

'It's never too early.'

'But we don't even have a relationship.' His foot is fiercely making circles in the patch of snow on the verge of the street.

'Oh. But, uh, you want one, right?'

He finally looks up at me. 'Oh, Tessa, I do!' His face looks so sweet, all lit up like a harvest moon, that I have to hide my smile.

I push my advantage. 'Then giving her those flowers is the best way to get one started. And as soon as you move your van, you can get on with it. Clara's home, I just saw her a short time ago.'

I've never seen him move so fast. He thrusts the flowers at me again and is about to open the door of his van when I see that someone has come from behind us and is opening the door of the Peugeot. I say, 'Guy, never mind, the man in front of me is moving. Here's your flowers, give them to Clara before you get cold feet again.'

He still looks indecisive so I give him a gentle shove towards her house. 'Oh look, you've got to go, she's seen you from the window. You can't run away now, Guy.'

This is a little white lie but I said I was a romantic, didn't I? And it works; he's walking up the path to her door, if not exactly like Lancelot than at least not too hesitantly.

I jump in the postal van, start it up, and wait for the man to get his Peugeot out of my way. There's nothing behind him (his car is facing me) and there's nothing on the road, but he's not moving. I look closely and see that he's on his mobile phone.

I count to ten, noting that he's got his seatbelt on so he must be going soon. Five minutes pass (I've counted to ten a zillion times) and he's still talking. His face is turned away from me and he seems not to see me, or is pretending not to. Finally, when it seems he'll be sitting there talking for ever, I get out of the van and walk over to his window.

It's shut, so I give an easy, friendly knock on the window. He looks up at me and shouts, 'What?'

I do a double take. I know this man. He's Mr Landers, one of the second homers in our village. He's had a house there for several years but no one calls him or his wife by anything other than their surnames; they made it clear they wanted no intimacy with us villagers as soon as they moved in. I've had a run-in with him before, when Marilyn's pet goat, Gruff, was being stubborn and sitting down in the hardly used road near their house. Mr Landers came by – he had a different car then; I haven't seen this one before – and instead of laughing about it as anyone else would, he had a mega hissy fit, shouting and hollering and threatening to report us.

So I am not well pleased to see him now. He's turning away from me again, as if I am too unimportant to take note of. I knock on the window again, this time a bit harder. He zizzes it down so hard it nearly takes my finger off. 'What?' he barks again. 'Can't you see I'm on the phone?'

I keep my voice sweet. Not because I'm such a goodie-goodie, but because I know it will annoy him. He wants me to shout back so he can yell even louder. 'Yes, Mr Landers, I do see that, but you happen to be blocking me in. I need to get on with my postal round. The Royal Mail always gets through, you know.' I give him a smile as I think, *except when blockheads like you stand in its way*.

He says, 'You'll have to wait. This is important.'

'So is the Royal Mail, sir,' I reply. Oh, I love it when I'm on my best behaviour with rude types like him. After a time they begin to get suspicious, not knowing if you're taking the mickey. It throws them, whereas shouting wouldn't. They're too used to shouting.

He turns back to his phone while I wonder if I should just give up and get Guy out of Clara's house to move his van. But why should I? Mr Landers is right there and for all I know Guy and Clara might just be on the brink of beginning that relationship Guy so wants. Who am I to thwart young love? Well, maybe not so young but never mind. I'm just about to ask him again to move when he cries into the phone, 'Don't you dare hang up on me you . . .'

Whoever it was obviously does, for he slams the phone down on the passenger seat, letting out a couple of swear words. I figure he'll go now so I jump back in the van, turn on the engine as he does the same. As I wait for him to reverse out – there is still nothing behind him – I'm jolted in my seat as he goes forward instead and rams into the van.

We're both out of our vehicles at the same time. I'm annoyed more than anything, as neither one seems damaged, maybe a few scratches that's all. The idiot was in such a fury that he went into first gear instead of reverse. Thankfully the damage isn't worse. I hope he's feeling properly shame-faced and apologetic – but not a bit of it. I can hardly believe what he's saying. He seems to be blaming me for the collision. 'You ran right into me,' he yells. 'Too impatient to wait for me to move. I'm going to report you.' He turns to look at the front of his car but there's not much there to look at. That doesn't stop him. 'You're going to damn well pay for this.'

I'm too shocked to be angry. 'Mr Landers, it was you who ran into me.'

He's right in my face, in my space, breathing down at me. He's not that tall but taller than me, ordinary-looking, maybe in his early fifties. 'It bloody wasn't. You hit me straight on. I'd swear it in any court.'

I'm so shaken by his bald-faced lie that I literally can't speak. He's going for his phone, looks at me with daggers in his eyes while he punches in directory inquires, asking to be put through to the main post office in Truro. He doesn't seem to be getting through to anyone so he throws the phone down again, starts on at me again. 'You've given me trouble before, I recognise you,' he says, no doubt meaning that incident with Marilyn and the goat blocking the road.

I finally find my voice. 'I've never given you trouble and I most certainly did not run into your car. You were the one who hit me.'

At this he blows, swearing and throwing another one of his temper tantrums. Really, the man needs either yoga or tranquillisers; he'll have a heart attack. I have to admit I'm losing my cool myself. 'I did not hit you. You rammed your car right into post office property. With me sitting inside, too. You could have injured me badly.'

We're at a stalemate. By now several of the villagers have come over to watch the scene. Guy is there with Clara, and Ginger, too, as well as Tufty from the shop. It doesn't take them long to figure out what happened. Mr Landers is saying again, 'I'll swear in court that you drove straight into my parked car.' He gets his phone, starts to punch in numbers again.

Guy, standing next to me, says loudly, 'And I'll swear that I saw everything, and that the post office van did not move.'

'Me, too,' echoes Clara, clutching onto Guy's hand.

There is a sudden, deadly silence. Ginger breaks it, saying softly but very clearly, enunciating every word carefully, 'I saw it, too. I'm happy to come to court as a witness.' And then Tufty and several of the other villagers join in, mumbling promises of support for me.

Mr Landers doesn't say a word. He looks from Guy to Ginger and then at me. We all stare back. He looks at Guy again, takes a step forward as if he's going to punch him. Guy, skinny awkward Guy, doesn't even flinch but also takes a firm step forward. Mr Landers, the brawny bully, is taken by surprise by this act of courage and obviously is not sure what to do. Finally, in a fury he turns, jumps into his car and violently starts the engine. I tense, thinking he's going to ram the van again but he reverses and drives far too fast up the road towards Treverny.

I'm totally shaken. I don't know if he'd been so angry at

whoever he was talking to on the phone that he forgot he wasn't in reverse, couldn't remember clearly, or whether he realised too late but was deliberately blaming me. I hope it is the first one.

Whatever, it's over now. The other villagers begin to disperse. Tufty says, 'He was in the shop a while ago, giving Melanie a hard time because she didn't stock the bottle of wine he wanted. Rude bugger, that one. Glad he doesn't live in Poldowe.'

'Unfortunately he's got a second home in Treverny,' I say. 'Not the most popular couple in the village, the Landers. Thank goodness they don't come down often. But never mind them now. I owe you three a big one, coming to my rescue like that. Thanks so much.' I give them all a hug, and an especially big one to Guy, thanking him for standing up to the man. Guy looks embarrassed, modest but proud. Didn't I say he was Lancelot? What a hero!

'What luck that you were watching.' I'm burbling now with relief that the whole sorry incident is over. 'All of you. And Tufty, too. He must have been watching from the shop window, saw the whole thing. Had you and Clara actually come outside, Guy, just before it happened?'

Guy looks a bit furtive. 'Uh, actually no. Clara and I were, um, talking, and we heard all this hollering so we came out to see what was up.'

'Me, too,' Ginger says. 'I'd been in the shop, didn't see what happened. Tufty couldn't have either; he wasn't anywhere near the window. We all rushed out when we heard the crash and then the shouting.' She giggles. 'I don't think any of the villagers saw a thing, y'know, just like we didn't. It's still winter, still freezing. Everyone was inside until all the noise and hubbub brought us running out.'

'But – but you said you'd go to court. Be witnesses.'

Now Guy is smiling, too, his crinkly face even more creased with fun. 'D'ya think I'd believe that bugger? If you said it was his fault, then it was, far as I'm concerned.'

'Same here,' Ginger says. 'And same as all the others who offered support. They know you, and they know him. He stops in here quite a bit when he's down from Up Country, to pick up bits and bobs. Always got his nose in the air. Her, too.'

I don't know what to say. Finally I stammer, 'But if it came to court, wouldn't you be perjuring yourselves?'

Clara, Ginger, and Guy are all shaking their heads. 'But don't you see, Tessa,' Ginger says, 'that it won't go to court now, cause we stood up to him. That's what it's all about, y'know. Life down here. Standing together, standing up to strangers who try to bully us about.'

I feel quite touched. 'And I don't even live in this village. But thank you all the same.'

Guy says, 'Don't matter what village. You're Cornish.' He grins. 'Well, sort of.'

What a great compliment – I'm sort of Cornish. I smile to myself all the way back to St Geraint.

CHAPTER FOUR

Doors Opening and Closing

The wintry weather is finally over and it's starting to feel spring-like, although it's only February. Light mists roll in from the sea in the early mornings, drifting in patches over the water and then up along the cliffs. With the gales and storms subsided, the sea has lost its white foam, and instead the water swells gently beneath the thin white fog.

Now that the snow is gone you can see the masses of snowdrops on banks and verges, and in the woodland. It's late for snowdrops, but after the hard winter there seems to be more of them than ever before. All the spring and summer flowers will be more glorious and plentiful this year because of the snow and frost; the plants will have had a chance to rest. There should also be more wild berries, blackberries and elderberries, sloes and rosehips. I'm not sure how I know this, or how I now know so many things about the countryside I never knew before, but thinking about it, I believe the knowledge and understanding has come by just living here. It's crept

up on me almost unaware. Today as I drove home I heard a
buzzard's cry, and recognised it immediately for what it was,
something I wouldn't have done even a couple of years ago.
In London I could tell if the sudden screech of brakes on a
traffic-filled street was that of a bus or a taxi, but I couldn't
recognise birdsong. Now I can tell when a songbird's chirping
turns to calls of alarm, followed by that sudden silence when
there's a sparrowhawk around. I love the way these things have
seeped into my understanding, rather like osmosis.

The flurry of activity at the end of the month when some
of the second homers return for half term reminds me that
it's time to get our house ready for the summer months.
We've decided that an easy way to supplement the family
income would be to rent our house for the holidays. I'm not
a huge fan of camping – I love my home comforts too much
– but the rest of the family is, and we had a fun camping
holiday on the north coast of Cornwall last year. I'm happy
to do it again for two or even three weeks, if it means raising
some income. Living here hasn't been easy, and still is a
struggle, financially that is. Ben has had a few acting jobs
and in between he works part time at the Sunflower Café in
St Geraint and also as a masseuse, for which he was trained
in London. He's being called more and more to the Roswinnick
Hotel in St Geraint, a gorgeous and very posh hotel, beloved
by both royalty and celebrities, to give treatments to some
of the guests there.

At least Ben and I aren't alone in this, trying all sorts of
things to make ends meet. We've discovered that in Cornwall
so many people are in the same position. The only truly rich
folk are the second homers; the other permanent residents are
usually like us, with several part-time jobs, struggling hard to

make enough money to keep going. Even those with huge houses are often land rich but cash poor. It gives everyone a feeling of solidarity, surrounded by people with the same money problems.

I get the idea of renting our house for the summer from one of my customers, a rather grand elderly woman who lives alone in a stunningly magnificent house on the coast. She's got a view of the sea to die for, and I sometimes sit on her terrace on a fine day enjoying the panorama with her. She's got a double-barrelled name but insists I call her Joanna. She's a widow with children all over the world, some in diplomatic positions and others writing important books about world events. She tosses scraps of information about them now and again, almost as an afterthought. I suspect that she and her husband had a rather aristocratic social life when he was alive. Occasionally she'll mention some lord or lady, and she always refers to the Prince of Wales as the Duke. But then everyone in the Duchy of Cornwall seems to refer to Prince Charles as that, as if he were just one of the locals.

Joanna is looking very elegant this morning, as she usually does, in a plain blue wool dress, immaculate but not new; I've seen her wearing it before. She has a number of similar outfits, all with plain colours, long sleeves, and beautifully tailored. She usually wears one or another with a pair of what used to be called court shoes, in quality leather with a small stocky heel. A plain rope of what I'm sure are very real pearls hangs around her neck. 'Tessa,' she says, opening the door as I'm about to post her mail through, 'do come and look at the sea. It's such a stunning colour today.'

I follow her through to some double doors to the terrace that runs the length of the house and around one side. There must be a fantastic view from most of the windows. We stand for a few moments side by side, admiring the way the sunlight, growing stronger every day, seems to be delving deeper into the ocean as the winter recedes, changing its colour from dark greys and greenyblacks, to lighter hues of blue and emerald. Joanna takes a deep breath. 'Ah Tessa, a day like today is a blessing. I do miss this sometimes, in the summer months.'

Because there were a few changes in our postal rounds last autumn, I didn't deliver to this area last July and August. 'Do you go away every summer?' I ask politely.

She turns to look at me. 'Why, of course. Everyone does. Don't you?'

I say cheerfully, 'Well, we camp for a couple of weeks, but that's about it. We can't afford to go away on a proper holiday, it that's what you mean. You know, planes and abroad and rented cottages or hotels and stuff.'

She looks perplexed. 'My dear, who can? I certainly can't, nor can any of my friends.'

Now I'm confused. 'But you just said you went away for the summer.'

'Yes, but not on holiday. I rent out my house, naturally. Quite frankly, I need the income. As do many of the people I know.'

I look at the sea. Tiny traces of the morning's mist hover here and there in patches, like receding ghosts. A fishing boat is chuntering out to sea with a flock of gulls in its wake, and a cargo boat sails in and out of the haze still lingering at the horizon. I think what a fortune it would be to rent a house like this for the summer. 'It's a brilliant idea. But where do you go?'

She smiles, gives a little wave of her hand towards the sea, as if it is there that she'll live in July and August. I notice the pale pink varnish on her fingernails. There's a tiny smudge on them: Joanna obviously does them herself. There are all sorts of ways to save money, even for someone who lives in a house like this. She says, 'Oh, I visit friends in the shires and the Home Counties, I have many in that area. And I reciprocate in the winter months. They often come to stay with me.' She smiles mischievously. 'Especially over the Christmas holidays, when they want to get away from their children and grand-children. Not to mention great-grandchildren. I often have quite a houseful, then.'

We talk a short while longer, and by the time I leave her, finish my round and get home, I'm buzzing with the idea of renting our house this summer. As soon as I walk through the door I'm looking around, trying to see the place with an objec-tive eye, wondering how our family home would look to poten-tial holiday renters.

It looks good, I say out loud. Even if I do say so myself. There are healthy house plants on windowsills and shelves, pictures on the wall, comfy chairs and sofa and cushions, soft lamps everywhere, flowers – the whole effect is, I think, quite pleasing. Friends who visit from London always say compli-mentary things about our house, and I've loved making a home out of it. Yes, the house will do well for a rental accom-modation, I'm sure of it. But as these thoughts go around in my head, another one surfaces. Strangers in our home? People who might not love it as we do? What if they break something precious? Our treasures are not expensive, not the kind that can be replaced by money, but things that mean something to us. A table lamp I found in a junk shop, just right for a corner of the living room. I searched months for the perfect one that we could afford. An exquisitely beaded cushion that

Annie brought me back from a holiday in Morocco, the cushion that goes so perfectly with an old armchair that belonged to my parents.

Annie. The phone rings and I have a feeling it's her. Since she's moved here we're either at each other's homes when we have a spare moment, or on the phone. We were like this before either of us married, and now here we are again. The great thing, too, is that Pete and Ben get on so well together.

'Guess what, Tessa?' she sounds excited. 'I've finally got some freelance work. A writer I met once through the BBC, does historical novels, two a year, can you imagine? Wants to try a different period from his usual Tudor stuff so I've got the job researching Victorian England. All stuff I can do on the net so I can work at home.'

'Should be fun.'

'And bring in some cash. Pete's salary is ridiculously low.'

I murmur sympathetic words. Agricultural rates in Cornwall are especially poor.

After some more chit chat Annie says, 'Listen, one of the main reasons I phoned was to say I've got two free tickets for a session with a crystal therapist in Truro, so let's go together.'

'What's a crystal therapist?'

'God knows. But it'll be fun. I'm all for trying alternative stuff and I know you are, too. It'll do us good, relax us.'

'You're stressed?'

She laughs. 'Not at all, I'm as contented as a cow. C'mon, let's give it a try. Have a girlie day out, just like the old days.'

Annie says she'll ring for an appointment and we hang up just as Ben comes in. I'm thinking about Annie and Pete, wondering if they could rent out their house for the summer, too. We could go camping together. 'It would be a laugh,' I say to Ben, 'roaming about all summer like gypsies, trying to find a place to stay.'

Ben stares at me. 'Tessa, what're you talking about? Who is going to be roaming about all summer?'

'Why, we are! The whole family. Though thinking about it, I guess Annie won't want to leave her home; she's only just moved in.'

He shakes his head. 'You've lost me, Tessa. Start all over again.'

'Oh, Ben, I'm sorry,' I give him a big hug. 'My mind is whirling again; I forgot I haven't even talked about it with you.'

We sit down over a cup of tea and I tell him about Joanna. He is as dumbfounded as I was when he hears the astronomical price we could get during the summer weeks. He quickly warms to the idea and starts getting as enthusiastic about it as I am. Then he says, 'But our jobs. We've got to stick around here.'

'I've thought of that. We always take a fortnight off to spend time as a family – remember our camping trip last year? We can camp near home and live in our tent while we rent out the house.' I'm getting so excited it's hard to sit still.

Ben tells me with a smile to calm down, reminds me that it's only February and a long time until summer. But he agrees that it's not too early to start making inquiries, for after all, people start booking their holidays soon after Christmas. So the next day I phone a reputable rental agency which, I've discovered, handles many of the properties in our area. I tell the woman on the phone about our home and we make an appointment for someone to come out next week and assess the house for possible lets. 'I think it'll be just what people would like,' I gush enthusiastically over the phone. 'We've tried to make it homey and comfortable. Our London friends think it's great.'

The woman clears her throat non-committedly. I've been waffling I know, but I love our home, and I'm proud of what we've created from virtually nothing. I want everyone to love it as we do. I ring off, saying lamely, 'Sorry to go on, but you'll see when you come here.'

The woman says, 'Oh, it won't be me, madam. It will be one of our rental consultants.'

Goodness, that's a bit formal, I think. But never mind. Someone is coming out and we're on our way. All we need to do is to find somewhere nearby to camp for the summer. I feel light-headed and buzzing, thinking what a blessing this added addition to our income will bring.

The next evening, Ben and I are invited over to our new neighbours' house for a 'light supper' as Kate tells us. 'Just us,' she goes on. 'Very informal, so don't dress up.'

I don't tell her that all our social life is informal these days, as it is with everyone in the village. When friends like Joe and Daphne, who farm on the edge of the village, come over for a meal, it's very much pot luck for food, and throwing on a clean jumper is as far as dressing up goes. It is the same with Annie and Pete.

We've seen Kate and Leon a few times since the day they arrived, but they've been busy settling in, so we've not spent much time with them. We're looking forward to getting to know them, having new friends right next door. I put on a new pair of wool trousers, new that is from a fantastic charity shop I know in Truro, and a cosy warm jumper that I've had for years. It looks a bit worn but it's a gorgeous deep blue colour, and after all, Kate did say casual. I don't like being cold, and I'm not sure what kind of heating they've got in their house now. The freezing weather might have gone but it's not fully springtime yet.

Leon opens the door, looking groomed and immaculate in black trousers and a soft grey cashmere jumper. Kate, behind him, is wearing a long skirt and a delicate fine woollen top with exquisite beading around the rather low-cut neckline. She has earrings to die for, silvery and long, like tiny moonbeams clustered in her long dark hair. This is casual? I take a deep breath, remembering they've just come from London. They'll change, adjust to rural life, just as Annie did. She, too, used to visit us dressed out of a fashion magazine, but now she shops like I do, looking at sales items and some of the vintage charity shops. I've also taken Annie to a couple of the clothes swaps I've been to in the past few months.

Women in this area have been exchanging clothes for years, but I read somewhere that it's now quite fashionable in London, since the economic downturn. Someone's even put a name to it – 'swishing'. Basically, we take turns holding the swapping party at each other's homes. Everyone has to bring at least one item of clothing that's clean, decent, and good quality. People bring nibbles, some wine, and we make a party out of it. One woman's cast-off clothes can be just what another one is looking for, and we swap. The catch is when several women have their eye on a particularly tasty item, but I have to say, everyone's been pretty laid back at the clothes exchanges I've been to, and graceful about not being too greedy. I have heard that in London, though, there are swishing parties that are not so amiable, when two or more women have their eyes on a designer item. Hostilities break out in some of the most benign circumstances, or so I'm told by old friends in the city.

When Kate compliments me on the unusual velvety scarf I'm wearing over my old jumper, I tell her about the parties, for that's where I got it. 'It's from Monsoon, never worn – the scarf still had the label on. The woman who brought it to the swap was given it as a birthday present but it wasn't her thing. Our swap parties are a terrific way to get new clothes, and all for free.'

Kate looks totally unenthusiastic but says, politely, 'I'm sure it's a wonderful idea, for those who can't afford to shop properly.'

Oh dear. I don't think Kate has realised yet that's me. She seems a very nice person, but I don't think the realities of Cornish life have sunk in yet.

The 'light supper', which at our house would probably be a Spanish omelette with our own fresh eggs, turns out to be a whole array of delicious titbits from Marks and Spencer that Kate picked up in Truro earlier that day. There are exotic salads, a huge variety of cold meats and cheeses, various sauces, and both hot and cold potato and pasta dishes. I'm sure she spent more on this supper than I do on a week's meals at home.

It's beginning to dawn on me that the Wintersons are not short of money. Kate's certainly not looking for a job; she's told me she's going to enjoy the next months doing up the house, getting used to country life. As for Leon, apparently he did something 'in the City', but he's now retired. How he can be retired when he's not yet forty, goodness knows, but I heard him tell Ben that he won't be looking for work just yet, except for some consulting work in the City. He wants to devote his time to hunting, apparently. 'I've just bought a new gun,' he says, eyes lighting up like a child's with excitement and pleasure. 'It's a Purdy. Haven't even used it yet. Let me show you.' He rushes out of the room and comes back with the shotgun. It looks new and shiny, expensive.

He doesn't notice that we don't say much apart from admiring the craftsmanship, which even I can tell is top notch. Leon strokes the gun lovingly. 'I've got a syndicate I shoot with,' he says. 'Pheasants, that sort of thing. I suppose you're quite good at it now.' He smiles eagerly at Ben. 'Let's have a shot at it together, when the season starts.'

Ben looks startled. 'Actually, I don't do any shooting.'

'Really? I thought everyone in the country did. But then you're not really country, are you. You're from the Big Smoke, like us.'

'Well, I'm country now. But actually none of the people we know around here shoot for fun. Joe, our farmer friend, has a gun but he only uses it for predators after his sheep. Cornwall isn't exactly hunting and fishing country.'

Leon looks rather doubtful but doesn't say any more, and the conversation turns to other things, including London, as it would naturally. All four of us had former lives there, and we have a fine old time reminiscing about it. We all agree, though, that we'd never go back again. 'I'm ever so happy here, even though it's only been a few weeks,' Kate says as we get ready to leave. I'm feeling a bit tipsy from all that superb red wine we drank with our 'nibbles', as Kate called them, but I'm quite sincere when I tell her that we're so pleased to have them for new neighbours.

'You're our role models,' Leon says, as we part at their doorstep. 'We want to become as much a part of this village as you have.'

'I'm sure they will,' I say to Ben as we walk down our quiet road towards home. There's a sliver of moonlight, just enough to see by, although we've brought a torch. The dark trees, bushes, and ground have changed dramatically since the snow and frost have gone. Our usual early spring has arrived with a riot of colour and bloom, the fields yellow with daffodils, the gardens dazzling with camellias. It smells like spring, too, rich and fertile.

Ben is thoughtful, and doesn't say anything. 'Don't you think Kate and Leon will settle soon?' I ask.

'Maybe. I hope so. But they're not like us, not like the other permanent house owners. They don't have to work, don't have to try to make do, like most of us.' We walk on in silence for a few moments, past the dark church, the leafless trees getting ready to come to life. Then Ben goes on, 'It can be divisive, being rich in our community. Unless you're a second homer. Everyone expects them to be loaded, and they've got to be to own a house in Cornwall and another somewhere else. But if you actually live here . . .'

I see what he means, and agree it might be harder for the Wintersons to fit in. But they will, I'm sure of it. And in the meantime, we've found some new friends. I'm already looking forward to introducing them to Annie and Pete.

CHAPTER FIVE

A Home is Not a Rental House

The magnolias are out in full now as spring gets under way, and I keep the van windows open so that I can catch whiffs of their scent, mingled with the sea air, as I drive around with the post. Signs of the season are everywhere with the greening of the earth, trees and plants. There's bird activity, too. Robins and various members of the tit family are scurrying about busily picking up twigs and grass to make their new homes. Stone curlews are getting ready to nest on farmlands and open fields. Daphne told me that one curlew nests every year in one of their arable fields. She swears they pick that particular field because Joe grows a wheat crop there, and the nest with the eggs and growing chicks will have shelter in the tall crops.

There's a wonderful human sign, too, that makes me feel that the long winter is over at last. As I drive around the lanes, walk around villages and towns on my postal route, I see, waving in the spring breeze, laundry pegged out on the clothes lines of Cornwall. What a sight! Now, this doesn't just happen in spring and summer. Usually all through the winter months, there are decent 'drying' days in every week. This winter, though, has been different. Because of the harshness of the past few months, clothes that were pegged outside froze on the line, so most were dried inside in front of wood burners or electric heaters, or tumble dried for those lucky enough to have them.

Not only do I love the smell of the clothes when they come off the line, but I feel great that I'm doing something for the environment. I read somewhere that if all households with a tumble dryer dried one laundry load a week on a washing line instead of using the dryer, they would save over 750,000 tonnes of CO_2 in a year. And so I'm pleased to see all the washing out today as I deliver the post. It's a perfect day – a bit of sun, but also plenty of wind. Over the last year I've become a kind of town crier of pegging. I get asked more and more often about the weather. 'Tessa, d'you think it'll rain this morning? Should I wait till afternoon to peg out my clothes, or do you think it'll get worse?'

I've taken to checking the local weather reports diligently to help with my advice, but more and more I notice I seem to tell instinctively what the weather will be. Somehow, I am able to read the signs, noticing things such as the way the sea swells, knowing that it means the rain is going to go a certain way; or when the seagulls fly inland, knowing there's a storm brewing. The way the birds are singing, the way the wind is blowing – all these things have seeped into my consciousness, and I seem to be more right than wrong these days when I try to predict the weather. Maybe this sixth sense makes up for my lack of green fingers!

One of my customers is actually pegging out her washing

as I drive up and head around to the back of her house where I usually leave the post. Her back garden faces the estuary with a breathtaking view of water, sky, woodland on the further shores, rocks and seabirds. The tide is out today and the few boats lie dotted on the sand, as if placed carefully by the Cornish Tourist Information Board to be as picturesque as possible. Even the sea debris – driftwood, clumps of watery turf from the river's edge, a dollop of seaweed – looks artistically placed on the damp sand, as if to show each to its best advantage. The heron, perched on one leg in the shallows, could have been posing there all morning, waiting for the first day-tripper to come and take its photo.

'Perfect drying day,' my customer calls out to me.

We both look up at the cloudless sky, feel the light but brisk breeze on our faces. 'Yep, perfect! I can't wait to get home and get my clothes out.'

She nods, a wooden peg clutched between her lips as she hangs out another garment. I approve of wooden pegs. There's something so satisfyingly old-fashioned about them that adds to the pleasure.

I tell her this and she agrees, removing the peg from her mouth and giving me a big smile. She says, 'You've got to have a proper washing line, too. No whirly things or plastic contraptions.'

We're really into this now. 'Oh, I agree,' I cry. 'And you should have a peg bag. Preferably something with sentimental value.'

'I made this one myself,' she says proudly.

'That's very suitable,' I admire her bag. 'Mine belonged to my grandmother.'

The next five minutes are spent very happily discussing the

advantages of wooden clothes hangers as opposed to plastic, and other such domestic things of fascinating importance, especially when standing in a delightful garden, filled with sea scents and birdsong, on a sunny Cornish spring day. Before I know it, I've grabbed a few pegs and together we're hanging out the rest of her washing, a few more towels, and some large items of bedding. 'Thanks, Tessa,' she says as we finish and I start to go. 'Those sheets and duvet covers are much easier with two.'

I'm humming and singing to myself as I drive along to my next village. Everywhere I look there is washing out on lines; most of my customers seem to be hanging out clothes. I chuckle as I realise that some of these items are familiar to me – I know the owner's clothes as well as I do them. Dodging the lines as I deliver their post, I know that the baker in one of the villages wears pristine white boxer shorts and has a pair for every day of the week. Today there are six pairs on the line that his wife has hung out – I assume he's wearing the seventh pair. The female doctor in the same village has extremely sexy lingerie in both black and red. What's great to see today is how many winter woollens are hanging out on the clothes lines. It's a sure sign that winter is gone for good – everyone is washing their heavy pullovers and cardigans, putting them away until next year.

When I finish work and arrive home, my new neighbour Kate is outside in her front garden talking to a tall man with wild-looking hair. As I get nearer, I see that it's Guy. He and Kate are talking earnestly and while they talk, Guy nods and some-times takes notes in a scrappy little notebook I've seen him carry around. Alongside his voluntary work for the Cat Protection Service, Guy, though a skilled carpenter, earns his rather precarious living doing odd jobs in many of the villages, as commissions for carpentry work are hard to come by. I guess that Kate has some employment for him, which he'll be glad of.

Kate calls me over to them, asks if I know Guy. After a few minutes chatting, she asks me in for a coffee. I accept happily and we start to walk towards the house. I'm assuming Guy is coming in, too, as the three of us have been talking about the work the Wintersons want done on their property, and it seemed as if the coffee invite extended to all. Guy must have assumed the same thing, for he's taken a few steps with us until he stops uncertainly. Kate says brightly, 'Thanks, Guy. I really appreciate you coming out today. And the job is yours, if you can start next week like you said.'

She says this warmly, but it's clearly a dismissal. Guy takes the hint, says he'll be back next week for sure, and says goodbye to us both. As we go inside Kate is chatty and happy, and I see that it never even occurred to her that Guy might be glad of coffee or tea before he set out on his next job. She obviously assumed he was in a hurry, I suppose, on to his next work place. It'll take her a while to learn that few people are in a hurry down here, even if they do have several jobs, a family, and a full life to live. I wonder if I should say something; maybe it's not too late and she can stop Guy from driving away. He did look dismayed when he realised he'd not been invited inside. But I decide it's not my place to say anything. Kate is a good person, and seems a sensitive one in many ways. She'll soon find out for herself.

'Tessa, good to see you,' she says as we go into the house. 'It's been hectic, trying to get the house right. Especially with Leon up in town.'

By town, she means London, where Leon goes at least once

a month for the consultancy work he mentioned. As we settle into her spacious kitchen, Kate enthuses about the work Guy is going to do on their house. Already a brand-new Aga has been installed in the kitchen, a huge gorgeous red one. It fills up the width of the room and is pumping out heat despite the warmth of the day. Kate makes me a delicious cappuccino from the machine glistening on the new marble surface and I drink it blissfully while she tells me about the insulation they're putting in, the Florentine tiles on the kitchen floor with the underfloor heating, and the wall-to-wall shelves for their collection of books, CDs, and DVDs in the sitting room. 'Guy says he can do carpentry, so he might be making our bookshelves. Leon collects old books so we want something suitable to display them. I've heard from some of the villagers that he's really good. What do you think?'

'He's excellent. I've seen some of his work. He's a fine craftsman.'

She's relieved. 'I did wonder if I should get someone down from London. Actually, I tried, but I can't get the furniture maker I know to come down here until mid-summer, far too late. It's a shame. He does such beautiful work.'

'Guy will be great,' I reassure her. I'm relieved she couldn't get her London carpenter. The locals wouldn't have taken kindly to the hiring of an Up Country workman when there are so many good ones down here in need of employment.

'I'm glad I asked you,' Kate says. 'I thought he was merely an odd-job man. I couldn't believe it when someone at the shop said he was a carpenter.'

'This is Cornwall,' I say with a smile. 'He does odd jobs, that's true; he needs the money like we all do. But he's also a terrific craftsman, like I said.'

Kate is going on with her plans. As she talks, a blackbird sings outside the open window. The two willow trees in the back are beginning to get that shimmering look trees get in spring, as if sprucing up for the great event of beginning anew. They're lovely trees, quite old. The name of the house, Treetops, obviously came from them, and the copper beech that stands at the end of their garden. Behind it is a grass field, now filled with sheep. Ewes and lambs placidly feed and rest, ambling contentedly in the warmth.

Kate follows my look out the window. We stop for a moment and listen to the blackbird, enjoy the view. Kate sighs contentedly. 'It's so lovely. It reminds me why we came here.'

As she speaks a raucous screeching sound pierces the sweet birdsong. Kate jumps. The sound comes again, louder and more grating. It's not very pleasant I must say, but it doesn't last long.

Kate cries, 'What on earth was that?'

'Oh, it's only the Humphreys' peacock. Have you met Edna and Hector yet?'

'No, not really, though I think I saw them getting into a rather ancient rusty-looking car one day.'

I laugh. 'That's their young friend, as Edna calls him. He's around eighty, takes them to the sea every so often. I'll have to introduce you.'

She looks doubtful but tries a wary smile. 'That peacock. Does it always make noises like that?'

'Well, now and again, I guess it does. They only got the peafowls last December, and with the cold weather, the peacock and hen have been inside a straw-filled shed all winter. Now it's warmer, they're out and about. And I suppose you hear the peacock's call more now that it's open windows time.' I look at her reassuringly. 'But you get used to it. I rather like it. It's nice to have a peacock in the village. Rather grand, don't you think?' Kate doesn't crack a smile at my light-hearted remark but looks quite troubled. 'Don't worry,' I say again. 'You'll get used to Emmanuel, honestly.'

'Emmanuel?'

Outside the peacock cries yet again. Really, he seems to be overdoing it; he sounds louder than ever. I do wish he'd pipe down for a bit and give Kate a chance to get used to the noise. 'That's his name, Emmanuel. Some Italian they met years ago was visiting England and looked them up. Apparently Edna and Hector stayed at his father's palazzo or something outside Rome for a time and the son wanted to see them again. Before he left, he gave them an early Christmas present. Hector's favourite carol is "O Come, O Come, Emmanuel", hence the name.' I burst into song, dragging out the Eee-man-u-el in an operatic manner.

Kate is not amused. 'A rather bizarre kind of present, don't you think?'

'The way I heard it, the Italian duke or whatever he was had peacocks wandering around his stately gardens, so his son wanted to give the Humphreys something to remind them of *la dolce vita* in Italy.'

'What?'

'You know, the good old days. Edna and Hector were thrilled. They love those two birds.'

Kate is still stressing about the noise so I change the subject quickly. Soon we start talking about a television drama we both saw the other night, forgetting the peacock and his mate for the time being.

When I leave, she walks me down the path in front of

her house. The front garden is not large but it's crammed with primroses. The ground is so golden around here at this time of year that it looks like reflected sunlight, all those primroses, bright wild daffodils and bigger cultivated ones. When I comment on the flowers, Kate says, 'Yes, they're lovely, aren't they? But we have lots more in the back. It's so large, our back garden. That's why we're getting rid of this one.'

'What?' I stare at her, dumbfounded.

She doesn't notice my surprise. 'Yes, that's what Guy is starting on next week. We're having the grass paved over. I've chosen some fantastic paving tiles from that huge garden shop outside Truro. The front garden will be our terrace; it'll extend around both sides of Treetops as well. I've ordered some amazing pots, made in Tuscany – oh Tessa, you'll love them, they're to die for! I'll put different exotic plants in them. I've got all sorts of ideas.' ·

I'm stunned. It sounds perfect for Islington perhaps, but not Treverny. It's also not very good for the environment. Apparently more and more people in towns and cities all over the country are concreting their front gardens to make more room, park their cars, whatever, and it's causing damage not only to the bird population, but also to the water drainage system. Because the rain can't drain away properly through a paved area, it causes flooding.

I can't tell Kate any of this, of course, though I'd like to. But she'd see me as being bossy and interfering, and would go ahead anyway. She's already made her plans, bought the paving tiles, and the pots. And she's so enthusiastic about it all, too. So I can't say how I really feel, but I do say, 'It's kind of a shame, isn't it, to not have this lovely front garden? It's full of wild flowers, you know, not only primroses; you'll see as the weeks go on.'

She turns to me eagerly. 'Oh, I love wild flowers, I truly do, but there are so many in the back, and all over the village. This will be something different.'

A bit of the city, I'm thinking. It's different only for our part of the world. She's bringing the city to her new home in the country.

Well, to each his own. Or her own. She's still turning out to be a good friend. I like her enthusiasm, her sense of humour. She's kind, too. She buys every new, well-reviewed novel that comes out, in hardback, and gives them away after a quick read to our village charity shop, as well as piles of children's clothes a nephew has outgrown but hardly worn. She's taken to giving me some of her better cast-offs, too, after the supper when I told her about our 'swishing' clothes swapping parties. I give her eggs sometimes, now that the hens are laying again. She tried to pay me for them but I wouldn't hear of it. 'That's what village life is like, Kate,' I told her. 'You give me some of those gorgeous clothes you don't want any more, and I give you eggs. It's a bit like bartering, you know? I do it with everyone. People give me their homegrown veg in summer, I give them a pot of damson jam I've made, or a pie, or whatever.'

Kate didn't look convinced. 'But cast-off clothes are different. I wouldn't sell them for goodness' sake, I'd give them to a charity shop if you didn't take them. Eggs are a commodity, you had to feed the hens, look after them, buy them in the first place – so you should sell your eggs. Here, take the money, please.'

'If I take it, I won't take your clothes. C'mon, Kate, I don't give you that many eggs anyway.'

In the end she accepted the gift of a dozen eggs, but reluctantly.

As we're talking, Kate continues walking with me down her path. Across the road, a woman is taking some flowers into the churchyard. Kate murmurs, 'There seem to be an inordinate number of deaths in Treverny. I've noticed how many people go to the churchyard with flowers. It's terribly worrying.'

'What do you mean?'

'Well, the radon gas, you know. I've heard some parts of Cornwall are quite badly affected, and Treverny must be the full of it. There must be more people dying here than anywhere else, judging from all the activity in the churchyard. I wish I'd known before we bought the house.'

'Oh Kate, Treverny isn't full of radon gas or any other lethal thing; in fact it's probably one of the healthiest places to live with all the sea air and unpolluted countryside. There are always people visiting churchyards down here, putting flowers on their loved ones' graves. It's not like cities, where people mostly die and are buried far away from their roots. Here people live nearby, so they can visit the graves often.'

She's so relieved that she gives my arm a quick, thankful squeeze. 'Oh I'm so glad we talked. You've no idea how it's been troubling me.'

As I go into my own home, I remind myself to warn Ben about the new paved garden next door. He won't like it either, but like me, he won't say much. It's their house after all, and what they do with it is their business.

Back home, I give the rental agency a ring. They were meant to be sending someone out a week or so ago, but they had to cancel for some reason. Too many homes suddenly being put up for rental, I suspect, but they assure me they need more, as Cornwall is even more of a holiday destination with all the Euro problems abroad, and many people forced to be more frugal. Campsites especially are booming, with many of them booked up already for the coming summer. It'll be no problem at all renting our house, I think as I look around it.

The woman on the phone jolts me by saying, 'Actually one of our consultants has just had a cancellation. She can be with you in half an hour.'

Suddenly my lovely home looks rather chaotic. Jake is lounging on his favourite armchair, the carpet looks a bit dog-hairy, and there are cushions on the floor where Amy and Will were watching television last night. There are also magazines and newspapers all over the place, not to mention a few play scripts Ben is reading, strewn around on several work surfaces, next to a batch of recipes I cut out last night from a favourite Sunday supplement and haven't put away yet.

But goodness, it's all surface stuff; I can tidy it away in minutes. 'That's fine,' I gush. 'Just wonderful. I'm ready to show you my house.'

The next half hour I rush around like a madwoman, even giving the sitting room floor a quick Hoover. By the time the rental consultant comes, my house looks perfect. Just the sort of place I'd love to rent for my own holiday.

The woman who knocks at our door exactly thirty minutes later is extremely businesslike. Navy suit, navy heels – high but not too high – crisp white blouse underneath her jacket, not too skinny. She's even carrying a briefcase. I offer her tea or coffee, which she refuses, but sits down for a moment in the armchair that Jake has just vacated. He's leaping around her in greeting but she ignores him. Thank goodness she's got dark clothes on and won't see the dog hairs that must be sticking to her trousers. I get the feeling she's not a dog lover so I put Jake out in the garden. When I get back, Ms Channing, as she's called, has pulled out a formidable sheaf of papers which she hands me. 'This is for you to read later,' she tells me. 'It gives you the requirements necessary for a rental property.'

We then go around the 'rental property'. She's taken a clipboard out of her briefcase and seems to be checking things as she goes along. I start off the tour bubbly and confident. 'This is my daughter's room. Amy's. We'll put twin beds in here, as well as in Will's room. His is smaller, but we can squeeze another bed in. That way the cottage would sleep six.'

'A good number,' she says, face non-committal. 'Don't forget that you have to have a bedside table and lamp by each bed. And a chair. Plenty of hanging space for clothes as well as a dresser. Oh, and a mirror for each bedroom as well.'

Goodness, all that? A bit fussy, I'm thinking, but OK, it's manageable.

She leaves the bedrooms and makes her way to the bathroom. 'You'll need to put a lock on that,' she says, indicating the door.

'Oh, right.' We've never had a lock on any of our doors inside. The family knows, and so do all our visitors, that if the door is shut, someone is inside, if it's open, the bathroom is free. So, a lock on the loo. Well, that won't be a problem either. So far so good.

'And you'll need locks on all the windows.' She's busy jotting things on her clipboard.

'Really? Here in this placid little village? Window locks?'

She nods. Seems a bit much, but I nod back. 'Fine.'

Ms Channing is very polite, quite nice actually, but I'm getting more and more uncomfortable as her eagle eyes begin to spot imperfections in our perfect home. Well, perfect to us anyway, but now I, too, am not so sure as she spots a couple of cracked windows at the back of the house, which we meant to get mended ages ago but never got around to. 'They'll have to be repaired,' she tells me as we go downstairs. Her eyes pierce the room, and all its hidden secrets. 'The sitting room needs repapering.' Oh dear, she's noticed the bit in the corner where it's peeling. But to repaper the whole thing? Really? 'I'm afraid so,' she says. 'Actually, the dining room, too. Make it look fresher.'

Next it is the windowsills. They've rotted slightly and need repairing as well. She looks out through the open window and I feel cheered. It's glorious out there again today, with spring at its best, flowers and foliage rampant everywhere, birds chirping away merrily. Ms Channing agrees when I mention it. 'Yes, it's lovely, really lovely. I do adore spring in Cornwall.' Abruptly she is businesslike again. 'Your gutters all need to be cleaned and drained.' She makes another mark on her clipboard. I imagine great big black Xs against our house. I feel like a schoolchild again, being marked down.

But I pull myself together. Those are only a few little things which can easily be seen to. Well, maybe not easily – glass is expensive, and new window panes won't be cheap – but it's all reasonable stuff. If it has to be done, it will be.

'I'm sure we can manage all those repairs before summer,' I say, confidence booming again.

She nods. 'Good. Now, can I see your equipment? Let's start with the kitchen.'

My confidence ebbs again. Our appliances are old and will need replacements. They're working perfectly well, almost perfectly, certainly they're good enough to do all the home cooking Ben and I do, not only for ourselves but for our many visitors. 'You'll need a microwave, of course,' Ms Channing is ticking her boxes furiously. 'Are you sure you don't have one?' She's peering around in cupboards as if we're hiding away the microwave for some strange reason.

'Yes, I'm sure we don't have one. I don't like the things.'

She looks up at me as if I'd said I don't like daffodils or little lambs frolicking in the meadows. 'Really? I couldn't live without my microwave.' She checks her list. 'Washing machine?'

'That's all right. We've had it for years and it's never given us an ounce of trouble. Works a treat. The clothes come out whiter than white,' I babble, sounding like a TV advert.

'Can I see it?'

She actually laughs out loud when she does. 'Far too old. And look at that bit of rust at the bottom. It'll never do. You'll have to get a new one.'

Seeing my face she adds kindly, 'Have a look later at the information I gave you. It tells you the high standards we require for our holiday cottages.' She's looking at all my mismatched cutlery, crockery, and glassware. 'I'm afraid none of this will do,' she informs me. 'Everything has to be matching.'

'Even eggcups?'

'Yes, even those.'

Goodness, whoever notices mismatched eggcups when they rent a cottage? We never did, when we lived in London and rented our holiday homes in Cornwall. Were the eggcups matching? Were the washing machines brand new? They worked, which was all we cared about with two young children, but we never noticed the age.

Still, the amount of money we can get for a week's rental is staggering, so we'll have to go along with it. We'll need to take out a bank loan to get the place up to scratch, but if need be, we'll do it.

However, there is more to come. As I walk Ms Channing to the car, she says, 'Oh, and you'll have to repoint this front path. I noticed on the way in that it's quite uneven.'

That's the understatement of the year. It's made up of large flat stones of various sizes. She doesn't say it, but I can tell by the amount of writing she's doing on her clipboard that the whole path will have to be redone. There is the less able, or the elderly holiday maker to consider.

When she goes, I sit down to look at the information she's given me. All the extra things we'll have to supply! A barbecue, a dryer. Cots and high chairs for babies, toys, games and books for older children. All the paraphernalia needed for a fire inside, for even in August the weather can be rainy or chilly, and besides, visitors like a cosy fire to settle in front of, even in summer. So that means supplying bags of coal, wood, tongs, brush, shovel, poker, fireguard, the whole works. The thought of strangers lighting fires in our house gives me the shivers. Will they be as careful with sparks and roaring fires as we are, especially if they haven't one in their own home? And, of course, the chimney will have to be swept professionally, and certified. The certificate has to be placed in a folder where the guest can see it. A fire blanket and extinguisher have to be provided. I'm getting more and more anxious about all this – good God, what kind of fires do holiday makers start, to warrant all this equipment?

By the time I've read all the information, I've gone right off the idea. When Ben gets home later, I tell him all about it.

'It'll cost a fortune,' he says.

'I know. We'd need a huge bank loan.'

'All the things we need to do! Not only will it take money we don't have, it'll take ages. We even need to get our LPG gas bottles checked and certified, even though they're outside. Our boiler has to be fully serviced and certified. There's so much more, as well.'

We talk it all through carefully. Finally we decide that, yes, we'll do it – in the end, it will earn us money. But we'll take it slowly. Getting all the things done will take time as well as money, and we want to do it properly, don't want to rush things. If we can't get our home rented before this summer, we'll go for the Easter trade next year to begin with.

We're both happy about this decision. 'As long as it doesn't change our place too much,' I say as we go into the kitchen, start to prepare the evening meal together. Will and Amy, home now and outside with their friends in the village, will be disappointed that we won't be camping out for a couple of months this year, but I'm secretly pleased. And who knows, maybe our cottage will be ready by the end of summer. But if not, there is always next year. As everything in Cornwall, there's no need to hurry.

Annie has booked the crystal therapy session for one of my days off. We set out together on a drizzly morning which doesn't damp our spirits in the slightest. We plan on a proper day out – an inexpensive lunch in a tiny café after our session, then a browse around the better charity shops.

There is a lurid purple sign outside the door of the crystal therapist's office which is tucked down a back street past the bus station. In bold black letters are the words CHAKRA READINGS and CRYSTAL HEALING. 'What are chakras?' Annie says as we knock on the door.

It opens so quickly that we both involuntary step back, nearly falling down the concrete step. An extremely tall, extremely skinny man with a wispy salt-and-pepper beard and long straggly hair dyed ebony black says, 'Chakras are the energy centres in the body. Come in, please.'

He ushers us into a long narrow room cut in two by a brown velvet curtain. The room has high ceilings which is just as well, for the man must be six foot six inches tall at least. He's dressed entirely in black which emphasises his skeletal frame, the pallor above his beard. 'My name is Gawain,' he says grandly, in what sounds vaguely like a French accent. 'Please sit.' He indicates two scruffy wing armchairs. 'You will excuse me, *s'il vous plaît*, while I prepare myself.'

He disappears down the corridor somewhere, shutting the door as he goes. Annie and I look at each other. 'Gawain?' she whispers. 'More like Gary, I bet. There's definitely an Essex twang there underneath that phoney French stuff.'

'Shall we make a run for it?'

'Too late, he's coming.'

Gawain enters the room, looking exactly as he did before except now he has a huge pendant around his neck. It's round and ivory-coloured with a black stone in the centre which stares out from the middle of his chest like a third eye. 'Creepy,' Annie mouths at me when his back is turned.

He takes a seat facing us and asks where we found out about him. Annie tells him about the two free tokens she found in the local newspaper and he can't hide the disappointed look on his face. Then he brightens as he says, 'But of course you must understand that one session might not be enough, especially if any of your chakras are blocked. Now, who would like to be first?'

Stifling a smile, Annie gives me a little shove. I shove her back. We engage in a silent tussle while Gawain pulls back the velvet curtain, revealing some kind of tall bed or massage table. Shelves on the walls contain crystals of various sizes, shapes, and colours. More velvet curtains cover the windows, blocking out any natural light there might be. A coloured lamp with a red bulb shines malignly in the corner, providing the only light. I wonder if the room doubles as a brothel after dark.

Gawain lights several tall candles. Now it looks as if he's preparing for a Black Mass. I don't know whether to laugh or to cry, and obviously Annie doesn't either, for she's clutching my arm and giving me odd pokes. I'm not sure if they mean 'let's get out of here' or 'what a hoot this is'. My poke back at her means 'how in hell did you get me into this?'

The next minute I'm lying on my back on the table, or bed, or whatever it is while Annie disappears behind the velvet curtain, though I'm sure she'll find a way to peek inside to see what's going on. Gawain plays some music on a small CD player and seems to have trouble adjusting it to the right sound, for a blare of noise nearly blasts me off the table before it quietens to a background hum of New Age sounds, high-pitched and eerie, with birds twittering in the background along with the rush of gentle waves. I guess it's supposed to put me in the mood but it only makes me wish I were walking on the beach with Annie instead of stuck here in this weird room.

Gawain takes a pink quartz the size of a fist and lays it on my forehead, letting it rest there while muttering something incomprehensible with a few French words thrown in. Then he does the same to my throat, my chest and my belly, changing the quartz for an amethyst somewhere down the line and shaking his head mournfully from time to time as if distressed by what my chakras are up to. He's obviously new at this sort of thing for his pendant with the Evil Eye hits me twice in the face while he's moving the crystal. Finally he takes it off with a very un-French swear word that he doesn't think I hear, for he turns back to me full of smiling charm once more.

As the quartz rests on my chest, Gawain tells me my heart chakra is ailing. But then it seems they all are, which naturally will entail more sessions, but, he assures me, he has a special offer of three for the price of two.

When my turn is over, Gawain once again leaves us 'to prepare for the next healing session'.

'He's gone out for a smoke,' I whisper to Annie. 'I could smell it on him last time. You have a sniff when you go in there.'

'Me, go in there? Not in a million years.'

Gawain, back again, says to Annie, '*Entrez vous*, madam.' Then, more prosaically, 'Your turn.'

Annie shakes her head. 'Oh Gawain, I'm so sorry but my friend here is exhausted after her treatment and I'm taking her home. Another time, perhaps.'

He frowns. 'The free offer only lasts until the end of the month.' Turning to me, he asks when I'd like my next appointment. When I say vaguely that I'll ring him when I'm ready, he knows he's lost us. He's barely civil to us as he sees us to the door, practically shoves us out. His French accent is totally gone. Annie was right, he's definitely an Essex man.

'Well, that was an experience,' I say, as Annie and I head for a café and a much needed coffee. 'Do you think we were his first ever customers?'

'His last, too, if he doesn't get his act together. He's been reading too many wizard books.'

'It's a shame, really. A man like that gives all alternative therapies a bad name, and some of them are quite good.'

'I'm sure crystal therapy is good, too, in the right hands,' Annie has found a café and is pulling me towards it as she keeps talking. 'I looked it up on the net before we came out and it's quite an ancient therapy. The Hopi Native Americans used it in Arizona, and the Hawaiian Islanders still do apparently.'

'Well, Gawain's hands were definitely the wrong ones.'

'Too skinny.'

'Chalky.'

'Bony. And did you see his fingernails? Far too long!'

We start to laugh. Inside the café I say, 'The poor man. Just trying to make a living, like the rest of us.'

Annie will have none of that. 'Fleecing us, you mean. I'm all for people making ends meet any way they can, even Gary from Essex, but not if they're fleecing others.'

She's getting so indignant that I remind her he didn't get a penny from us. 'He must think he's good,' I muse, 'giving away free sessions. He must really think people will come back for more.'

'Poor Gawain.'

'Poor Gary.'

Later after lunch, some retail therapy at the vintage second-hand shop, and a great many laughs, Annie puts something in my hand. It's a tiny pink quartz stone, no bigger than a finger-nail. 'A souvenir,' she says. 'I picked it up in that tiny gift shop opposite the store where you had gone to buy some socks for Ben. A memento of another successful girlie day together. I feel my chakras are positively glowing.'

'Mine, too. Positively radiating,' I say, as arm in arm we head back to the car and our respective homes.

CHAPTER SIX

Roosting Rooks and Piercing Peacocks

I can hear the screeching as I walk down through the village towards the Humphreys' house. 'Goodness, Tessa, what's that?' Kate Winterson has come rushing down the road after me, looking a bit panicky.

Another raucous noise, even louder than the first screech, nearly drowns out my reply. Kate cries, 'What did you say?' She's stopped walking towards the sound, clearly terrified.

'It's only the peacock,' I shout. 'Emmanuel, remember? I told you about him a week or so ago, belongs to Edna and Hector at Poet's Tenement. You've heard him before.'

'Oh, God! The peacock? Are you sure? The nasty creature is sounding louder every day. I thought it was human. Someone being attacked.'

'This is rural Cornwall, not London,' I say cheerily, trying to get that anxious look off her pale face.

She looks doubtful. 'Isn't some kind of panther supposed to be stalking the countryside?'

'That's Dartmoor. Or Exmoor. Take your pick. Maybe even Bodmin has rumours of those things, I'm not sure. But even if they exist, Kate, we're nowhere near any of those places. And if they do exist, they certainly do not attack humans.'

She still looks uneasy, but she's now walking down the road with me instead of stopping in the middle and refusing to go on.

'You still haven't met the Humphreys, have you?' I ask. 'Lovely couple. C'mon, I'm going there now. I'll introduce you to them.' I smile. 'And to Emmanuel.'

'That's the last thing I want to meet. Sounds like a dozen peacocks over there.'

'Only two. Emmanuel and the peahen. The Duchess, she's called. But it's only Emmanuel who makes that noise.'

We've walked through the churchyard where the magnolias are out, full and white and pink. Everything is fresh and sweet smelling. 'Isn't it gorgeous?' I say, but before I finish, Emmanuel shrieks again, sounding louder as we get nearer. 'He's quite mature, I believe, in full feather. He's magnificent when he fans out his tail. All that iridescent blue and green, stunning.'

'I know what a peacock looks like,' she says, snapping at me. This isn't like Kate. She might be a bit nervy and over-anxious, but never snappy. 'I hope the ridiculous bird doesn't carry on like that all spring and summer.'

I try to answer but another cry from Emmanuel drowns me out. Kate moans, 'Who in God's name can live with that?' She puts her hands over her ears.

'Well, I guess we all do. I admit when Emmanuel and the Duchess were first let out, his cries were a bit jarring. But you get used to it. We have, anyway.'

'Does he let up, then?'

'Uh, I'm not sure. Though I'm certain he will once he gets used to living in a new place. You'll hardly notice his cries soon, trust me. We don't any more. It's just part of living in a rural area, like the noise of tractors, or lambs bleating for their mums.'

She looks doubtful and I can't blame her. I don't have the heart to tell her that the peacock's cries are completely unpredictable. At least Emmanuel's are. Like geese, he squawks when someone walks into the Humphreys' garden, carrying on until they reach the door. 'Better than our old brass door knocker, Tessa,' Hector told me proudly a few days ago. 'We know when anyone is there. It's wonderful!'

Not so wonderful for the rest of the village perhaps, though I didn't say so. But the Humphreys are so well liked, and have lived at Poet's Tenement for ever, or so it seems, that everyone is putting up with the bird's shrieks. And it's true what I said to Kate, that you do get used to the sound after a time. Besides, Edna told me that he'll calm down when he gets used to being outside. 'It's the joy of spring in his veins, Tessa,' she beamed at me through her thick specs. 'It's the newness of everything. Once summer sets in he'll be quiet as a mouse, I'm sure of it.'

I have my doubts, but what do I know about peacocks?

I ask Kate again, 'D'you want to come to meet Edna and Hector?' She has walked me as far as their house, where the clematis, scrambling all over it, is out in bloom. Some of the upstairs windows are covered over with fronds of leaves and flowers. Doug tried to remove it once when he was doing his weekly gardening for the couple, but neither of them would let him. 'Better than curtains, maid,' Hector had said. 'Lot less bother.'

Kate definitely does not want to meet them. 'Maybe some other time,' she says evasively. 'I don't want to face that creature with the feathers,' she shudders.

'Kate,' I protest, 'Emmanuel doesn't bite, nor does his Duchess. She's ever so quiet, by the way. He's loud and bossy, but he doesn't go for people. I think the Italian man got them from a zoo. They weren't caged or anything, but wandered around the public paths and the picnic tables. They're used to people.'

But Kate isn't convinced, and we say goodbye, planning to meet one evening the next week, the four of us. I hope by then she'll have got used to the peacock's cry.

Edna and Hector are in their front garden, both dressed in baggy cotton trousers and some kind of striped kaftan on top. One of them has purple and yellow stripes going horizontally, the other has red and pink vertical ones. Both look faded and are patched in places. I'm no longer surprised at the bizarreness of their clothes, all the bits and pieces they've picked up over the years. Emmanuel greets me with his usual cry and then ignores me while Edna feeds him morsels of cheese. 'I've tried so hard to wean him from cheese,' she says with a sigh. 'I'm not sure dairy food is that good for him. But the children at the zoo fed him their cheese sandwiches; he's quite addicted to it.'

'And the Duchess?' I ask.

'She's more partial to ice cream, I'm afraid. We do treat her to a scoop of Cornish vanilla now and again, since it's got warmer. She's such a sweet thing.'

When the peafowl realise there is no food left, they strut away to the back garden. Emmanuel is mercifully quiet. But now there is another noise. Some rooks are having a conversation in the holm oak. We watch them for a few moments then I ask, 'Have you had someone look at the tree?'

They are both silent for a few moments until Edna says, 'We contacted the tree surgeon you told us about. One of your customers, I believe. William Woods.'

'Yes, that's right.'

She beams. 'Such a lovely boy. I asked him if he had an older relative called Sydney with the same surname. It turns out to be his grandfather. Dear Sydney, such a nice young man, he was. But William said he's become somewhat reclusive.'

As usual, it's a small world in these parts. We go back to the topic of the oak. I say, 'William, or Woody as everyone calls him, is fantastic. He knows everything about trees.' I'd met him and his girlfriend, Holly, last year, after they finished training at a college in Devon, when they moved into a caravan on a half-acre of land on one of my routes. Woody is Cornish born, another young man who can't afford to buy property in his home county, with house prices still sky high despite their falling dramatically in other parts of the country. The caravan belongs to his grandfather, the same Sydney that Edna mentioned, as does the land and a small tumble-down cottage. Woody and Holly shouldn't be there; the caravan is supposed to be a holiday let only, but so far no one knows they're living there permanently. That is, most people know, but no one tells the authorities. Too many people are just about getting by these days, not only in Cornwall but everywhere. Here at least, most keep silent about what others are doing, as long as it doesn't hurt anyone or infringe on anyone else's rights. Anyway, neither Woody nor Holly want it to be permanent, but so far they don't seem to have any other option.

'So what did Woody say?' I persist. 'He came over, then? Saw the tree?'

To my surprise, Hector's reply is gruff. 'I don't want to talk about it, maid.'

That's so not like Hector, to be abrupt like that. He's already turned his back from me and is walking around the tree, looking up at its branches, feeling the trunk.

Edna says, 'We phoned this Woody, and he came out to take a look at the tree. We hoped he'd tell us the tree had some kind of curable disease, but we knew in our hearts it was worse than that. He said it looked poorly, "staggy headed", he called it. Some of the branches have died, and look at the leaves.'

I stare up at the tree and see that many of the leaves are looking slightly droopy. 'So what was the verdict?'

'He confirmed what we knew all along. Our wonderful tree is dying.'

Edna's eyes fill with tears. We don't speak for a moment then I say, 'Could the hard winter be to blame?'

She takes out a bright blue hankie, takes off her owl-like glasses and wipes her eyes. Putting the spectacles back on she says, 'Holm oaks don't like frost, so the winter didn't help. But it's old age. This tree is ancient, you know.' She gives a rueful smile. 'Like Hector and me.'

It's the first time I've heard either of them make any reference to their age. As long as I've known them, they've not seemed to make any concession to it either, carrying on in much the same way they did when they were younger, according to the locals. They don't travel now as they used to, that's the only difference. They still read copious amounts, newspapers and books, quite hefty ones on history, politics, nature, and a few novels in between. I've seen them lying open on the kitchen table, heard Edna and Hector discussing passages. They also play chess every evening. And of course their daily walk in the

garden for a good half hour, rain or shine, keeps them physically fit. Not to mention the tai chi that Hector tried to
demonstrate not long ago in their kitchen.

So I'm quite thrown to hear Edna calling herself and Hector
ancient, even though of course it's true. But then she pulls
back her fragile shoulders, looks me straight in the eyes through
her thick glasses, and says firmly, 'But of course we have
weathered the winter cold and frosts far better than our poor
old oak.'

Hector has made a full circle of the tree and has come
around to stand in front of us. His face, wrinkled and pale
like a scrunched up sheet of white paper, looks sad. 'I shall
miss that tree. But I don't believe it is dying. Or rather, of
course it is, we are all dying in a manner of speaking, but like
me, I believe the tree has at least a bit of time left.' He takes
a deep breath and adds, 'I've always believed that one is never
so old that one cannot hope for another day. So we shall see.'

I look up at the tree again. It's massive, the branches heavy
with dark green leaves. For the first time I notice just how
close it is to the Humphreys' house. If it fell, it would crash
right through the roof.

The thought gives me the shivers. I say, 'But – what does
Woody think? Isn't it dangerous, leaving the tree and just waiting
for it to die? What if it keels over and lands on Poet's
Tenement?'

Edna says, 'Nonsense. It won't happen that quickly.'

Hector agrees. 'Anyway, even if there was that chance, we
couldn't have it taken down. We wouldn't dream of disturbing
the rooks.'

As if they understand this, the birds start crying out to each
other again. From behind the house, Emmanuel, who has been

quiet for a change, adds his voice to the din. When it quiets down Edna says, 'Hector is right. The rooks have lived here for years.

Hector nods. 'I can't remember when there wasn't a rookery in this tree. It's one of my earliest memories. As long as the rooks are here, the tree stays.'

His wife's head is bobbing up and down in agreement. 'Hector is right,' she says solemnly. 'We can't let the rooks down. This tree is their home, just as Poet's Tenement is ours.'

As she finishes speaking, Hector takes her hand. The two stand there holding hands tightly, looking at me almost defiantly, as if I were about to uproot the old tree right there and then. 'But,' I begin, before hesitating, not quite knowing how to go on. 'You said a month or so ago, that the rooks knew something was up. They were getting restless, you said.'

'So I did, maid,' Hector says. 'And so they were. They knew their old tree wasn't quite right. But Edna and I, we've talked to them, reassured them that as long as we're here in Poet's Tenement, their home in the oak is secure.'

I can't say anything to this. It's their life, their house, their tree. And, I could add, their rooks, if wildlife can be owned. Certainly this rookery has been part of Poet's Tenement for generations. I take my leave of the Humphreys, promising to drop some eggs off to them before I make my way home.

As I throw some bread to my hens, Pavarotti, my cockerel, crows loudly with the joys of spring. I throw him a fat crust and mutter, 'Fine, it's a gorgeous day, I agree, but pipe down a bit, please? The peacock is making enough noise for one village these days; don't add to it.'

I see Woody the next day. As I drive along the dirt track towards the caravan, I see him digging at the edge of the field. I want a word with him, so I stop the van, grab his post, and walk up to him. It's actually addressed to his father's house, as officially no one lives in the caravan, but I'm happy to deliver there.

'Thanks, Tessa,' he says as he takes a couple of letters, glancing at them. His face falls. 'Nothing interesting, though. I got ten quid in premium bonds and I keep hoping, but my number never comes up.'

'Maybe next month, right?'

'Yeah, right. Mebbe. Pigs might fly, too,' he shrugs his shoulders.

'That looks like hard work, what you're doing.'

'Making an allotment. Trying to anyway. Not easy when there's nothing to begin with but a grass field.'

I see that he's already edged out a good-sized plot with the shovel and is now digging up the turf. He follows my look and says, 'This is only the start. Next is getting out the fork, breaking up the turf and earth, picking out the weeds. I want to have it done so Holly can get some veg in. We thought we could start a bit of a business, see? Eventually sell the veg and stuff up on the road, for all the folk that come down here renting cottages and all.'

'Great idea.' I try to sound more enthusiastic than I feel. I don't tell him about all the others I've met who have the same idea. Starting market gardens, selling eggs, goat's milk, and what have you. Still, why can't they all make it work? More people are having 'stay-cations' as the newspapers have coined it, staying in England what with air travel unpredictable with volcano dust, strikes and terrorist scares, not to mention the high prices abroad now. The joy of staying in England for a holiday is becoming more and more appealing, and as usual, Cornwall is the first choice of many.

Woody talks about his new project for a while and then I get a chance to ask him about the Humphreys' tree. 'Yeah, I went out there, had a look. Funny old couple, aren't they? Kinda old-fashioned but with-it at the same time, if you know what I mean. They had on the oddest clothes, too. But they were friendly-like, I couldn't help liking 'em.'

'Good, I like them, too. So what's up with the tree?'

'Oh, it definitely should come down. No telling how long it'll last, could be a few years, could come down next winter. The hard frost didn't help, lasted too long. Holm oaks don't like bitter winds or below freezing temperatures much, that's why it's lived so long here, right near the coast. We don't usually get 'em like we did this year and the end of last. Mental, that was. I never saw so much ice and snow.'

'Woody, did you tell the Humphreys what you just told me? That the tree is dangerous now?'

He looks almost offended at this, as if I've injured his professional pride. 'Of course I did. I told them it should come down immediately, actually. Which is true. You know we get these fierce summer storms sometimes. One of those could take that tree right down onto their house. I told 'em sure enough.'

'Oh dear.'

'What's the matter?'

'I was hoping you could convince them that the tree would have to come down, but it sounds like you've already tried. They told me they were worried about the rooks.'

Woody nods. 'Yeah, they talked about the rooks to me, too. Said the birds were nesting now and they wouldn't hear of taking down the tree when they were laying eggs and all that. I hear what they're saying, but it's still a safety issue. Summer storms, as I said.' He rolls his eyes towards the heavens as if a wrathful wind sent by God himself was about to blow down on us. 'But it's up to them, I told 'em. If they want to wait till the chicks fly outta the nest to take down that tree, that's up to them. I told 'em to give me a ring when they're ready. Can't do more'n that, right?'

'Right,' I agree. 'You've done all you can. Well, fingers crossed we have a calm spring and summer.'

By the time I get back to the postal van, Woody is digging away. I silently wish him luck on his new project. I drive up the potted lane to the old farmhouse where Sydney lives. He's outside, waiting for me like he often does, winter or summer. Despite having his grandson and Holly in the caravan, I know he gets lonely, living a Spartan existence in his bachelor household. His wife died decades ago and his daughter married a Welshman, moved to Cardiff, and as far as I know, Sydney has no relatives other than Woody in Cornwall. There are no near neighbours either, and no one to chat to over the garden fence. I know Woody and Holly keep an eye on him – he's in his eighties and has problems with his heart – but they're young, and busy struggling to make a living.

Sydney smiles eagerly when he sees me. He's a nice-looking man with a head of thick snow-white hair, a pleasant wrinkled face, and a tall broad body in pretty good shape for his age. As usual he's dressed immaculately in a checked cotton shirt, the kind you buy in stores that sells goods to farmers, and a plain blue tie. Sometimes the colour of the shirt or tie varies, but that's about all.

Except today. Despite the warmer weather, Sydney is wearing a pair of fingerless gloves, a rich chestnut colour with a bright fuchsia stripe across the knuckle and around the thumb. It's those gloves again, the same ones that Melanie and Tufty wear in the shop, knitted by Tufty's mother. I've never seen Sydney wear anything like them before; in winter he wears plain old-fashioned brown leather gloves with all the fingers intact.

I've got to ask him about them. 'Oh, Holly got the gloves for me. She saw the shopkeepers in Poldowe wearing them. Holly told them about my arthritic thumbs so that nice Melanie woman gave her a pair for me.' He goes on to tell me that even in summer his thumb joints ache, and the gloves have been a godsend. I smile quietly to myself thinking how they are spreading amongst my customers.

We chat about Woody and Holly, their market garden venture, and the fact that there's not much work for Woody with trees. 'He got all qualified, thought he'd be made, but there don't be much call for a tree surgeon round here.' Sydney looks quite low, thinking about this.

'It takes a while,' I reassure him. 'Word has to get around. He'll start finding tree jobs as people get to know about him.

He cheers up, and asks me in for a cuppa. I decline but would love a drink of water. We go into the kitchen which is bare, clean and functional, but rather depressing. There is an old-fashioned white and blue dresser, the kind that was fashionable in the 1950s, with smoky windows on the cupboards that house a few plates, some cups and bowls. That, and a plain pine table, with three chairs, are all there is in the room other than an ancient cooker and fridge, and a sink with a couple of taps. There are no kitchen implements in sight, no saucepans, cookbooks, pictures – only bare walls painted a dull green. Everything seems lifeless. There's nothing living here but Sydney, who seems to be only half alive himself, functioning on a very basic level. There's not even a houseplant anywhere.

Having a sudden brainwave, I blurt out, 'Sydney, would you like a cat?'

He looks at me as if I'm mad, making a suggestion like that out of the blue. I hadn't thought it through before I spoke, but suddenly a plan forms in my devious mind. Sydney needs something warm and alive in his house, to warm and energise him. And Clara needs to find a home for some of her cats. What could be simpler than that?

A few days later, when I drive up to Sydney's cottage he's not out front waiting for me. I'm instantly concerned. Is he ill? Has he fallen? Woody and Holly aren't in their caravan or out in the field – perhaps Sydney is in hospital? I go up to the house and am relieved when the door opens and Holly grabs me, pulling me inside. 'Quick, c'mon in, can't leave the door open or the cats will escape. Clara says they need to stay inside for a few days until they get used to their new home.'

Cats? More than one? My plan has been even more successful than I'd hoped, for indeed there are two half-grown felines, one black and grey, the other a multi-coloured tabby, swishing their tails at me from under the kitchen table. Sydney is actually crouched on the floor, calling out to them, making soft mewing noises to entice them from their shelter. Holly, who is pert and tiny, with red and green streaks in her mass of hair, shakes her head in delight as she nods towards the elderly man. The half dozen silver and bronze earrings in each ear shimmer and sparkle in the hazy sunlight coming in through the kitchen window. The sad house of a few days ago is bursting with light and life.

'Look at Sydney,' Holly whispers. 'Totally changed since that cat lady, Clara, came out with the bloke who drives the van. They brought the cats and Woody's granddad has been over the moon.'

Woody, who has been helping Sydney try to coax the cats out, says, 'They're really quite tame, just nervous every time a new person comes into the house.'

Sydney is standing by now and greets me with the happiest smile I've seen yet on his face. 'I got to thank you,' he says to me. 'Clara phoned right after you gave her my number. I didn't expect her to do it so soon, y'know, after I told you I'd be willing to help out, give one of the strays a home. I didn't know there are so many. After we talked, I said I'd have two. They're from the same litter, y'see, so I sort of thought they shouldn't be split up.'

'Quite right, too. I know Clara and Guy will be pleased they've come to such a good home.'

'Oh, I hope so. Clara said they'll come out later, to see that we're all getting on just fine.' He looks fondly at Holly as he goes on, 'This maid here went and made some scones for me, so's I can offer it to the cat people when they come out.'

Holly looks at me and winks. Not only cats for company, but Clara and Guy, too. They're sensitive souls and could obviously tell Sydney was lonely.

When Holly walks me out to my van, I notice her fingerless gloves. Bright pink with a deep silvery stripe in the usual two places. She sees me looking, takes them off sheepishly. 'Yeah, far too warm this time of year, I know, but I got them from the shop in Poldowe for Sydney and couldn't resist this pair for me. Aren't they cool? Will be great in autumn. I only grabbed them now as a protection against cat scratches. Tessa, that was an ace idea. I thought of a dog, but Sydney lost his favourite dog five years ago and vowed he'd never have another. I never thought of cats.'

'Well, I deliver post to Clara, so I know she's always needing homes for them.'

'Brilliant plan, absolutely brill.' Her animated face suddenly turns pensive. 'It'll give him something to worry about, other than me and Woody. He frets about us constantly, especially me. He likes me about, but is scared I'll leave cause I can't get work.'

'Would you? Leave?'

'No way, I love Woody, love living with him,' she sighs. 'But it's tough. I do need a job.' Her pixie-like face, a perfect oval with huge blue eyes, the red and green streaked fringe of hair covering her eyebrows, brightens again. 'Still, we've got the allotment. Mebbe I'll be a whiz at growing veg!'

'I hope you're better than I was,' I laugh. As I get into the van, I see that Woody has come out. He has one arm around Holly's shoulders and he waves goodbye with the other. Sydney comes out, too, making sure the kitchen door is tightly shut, and stands next to the young couple. They seem happy and together, and I hope it lasts a long time.

March continues to make up for the hard winter by being even more mild than usual, and every week feels warmer. In this part of Cornwall, spring always comes earlier than anywhere else in England, so it is magical now. Going to work is almost blissful, the dawns are stunning over the sea and surrounding countryside. Birdsong fills the morning sky: larks, blackbirds, and robins join the chorus, and before that there are owls crying and calling in the starlit nights. This morning, as I deliver my post, I see six buzzards flying over a wooded copse, making their distinctive high calls. They look so graceful, gliding as if free-falling on those massive wings. I've noticed so many more around this year, noticed, too, how the rabbits, on which buzzards feed, have increased in numbers as well. Familiarity with the countryside we've made home has grown with each year. At first it was all new and wondrous, and although the wonder is still there, in place of the novelty of everything has come a deep sympathy with the land and the creatures that inhabit it. The connection between all things in nature – human beings included – has become so much a part of me since settling here. Nothing lives and dies in isolation: foxes are killed so rabbits increase, rabbits mean more food available so the buzzards increase. And so the cycle goes on.

This fresh spring morning is full of things I never knew before we moved here. I couldn't even have identified the buzzard I see nearly every day sitting on the same telegraph pole. I pass a meadow of fine-looking sheep and stop to admire them. Many of the ewes are pregnant, and now I can tell which are carrying young and which are merely carrying too much fat. I also know what that blue mark is on a ewe's back, something I used to wonder about when we lived in London and only holidayed in Cornwall. It lets the farmer know which ewes the ram has serviced when he's put in the field with them. The ram's chest is marked with the special blue paint and when he mounts a ewe, he leaves his mark on her fleece.

I've grown more familiar with the sea, too. As I deliver the post in Morranport on this fine day, I watch the way the waves are moving and somehow I know, without knowing how I know, that the light wind freshening the air is coming from the west. The tide is high, too; it's a spring tide, lapping right up to the sea wall. The scent of it is heady with seaweed and salt. I know it's a spring tide rather than a neap tide because the moon was full last night. I'd never heard of a neap tide before, and now I know that it's a kind of a low high tide, which, like all tides, is governed by the moon. A neap tide only occurs when the moon is a quarter or three-quarters full, so that's how I know this must be a spring tide. I haven't looked up such facts in a book or googled them – this seems to be knowledge I've acquired by listening to those who live by the sea, fishermen, their wives and children, and others who were born and grew up on the Cornish coast. I've also learned that during the low spring tide is the best time to find unusual shells and strange, tiny sea creatures that are revealed when the sea peels right back from the beach.

The post office and shop in Morranport is run by a feisty eighty-something-year-old who makes me realise, encouragingly, that eighty is the new fifty. Nell is a fun, flirty, buxom Cornishwoman who has been running the post office for years but has been threatening retirement off and on for a decade or so, according to the villagers here. The year I arrived, I took her seriously, and was happily surprised when she was still there months later. Nell is wearing a bright yellow fluffy jumper that matches a paper daffodil she's tucked into her short, unruly white hair. This is something new, and I wonder what's up. Perhaps, like me, she's celebrating the joys of spring. I'm about to ask when I see she's talking to a man of about the same age, though I can't quite recognise him as he's half hidden by a shelf of postcards.

'Sydney, you best be off now,' she's saying to him, though her body language is saying otherwise. She's smiling flirtatiously at him.

I recognise Woody's granddad now. He's saying shyly, 'There's not any customers here, Nell.'

Nell pushes him away in a gesture of mock annoyance. 'Are

you saying that I don't work when the customers be gone? Why, if you could see the paperwork, and the stocktaking, and organising, and managing, you'd be wondering I had the time to wish you a good morning. Shame on you, Sydney.'

Her words, combined with her body language – Nell hasn't made a move away from Sydney – are confusing him, though he's obviously enjoying her banter for he's not moving either but smiling sheepishly at her. Finally, Nell notices me looking at them. 'And what you be grinning at, my maid? Are you thinking I be wasting the post office time instead of working?' She glares at me, but I know her well, now. She's a sweetheart underneath her stern looks and gruff words, and we get on just fine.

'If everyone worked as hard as you did, Nell, the Royal Mail would be rolling in money. This must be the busiest post office and shop in Cornwall.'

As if to prove my words, the place fills up and there are now a couple of people waiting at the little post office window. Nell goes off at once to serve them and have a pleasant exchange of gossip, while I say hello to Sydney who is looking quite sprightly, clean shaven, and with a fresh haircut. 'How're the cats?' I ask after we've talked about the glorious weather. 'I didn't see them about when I last delivered your post.'

'Oh, they'll have been sunning themselves out and about somewhere. Dear'ums, both of them. Such friendly creatures. They don't half eat, though. Seems I been popping out every day to the shop here to pick up another tin of cat food. Nell has been such a help. She's had cats for years, knows the kind of grub they're partial to.'

Aha, I'm thinking, so that's how this flirtation has started, for that's definitely what it looked like, that little exchange with

Nell. Morranport is Sydney's closest village, and about as far as he goes these days in his ancient Mini, so of course he'll get his provisions here. I chuckle to myself, thinking that the cats have certainly cheered him up, got him out of the house more often. From the look of it, he's been a frequent visitor here lately.

By now the shop is even more crammed with people buying provisions for a picnic, a bucket and spade for the little ones, cold drinks, and various other odds and ends. Sydney says, 'Nell's right, you know. The shop seems to be getting busier and busier, and it's not even the Easter holidays yet.'

'It will be in another week.'

'She'll be run off her feet, poor woman.' He looks truly upset at this.

'Oh, Nell can handle it,' I say to reassure him.

He looks even more distressed. 'But she shouldn't have to. That's why I suggested Holly.'

'What?'

He takes my elbow gently, leads me to the tinned tomatoes and baked beans in the corner of the shop to keep out of the way of customers who keep bumping into us as they browse around the tiny space. 'You know – Holly, Woody's girlfriend. Such a sweet little maid.

'Yes, I know who you mean, Sydney, I was asking what it was you were suggesting to Nell about her.'

He takes my elbow again and leans his face down towards mine. I get a whiff of aftershave. It smells like something he's had in his bathroom cupboard for decades, but at least it's not too overpowering. He has to stoop down to make sure I hear, for his voice has dropped to a whisper. 'Holly needs a job, and Nell needs help in the shop. You see what I'm getting at?' He straightens up triumphantly, looking as if he's solved several world problems in one go.

I say, 'Have you mentioned this to Nell?'

He nods. 'The other day.' His look of triumph falters. 'She acted like she didn't hear a word I said. She's a wonderful girl, our Nell, but she can be a mite stubborn at times, y'know.'

Nell, stubborn? The understatement of the year, I nearly said. And I've never heard her described as a girl before. Sydney is going on, 'Any chance of helping me in this, Tessa? Nell likes you, she'll listen to you.'

I tell him I'll try, because I think it's a good idea. Morranport, as well as St Geraint and all the coastal areas of Cornwall, doubles or even triples in size during the school holidays and summer months, and Nell certainly is run off her feet. She still has the locals who come into the post office with pack-ages to mail, stamps to buy, cars to tax, and all the sundry services post offices continue to provide, despite the Internet taking over many of these things. The villagers like the face to face contact, the chats, the walk to this tiny post office perched practically on the sea. For some, it's their only contact with other people except for their post deliverer. So Nell has these to deal with, along with the extra visitors buying shovels, spades, and fishing nets, and day-trippers buying ice creams, cold Cokes, and the Cornish pasties Nell gets in from the bakery.

I get a chance to talk to Nell alone before I leave. For a few moments the shop is clear and I jump at the opportunity. Nell hardly hears me out before interrupting, 'You be saying I'm too old for this job? That it's time I be put to pasture? Retired? Or just shot and dumped into the pond, like they used to be doing with lame horses in the old days?'

'Oh, Nell, of course not. Listen, not even I could handle all the people who come in here in summer, and I'm about thirty years younger than you are.'

'You got some cheek, maid, thinking you be knowing how old I be,' she glares at me, but her eyes are dancing with fun.

She's in a mellow mood now so I push my advantage, talk to her about help, at least from now until summer's end to start with. She knows Holly, and likes her, so that's no hurdle, but she still stubbornly insists that she absolutely does not need any help at all in the post office or shop.

I'm about to give up the campaign when I have a brainwave. I say enticingly, 'Sydney's so fond of Holly; she's like a daughter to him. He would be so happy if she found work, especially here with you, Nell. He thinks the world of you.'

She looks pleased even though she's doing her best to look stern. 'Hmmph,' she says. She's not usually a woman of few words so that's encouraging.

I go on, 'One thing does worry me. With Holly here as well as you, you'll never be able to get rid of Sydney. He'll be hanging around the shop even more than he seems to be doing since he got those cats, always in your way. Nice as he is, I know you wouldn't want that.'

Nell clears her throat, 'D'you know, I be thinking while you be nattering away, that I have forgotten how crazy it be in summertime. Why sometimes so many folk are crammed into this little place that drawing a breath be near impossible.' She waves me an offhand goodbye and I leave with my bag of post for the residents of Morranport.

I see her again a couple of hours later, back at the post office. 'Oh hello, maid,' she greets me with a smile. 'I phoned that nice Holly to help out in the shop when we be getting rushed. Thought I'd be telling you before someone else blabs it to you, seeing as since you're the postie here.'

I smile to myself as I walk out the door. Diplomacy and general animal cunning are as necessary here in rural Cornwall as they are in London, sometimes.

Before I leave the post van in St Geraint I stop at the tiny cottage belonging to Tufty's mother, Angela, the knitter of those colourful fingerless gloves. She wasn't home when I tried to deliver a package to her earlier, and she'd forgotten to leave the porch door open as she usually does when she's out. There's a letterbox for the thinner mail, but this is a bulky package that I didn't want to leave outside. It's no problem calling again, as I pass close to her cottage on the way to the boat yard car park.

She's home this time, pottering in her front garden which is wild and wonderful, a patch of uncut grass filled with flowers. Bright spots of blue, yellow, pink, and deep red poke out between the grasses. White wood anemones crouch between tiny wild daffodils and delicate violets, plus a host of other flowers I don't recognise.

Angela's white hair is standing straight up on top of her head as it often is, unless she remembers to smooth it down. She has this habit of running her hand through and then forgetting to pat it back down again. She's sweet and cherubic, rather old-fashioned in her manners and dress, hardly ever going out, not even having a television, as Tufty once told me, but preferring to reread again and again all Jane Austen's novels.

So it's a huge surprise to me when she cries, 'Oh how marvellous! My wool has arrived, and I only ordered it from eBay a couple of days ago. God bless the Royal Mail.' She smiles her sweet matronly smile, 'And eBay, of course.'

Right there and then she opens the parcel and out tumble a rainbow of colours, balls of wool that look like the neon lights of a huge modern city, bright and glowing and magical. Some sparkle in the sunlight, others smoulder like embers with their fiery colours. 'Aren't they wonderful?' Angela enthuses. 'Such vivid colours! When I discovered these on eBay, I was thrilled. I've found a steady supplier, too.' Her gentle smile turns slightly sly. 'I hope you don't mind if I don't tell you the name. It's a very small outlet and I seem to be taking all of his stock of this type of yarn.' She looks slightly embarrassed. 'Though I have to say, I've already bought far more than I can use. I can't seem to resist.'

I assure her I wouldn't dream of asking about her supplier. 'But Angela, have you ever thought of selling your gloves? I see they've spread out of Poldowe. It's not just Melanie and Tufty wearing them now, but others, I've noticed lately.'

'Oh, I couldn't ask money for them,' she looks shocked at the thought, then turns wistful. 'But it would be a treat to see other people wearing them. They are a bit of fun, don't you think? I sometimes imagine Jane Austen in a pair. She had quite a mischievous streak, you know.'

By the time I leave, I've convinced her that if she sold some of her gloves, it would pay for the knitting materials, and more importantly, bring delight to loads of people. In the end, she insists on giving me five of her 'best' pairs to show some of the village shopkeepers. I've got my eye on a deep orange pair, the colour of a mature pumpkin or a harvest moon – perfect for Halloween, especially with the silvery black trim. I'll buy them surreptitiously from one of the village shops; if I admire the pair too much she'll give them to me then and there, and I know she struggles to live on her small pension.

I spend an hour on the way home stopping at a few village shops to ask if they'll take some of Angela's gloves in the autumn. They all agree. The St Geraint post office shop will take at least ten, feeling sure they'll sell them all during the half-term holiday. I negotiate a fair price (Angela asked me to do this) and I finally make it home feeling quite pleased with life. From this small beginning, who knows, a whole empire can grow, I say to myself. That's how Laura Ashley started, that's how The Body Shop began, organically and growing upwards from the roots. Laughing at myself for my crazy dreams for other people, I quickly come down to earth, remembering that's the last thing Angela would want. Maybe a small cottage industry would do, rather than a multi-national company.

Though it's far too warm for gloves, I pull on the ones I purchased from the Treverny shop, where I left the five pairs. Well, four now. I hold them up to the sunlight which catches the bright orange and they gleam joyfully like a sunset over a late autumn seascape.

Annie rings me one morning on my mobile. 'I can't remember if you're working or have a day off today,' she says. Her voice sounds strained.

'I'm off. What's up?'

'Look, can we talk? I'm free now if you are.'

I've got a dozen things to do but I'll put them all off for Annie. Something must be wrong; we met only a few days ago. Ben and I went to their place for an evening of fish and chips, and a DVD, though we never did get around to watching the film as we were too busy talking.

She's here in less than half an hour. We seat ourselves at the kitchen table and I say straightaway, 'So what's up?'

'I don't know how to tell you.'

'Tell me what?'

She looks at me, worry and concern written all over her face. 'We're moving. Pete and I. Leaving Cornwall.'

I'm so stunned I can't answer. Annie rushes on. 'We had a phone call, the day after that evening with you and Ben. Pete's uncle, the one who has a small farm in Devon. You've heard Pete talk about him.'

I nod. I still can't find my voice.

'He's just turned sixty and wants to turn his life around. Travel, see the world. He's got no children, no wife – they divorced years ago – and Pete is like a son to him. But he doesn't want to sell up, loves his farm, the animals. He just needs a rest from them for a few years. So he wants Pete to take over. He's been thinking about this for months.'

I finally speak. 'So how does Pete feel about all this?'

Annie smiles for the first time. 'Oh Tessa, he's so happy! It's his dream to run a farm of his own. He's been in agricultural supplies for so long and this is a chance in a lifetime. And he loves that farm; he spent all his childhood summers there, helping his uncle.'

'Annie, I'm stunned. I don't know what to say,' I still haven't taken it in. 'How do you feel about it?'

Her smile fades. 'I wouldn't choose to leave Cornwall, you know that. I've been so happy here. And having you nearby again has been such a treat, such a bonus to my new life.' She sighs. 'But I want to give it a go. Because of Pete. How can I say no?'

I understand, of course I do, but my heart is heavy. 'When would you start?'

'As soon as possible. His uncle wants to be gone before

summer. Pete's giving in his notice at work today. We've been talking about nothing else all week, listing the pros and cons. We only decided late last night. Pete wanted to make sure I was up for it. He said it was up to me, in the end.'

'And are you? Up for it?'

Annie's eyes fill with tears. She looks vulnerable, uncertain. 'I don't know. But I've got to try, for his sake.'

I lean across the table to give her hand a squeeze, blinking back my own tears. 'Of course you do. And you'll be fine.'

'Will I? I'm not a starry-eyed twenty-year-old any more, Tessa, I'm double that. Maybe I'm too old to start a new life as a farmer's wife.'

'You started a new life here.'

'That was different. A little house in a village, my best friend nearby – it was easy.'

'It was easy because you had Pete. And you'll have him wherever you go. Hold on to that.'

She's smiling now and crying at the same time. 'I will. I do. I love him to bits, you know.'

That evening, I tell Ben the news. He's sad about it, too. The four of us have had such treasured times together since Annie and Pete met. 'But you'll miss Annie the most,' he says to me.

I nod. I've already had my little weep, my bit of grieving, and I'm determined to be optimistic about the move. 'I will miss her, but at least Devon is loads closer than London. Think of the fun times we'll have visiting them. The farm is right on Dartmoor, apparently.'

'Lots to explore around there,' Ben agrees.

'And look how lucky we are – our old friends are moving, but we've got new friends now, right next door, who we seem to have lots in common with. I know Leon and Kate could never take Annie and Pete's place, but you know that old cliché – when one door closes, another opens.'

Ben and I talk for a long time, long after we should have been in bed as I'm up early again tomorrow. But it takes a while to digest the news, and then we end by reminiscing about Annie, about how long she's been in our lives, and from there, on to other friends throughout the years. And still I lie in bed for an age before I fall asleep, thinking of how life always manages to surprise us with the things we least expect.

CHAPTER SEVEN

The Trumpeting of Angels . . .

Easter week and Cornwall is brimming with visitors. The weather is still totally perfect – what the English always imagine the whole summer will be like after one idyllic sunny weekend. Everywhere people are planning camping trips, garden parties, fetes, barbecues, regattas, and a host of outdoor activities for the months between now and the end of August. How we forget, those first sunny warm days or weeks, the idiosyncrasies of weather in Britain.

Today it feels as if summer will go on for ever. A host of blue tits are pecking away at the bird feeder and hardly move as I go outside, they're so used to me. Guy waves to me from the front of the Winterson's house where he is finishing the pavement he's laid, covering the entire front lawn just as Kate and Leon had asked him to. Guy seems distracted, frowning at his own work as he stands looking at it.

'You've done a great job,' I call out. It's true, the paving stones are perfectly laid, and it all looks quite grand and elegant.

Perfect for a town house, but, as we'd feared, totally out of place in the country. Who needs perfect paving stones when we have such stunning rock formations by the sea or on the moor? And who needs potted azaleas when we have an abundance of wild flowers and woodland?

Guy feels the same, for he only shrugs despondently at my compliment. He tried to talk Kate into leaving a border around her terrace to plant shrubs, or some flower bulbs, but she barely listened. She's thrilled with it all, and has decided to lay more paths and paving slabs in the back. More grassy spaces lost.

Kate comes out as I'm admiring Guy's workmanship. I'm taking Jake for a walk in nearby woodland and ask her if she'd like to come along but she declines. 'Too many things to do,' she tells me. 'I've got a furniture maker coming from Bristol to measure the wall for my bookcases. I also want him to make some kitchen shelves; those old ones are so tatty.'

I can't hide my surprise. 'But I thought Guy was doing them. You asked me about him. Is there something wrong with his work?'

'Oh no, it's fine, just fine, and Leon and I have told him so. But we had second thoughts about something as intricate as the kind of woodwork we want done. He's only an odd-job man after all.'

I'm nearly speechless. I stare at her, wondering if this is some kind of joke. Jake barks, impatient for his walk, but I need to find out more. 'Kate, we're all odd-job men and women around here. We've talked about this before. There's so little full-time work in Cornwall that most of us make do with all sorts of employment, Guy included. He's a brilliant carpenter, I've seen some of his work. And he's local.'

She looks embarrassed but starts talking at once, eager to either reassure me or to justify herself. Probably both, I decide. 'Don't worry, Tessa, he's fine about it. I've already told him and explained.'

I remember Guy's glum look when I greeted him, and now I know the reason. She's going on, 'I told him this man in Bristol has been highly recommended, has quite a business in his area, but he'll work down here.' She brushes some of Jake's hair from her pale linen trousers distractedly; he's been rubbing against her, trying to get her to stop talking to me so he can have his walk.

Kate continues explaining. 'He charges a fortune, this furniture specialist, as you can guess. But we've got it, so why not spend it? And the house will look stunning when it's finished.' She brightens up. 'We'll have a huge house-warming party, maybe at the end of summer. Live music, a marquee in the garden, dancing, loads of our friends from London. I can't wait for you and Ben to meet them.'

'Sounds fun. The villagers will love it.'

She looks a bit taken aback. Surely she'll invite at least some of her neighbours? She says, reading my thoughts, 'We haven't really got to know anyone but you and Ben very well yet. We're so lucky we happened to move in right next door to people like you, who share the same ideas about things.'

I'm having a niggling doubt about this all of a sudden, despite what I said to Ben about us having lots in common with the Wintersons. It's all very well talking about theatre in London, and what's going on in the city, but we've left all that behind, by choice. What's important to us now is this village, this community, our life with the people here. It doesn't seem to be getting that way for the Wintersons. But then I think, yet again, give them time. It's not easy, they just need to settle as we have.

Kate walks with me to the little pond by the village green that is a colourful riot of primroses, flowering shrubs, and trees. We lean over the narrow wooden bridge watching the ducks playing in the water, quacking loudly to each other. Kate shudders. 'More bird noises. That peacock up the road – it's driving me crazy, Tessa.'

'Still? I didn't think he'd been quite so bad lately.' It's true, I can't remember when I heard him last. But then Emmanuel's daft cry doesn't bother me, so perhaps I just haven't noticed.

'Leon and I were talking the other night about it. We feel we have to do something.'

'Like cover his head with a sack?' I say lightly, thinking she's joking. Kate doesn't answer for a few minutes and we walk along silently, looking at the willow tree at the edge of the pond. Its branches are perfect, draped like an elegant curtain down to the water's edge, and it has that fuzzy pale green shade that occurs just before the leaves burst out of their buds. Willows are amazing trees, I've learned since coming here. Their bark produces a compound called salicin, which we use in aspirin. Willows are mentioned in several ancient texts, too, according to the tree book I've taken to carrying around with me when I remember.

Kate isn't even looking at the pond, the ducks, the willow tree. She's biting her lip in that kind of anxious way she has. She doesn't seem any more relaxed than she did when they first moved here. And now she's talking about the peacock again. 'Tessa, I think we villagers should take a stand. Complain about that bird. I'm sure it's illegal, keeping a thing that makes all that noise.'

I'm stunned. Surely she's not serious? 'It's not that bad, Kate. Even if it was, Emmanuel is special, belonging to the Humphreys. Those two are the village elders, for goodness' sake, they're well respected by everyone. Loved, too.'

'Oh God, I'm OK with that, and I'm sure they're very nice people. That doesn't mean they can thoughtlessly disturb the peace and quiet of the whole village.'

'Who's disturbed? I've not heard anyone else mention it.'

Kate says curtly, 'Well, maybe they're all too frightened of the Humphreys to say anything.'

'That's ridiculous. No one's frightened of them.'

'Well, let's see, shall we? I'm starting a petition about that peacock, saying it's a nuisance to the community and asking for them to remove it.'

Once again I'm shocked. 'Kate, I don't think that's a good idea.'

'Look, I don't want to do it. I came here for peace and an unstressed life, not to do battle. But I'm really going crazy with that noise.' She looks as if she's about to cry. 'I'm sure Leon and I aren't the only ones here who feel like that. I'm sure everyone will thank me for it when that wretched bird is finally removed.'

I'm about to disagree with her when the wretched bird gives such a blood-curdling shriek that it silences us both for a few moments. Finally Kate says, 'You see, Tessa? Sign my petition. You'll be glad of it.'

I shake my head. 'Sorry, Kate, I could never sign anything like that. Neither could Ben. Edna and Hector have been here for ever, and who are we to say what they can and cannot do on their own property.'

There is another moment of silence between us, not a

comfortable one. She puts her hand on my arm in a placating gesture. 'Look, let's not fall out over a peacock. That's fine if you don't sign, I'm sure others will.' She smiles. 'Let's agree to disagree, like friends do about politics and religion and other touchy subjects.'

I smile back. 'I don't fall out with people, Kate.'

She looks relieved. 'So we're still invited to dinner at your place tonight?'

'What a question! Of course you are. We're both looking forward to it.'

Kate is smiling now. 'We're looking forward to it, too. We'll bring wine, but anything else? I'm going into Truro later, I can do some shopping for you.'

'Thanks for the offer, but we're fine. Ben's cooking. He's a brilliant cook.'

'I'd better go, then. Oh, I suddenly remember, I've got to ring that furniture maker in Bristol, set a date for him to come down here. See you later.' As she starts to rush off she adds, 'And don't worry about Guy. Leon gave him a very generous bonus when we told him that we've decided to get an out-of-town craftsman. We told him this man had been highly recommended by friends of ours, which is true. And we're paying Guy quite well for the work he's done outside. Well over the local rates.'

Oh dear, I think as I walk with Jake, Kate just doesn't get it. Yes, Guy needs the money, but it's so much more than that. It's his professional pride at stake, that and the fact that the Wintersons won't even give him a chance though he's right on the spot and has had good reports about his work from us and others. The villagers aren't going to like it either, a good local man turned down in favour of someone from Up Country.

Well, none of your business, Tessa, I tell myself firmly. I put Kate and Leon out of my mind and bring myself back to the fresh air, the warming earth under my feet, the profusion of trees and wild flowers, with pink campion and yellow buttercups everywhere I look. Jake finds a little stream and leaps into it, scaring any tiny fish or water creatures lurking there. The rocks at the edge are bright green with moss and the bark of the trees is encrusted with lichen. So many trees – beech and oak, a few conifers, and birch. There is a holm oak that reminds me of Edna and Hector, and I wonder what, if anything, to do about their dying tree. Not that I can do much, and not that I want to interfere, but if the tree is dangerous, I'd never forgive myself if it came crashing down on them or on their house.

And so the next day, when I see Woody at his caravan, I ask him about the holm oak again. He's outside sitting on a rickety canvas chair, Holly is lying on a torn blanket spread over the grass. 'Can't get enough of this sun,' she murmurs, patting the empty spot next to her. 'Come grab some rays, Tessa,' she says to me, then grins. 'Hey, how cool are those shorts?'

I grin back. 'You're just jealous because you don't own a pair of baggy Royal Mail official shorts.'

Holly is wearing shorts, too, tight denim ones, and about eight inches shorter than mine. She's wearing a tiny halter top with ropes of coloured beads hanging around her neck. 'This weather is awesome,' she sighs. 'So warm, and only April.'

Woody, in shorts, too, and with his shirt off, brings me an ice-cold lemonade and insists I take the canvas chair. 'Sit down for a bit,' he says.

I do. What's the point of living in a place like this if I don't take advantage of it, especially when the sun shines like it is today? I say this to the young couple. Holly nods. 'Yeah, well that's what I'm doing for sure. Taking advantage, before I start work this weekend.'

'At the post office in Morranport? I heard Nell offered you the job.'

'Yep. Part-time at first then full-time during July and August.'

'Are you pleased?'

'Dead right, I'm chuffed. I like the old girl, and working in a shop'll be fun.'

I drink the refreshing lemonade gratefully and get up to go, first asking Woody about the Humphreys' tree. 'I know we've talked about this, but I still can't help worrying about it. I know nothing can be done while the birds are nesting, but maybe you could go around again, convince them that sooner rather than later the tree has got to come down?'

'Oh, I've already done that. I called in a week or so ago, had a morning's job in the village and thought I'd stop by, have another look at the tree. Mrs Humphrey – or Edna as she said to call her – and Hector, they were great, brought me out some tea and cake,' his face takes on a bemused look. 'The tea was kinda odd, tasted strange, but the cake was delicious. Edna gave me some to take back to Holly.'

I chuckle to myself, thinking of some of Edna's teas that I've drunk over the past couple of years. Sometimes I'm lucky and get ordinary English breakfast, or something incredibly tasty she's concocted out of various herbs, but sometimes it's disastrous, as she's always experimenting with plants and seeds. I used to worry that they might poison themselves, but I've realised that despite the taste of some of the brews, they're all harmless.

Guy is still talking. 'They'd like to meet Holly. I told them all about her, how she's moved into the caravan with me and we're going to start this market garden.' He turns to Holly, who is standing now at his side, listening to us. 'That was before you got this job at Morranport,' he continues. 'Guess you won't be able to help out much once you start there.'

Holly takes his hand. 'I'm only part-time to start with, so I can help with the planting and stuff. Think of the money, Woody. We can buy fencing to keep out the rabbits, for a start.'

I bring the conversation gently back to the dying holm oak at Poet's Tenement. Woody says, 'Yeah, I looked at the tree again. Definitely staggy headed, not too good. I figured that mebbe I could call in every now and again, warn them about that tree, and slowly get them to come around to the idea that it's got to come down.'

'That's nice of you, Woody.'

'Well, I like'em, y'see. And I like that ole tree. I don't like it coming down any more than they do. But if it gotta be done, I figure that if Edna and Hector get to know me a bit, they won't mind so much when the tree goes. At least it'll be a friend and not a stranger taking it down.'

I'm touched by this sensitivity but not surprised. Living in a close community, sharing both good fortune and hardships throughout the decades, the locals seem attuned to each other in ways you don't often see in cities. There is something else I've noticed, too. Since living here, I've been struck by how the various tradespeople hate to see money being spent unnecessarily, even if they're the ones who would profit by it. When the local electrician came to do up some of the dodgy wiring we need to repair if we're going to rent out our house, he kept thinking of ways we could cut costs by doing one or two things differently. Our local garage man takes real pleasure in finding parts like a wing mirror for me on eBay instead of ordering a new one. This desire to be frugal is, I think, one of the great legacies of Methodism, which flourished in Cornwall over two centuries ago.

Just the other day I met a very grand elderly lady at Joanna's house, who was obviously a great friend of hers. Joanna called me in to introduce us, as if I were a dear friend instead of the local postie. The two women were drinking tea from delicate china cups, gazing at the sea from Joanna's magnificent terrace. You might have thought they were sitting at Buckingham Palace, they were so tidy and refined, sharing some kind of fancy biscuits laid out in an orderly manner on an exquisite antique plate.

'Do have tea with us, Tessa,' Joanna invited me that day, as she often does. 'Or would you rather have coffee, since it's not exactly tea time yet? Lillian and I don't drink coffee, I'm afraid, but I can quickly make some for you. It's no trouble.'

Lillian, looking remarkably like Joanna, with the same type of neatly permed hair, same court shoes, added, 'After seventy, coffee tends to disagree with one. I never touch it now.'

I refused a drink and biscuit but I sat for a moment to talk to Joanna and Lillian, as Joanna wanted to hear all about my house-renting escapades. She feels quite elated that I've taken the idea from her. 'Very sensible,' Lillian said as I told them about the various repairs we are slowly making to the place. 'Especially as you say your husband is doing most of the handiwork himself.'

'Yes, except for electricity and things like that – the central heating, for instance.'

'Central heating?' Lillian looked as though I'd told them we're putting in a dungeon in the basement. 'Whatever for?'

'Well, it does get chilly sometimes in August, as the estate agent said. We've got to have it to be able to rent.'

'That's true,' Joanna confirmed. 'I had to install it here. Never use it myself.'

Lillian looked thoroughly disapproving. 'Of course not. You've got a perfectly sensible wood-burning stove, as I have,' she turned back to me. 'Central heating is quite unnecessary in Cornwall.'

'Perhaps. The point is, whatever we prefer ourselves, we need central heating to be accepted by the rental company.'

Lillian sighed theatrically, turning to Joanna, 'You see now, why I could never rent like you and others of my friends do?'

Joanna nodded and said to me, 'Lillian has a beautiful house. Very large, very grand.'

'But without central heating. Good heavens, no one expects to be warm in winter, do they, Joanna?' Her friend shook her head in agreement. Lillian went on, 'In winter, even a winter like the one we have just experienced, we heat one room. To do more is an incredible waste of money. One room is enough for any family, in the winter. At night, we scuttle upstairs as fast as we can and undress under the covers. Hasn't done us any harm, has it, Joanna?'

Joanna shook her head again, in total agreement with her friend. Lillian looked me in the eye and said, kindly, 'Be careful, young lady, and think of what you're doing, before you start heating your bedroom. No good will come of it.'

I promised solemnly that I would give the matter grave consideration. As I left the two of them, Joanna called out after me, 'My dear, I suggest that if you really feel the cold in winter, get an electric blanket. It's a luxury I admit, but I finally bought one for my nine-year-old grandson to use when he stays. I'm afraid his parents have coddled him. He complained his fingers and toes would freeze in the night when he stayed with us over the last Christmas holidays. Silly boy. But I indulged him. After all, he's my only grandson. A bit of spoiling is allowed.'

Later, I tell Annie about this conversation when I meet her in St Geraint for lunch. I haven't seen so much of her since she told me her news, as she and Pete have been dodging back and forth to Devon, staying with Pete's uncle, learning the ropes of his farm for the takeover in May. She seems to be looking forward to it now, perhaps caught up by Pete's enthusiasm, and I'm happy for them both.

Annie is amazed as I tell her about Joanna and Lillian. 'Honestly, these old-timers, put us to shame. I froze in Pete's cottage during the winter, even though we have a wood burner in the sitting room, an Aga in the kitchen, and an electric fire in the bedroom. I would have killed for central heating.'

I laugh and say, teasingly, 'Hah, City Mouse, still the same. Used to your luxurious city life.'

'When it comes to freezing winters, too right. Give me the centrally heated city. Anyway, don't go all righteous on me. I know you can't wait to get that central heating in. How are plans going, by the way, for the house rental?'

'Not that great. There's so much to do to the house, not to mention all the new things we have to buy. It seems such a waste of money, spending it on matching crockery and replacing a perfectly good, if old, washing machine. It's painful, when usually every penny we spend has to be for something we really need,' I shake my head. 'To be honest, even taking out a bank loan, we still won't be able to get everything ready for renting this summer. It's such a disappointment.'

'What a shame.'

We're sitting outside a new café that opened at the beginning of the month, right at the edge of the water, not far from the boat yard. Annie's been gazing out to sea with a slight frown, which I know means she's thinking furiously. 'Annie, what's up?'

She looks at me again, saying excitedly, 'Look, you want to rent out your house this summer but you're not ready to get involved with a rental agency, right?'

'Well, sort of right. We're ready but the house isn't. No agency will take us until the place is up to scratch. And we've got no money to do that.'

'Tessa, I know at least half a dozen people in London, friends from my old BBC days, who love coming to Cornwall for holidays and would love renting your house.'

'Without central heating? Or a new washing machine?'

'Just the way it is, mismatched crockery and all.'

'But – how do I find these people?'

'Easy, I will. I still email old friends there, and phone them, and they visit, you know. The thing is, Tessa, you can't charge what the estate agent would charge for the matching crockery and smart barbecue and all that frippery.'

I'm getting as excited as she is now. 'Of course I wouldn't charge as much, if they take the house as it is. Oh Annie, even if it's just for a week or so, it'd be brilliant. And a great way to get used to strangers using our house.'

Annie's eyes are gleaming with plans. 'The great thing is, they won't be strangers. Well, maybe to you, but I'd only tell the people I know and like about your house. Lots of them know all about it already, from all the times I came to visit you before I met Pete and moved down here.'

A discouraging thought hits me. 'Annie, remember that the

estate agency said our house wasn't up to par for renting. I don't want your friends disappointed.'

She's already got out her mobile phone and is trying to contact someone who said he wants to holiday in Cornwall this year. He doesn't answer, so she leaves a quick message and gets back to me. 'But that's the point, Tessa. The kind of people I'll put your way are the kind that don't want some sterile holiday house with everything perfect. They'd prefer to stay in a real Cornish home, like yours. It's a lovely place, it's warm and cosy – they'll love it.' She grins mischievously. 'And they'll love it even more when they know they're getting it loads cheaper than it would cost from an agency. And Tessa, you and Ben won't have to pay agency fees.'

I'm so uplifted by this that I practically dance all the way back to my car. Annie adds, as we say goodbye, 'I'm only doing this for selfish reasons, you know. If you rent your house, you can spend that time with us up on deepest darkest Dartmoor.'

'Only if we can help.'

'I'm sure there will be loads of things to do. The house is sprawling and pretty ramshackle, but there's plenty of room and there's a good feel about the place. I'm actually beginning to look forward to going there, much as I'll miss Cornwall, and you and Ben and the family.'

'I'm so glad, Annie. How's Pete, anyway? Still as excited about the move?'

'Oh, even more so, since he's been up at the farm on week-ends.' She gets that dreamy expression I've seen before. 'Oh Tessa, he's so fantastic. He's a darling, he really is.'

'So you've said. Many, many times.'

'I know. But Tessa, he really is the best husband. You know what he did yesterday?' I try not to let my eyes glaze over as

Annie tells me another wonderful thing that St Pete did, something really quite ordinary – bringing her some flowers – but
to Annie, a heavenly act comparable only to the trumpet call
of angels. I smile tolerantly, and listen. She's a newlywed after
all. Anyway, I feel the same about Ben, and we've been married
ages. But the real difference between me and a newlywed is, I
don't have to talk about it all the time.

That evening Ben comes home late, after the children have
eaten and gone to bed. He's had some work lately doing voice-
overs, and had to go to Bristol early this morning for the job.
Luckily he'd met Leon at the train station in Truro, coming
back from one of his stints in London, and Leon drove him
home. Ben says, 'Of course Leon was in first class, but I spotted
him before he left the station. It meant you didn't have to
come pick me up.'

He opens a bottle of wine he's brought home, a celebration
for the finished job, while I put the flowers he's brought me
into a chunky white vase. They are gorgeous red tulips. 'A
woman came along the train in Exeter selling them,' he tells
me. 'I've never seen that before, don't know if it's legal or
whether she was thrown out at the next station. But I got some
for you anyway.'

They're beautiful. 'You are wonderful,' I say. 'Like the trum-
peting of angels in heaven.' I give him a hug, kiss him soundly.

'You've been around Annie too much,' he teases me. 'That
sounds like the kind of things she says about Pete.'

'How'd you guess? Well, let's hope she's still saying them
when they've been married as long as we have.'

We drink the wine, reminisce about Annie and Pete's wedding
in Cornwall last year, then go on reminiscing about our own.
It's late when we get to bed and I'll be groggy all day at work,

but *c'est la vie*. That's the nice thing about being a postie, I can take things slowly if I need to. As long as the post gets there on the day it should, at more or less the time it should, I'm all right.

It's the more or less that I love. It's what makes living here so wonderfully relaxing.

CHAPTER EIGHT

A Mermaid's Ear and Other Wonders

I'm in Poldowe a week or so later, delivering to the main street of the village, when a van screeches to a stop next to me and Guy jumps out. 'Tessa, hey, all right then?'

'Fine, Guy, how about you?'

'I'm good. Uh, you got any post for Clara? I thought I could pop it down to her. Save you a trip, y'know.'

'Are you on your way there, then?'

'Well, um, yeah. Or no. That is, I've not picked up any cats lately. Not been any about, things have been slow on that front. So I haven't seen her, y'know? Not in the last week or so.'

'Guy, you don't need the excuse of cats to call on her, do you? I thought you were friends?'

He blushes, looks down, mumbles something I can't hear. Oh dear, he's in a bad way. 'Guy, what's up? I can't understand what you're saying.'

He speaks up, and a garble of words rush out. 'Well, that's

the thing. We were. Friends, y'know. I used to drop in on her all the time, even without cats. Just to chat, y'know?'

'Yes, I do know, Guy. I used to see you two at her place, when I dropped in the post. So what's wrong? Aren't you friends any more?'

He's blushing and twitching and staring at his feet again. Goodness, he really is in a state. To save him from more misery I say gently, 'Here, Guy, here's a leaflet about eye tests or something you can give her, that's all the post today. But it's something.'

He takes the junk mail with such joy that I think he's going to swoop me up and swing me round. He gibbers some kind of thank you and starts heading towards Clara's house but instead turns in a rush, scaring some sparrows pecking on a grassy lawn nearby. 'Tessa, you've been such a great friend to us, to me and Clara. I got to tell you, you'll think I'm bonkers though.'

'Not at all,' I say in my kindest, most understanding voice. 'Tell me everything,' I say, even though this isn't exactly the right spot for a chummy conversation, on the main street of a small village with the locals walking about, eager to start a friendly chat. As we've been speaking, a couple have already greeted us on the way to the shop and it won't be long before someone joins us, I'm sure.

Guy obviously feels the same way for he grabs my arm and pulls me across the road to the church, mumbling something about getting a bit of privacy. Just in time, too, for out of the corner of my eye I can see Ginger lurking in front of her house, glancing surreptitiously at us. More than one of the windows of the nearby houses have curtains twitching, too. Not that I blame them. Guy is so noticeable with his wild bushy hair and wide smile that you can't help but look twice when he passes. And for the last ten minutes he's been twitching and tapping his feet and looking totally agitated as we've been standing and talking.

The two of us perch on an ancient tomb in the churchyard. I try to see whose grave it is, but the engraving has worn away, it's so old. I spare a quick thought for the bones beneath, wondering what life, what dreams and hopes the person had, before turning my attention back to Guy. 'So tell me what's up.'

He runs his big hand through his thick hair and it stands up even more than usual, giving him a look of surprise or shock. 'Y'see, you're right. We *were* friends. Great mates, for a couple of years, ever since Clara started this cat business and I kinda got to helping her out. Gave me something to do in between jobs. I had the van, you see, and could sling a cat basket in there easy like, cart the cats around, help deliver them to new homes.' He stops twitching and for a moment starts to relax, thinking of Clara and their friendship. He gets stuck in his reverie for so long that I have to gently prompt him, for I still have a batch of post to deliver. 'So what went wrong, then? Did you fall out with her?'

He stares at me with a horrified look. 'No, no, no, of course not. Never! Clara and me, we get on like a house on fire. Fall out? No, no. Whatever gave you that idea?' And off he goes in yet another trance, staring out over the churchyard – which is quite beautiful with budding shrubs and a stunning magnolia tree at one end, and the ground covered in bluebells – musing on the impossibility of ever arguing with Clara.

I really do have to get on with the post. 'Guy,' I say, less gently this time, 'do tell me exactly what the problem is.'

He looks at me gloomily. 'The problem is, I started to fancy her. Sudden, like. Over the cat. The kitten, you know, you were there – the one we took to Marilyn for her birthday, in the snow. It got away, remember? We found it in your car?'

'Yes, yes, I remember. You started to fancy her then?'

He's standing now and pacing about in front of me. 'Yeah. Couldn't help it, Tessa. Suddenly I saw how great she looked, how great she is, how terrific really, and . . . well, you know.' He looks as if he's about to cry.

'I do know, Guy. Perfectly normal, she's a lovely person. So why are you so miserable? From what I saw that day, it looked like she was starting to fancy you, too.'

Guy sits down again and his whole body slumps over the tombstone. 'She does,' he wails, 'that's the trouble.'

'You've lost me, Guy. You fancy her, she fancies you, you're both single, what's the problem?'

For the next ten minutes, while a robin sits on a nearby tombstone staring at us, Guy tells me what the problem is. It seems he is painfully shy when it comes to love and romance, and all the rest of it, and feels too awkward and anxious to just pop in on Clara like he used to. ''Cause we're not mates any more, get it? It's different.'

I listen to all this patiently but now I've really got to get on; we've been talking for ages. 'Guy, believe me, you can be mates with someone as well as being lovers.'

He looks amazed at this. 'How?' he wants to know.

I stand up, brush some moss from my uniform. 'Go see her. Now. Without the post, without any excuse. Go and tell her how you feel, for goodness' sake, it'll make it much easier for her, too. I'm sure she knows it anyway, and is wondering why in the world you've stopped coming around. You've probably broken her heart, actually.'

Now he is truly horrified. 'I haven't! Have I? Crikey, what should I do? I'd never hurt her, never ever.'

Brisk measures are called for here. I pull him up, or rather urge him up with a few brisk military-like gestures and pushes, and march him out of the churchyard. 'You're going to see her right now. Forget about yourself and your shyness and everything else, and think about poor Clara, in there, heartbroken. She's probably seen your van, knows you're in the village and haven't been to see her. How do you think she feels about that?'

Pulling him across the road, I half shove, half drag him to the front of Clara's house. I really hope she's not at the window watching this. 'Just get in there,' I order in my sternest voice.

He straightens his shoulders for a moment then immediately slumps. 'I can't. I'm terrified. What if she laughs at me?'

So that's his problem. He looks so forlorn, so dejected and afraid, that I take both his hands and squeeze them gently. 'She won't, Guy, I promise. You're a lovely man, good-looking, kind – what more could a woman want? You know she fancies you, too, she held your hand that day with the kitten, I saw it. Don't blow it now. Don't break her heart.'

I squeeze his hands again for moral support. He straightens up, looks me in the eye, nods, then turns and marches up to Clara's front door. He doesn't look back once, not even when she opens the door, smiles hugely, and they both vanish inside.

What a relief, I think as I carry on delivering the post in Poldowe. I feel quite cheery, young love always does that to me. Well, not exactly young, but young enough. Clara can't be more than forty, still time to have a baby if that's what they want . . .

I stop myself. They haven't even gone out on a date yet, and here I'm imagining babies and whatnot. Always the incurable romantic. I'm grinning to myself, thinking about Guy and Clara, my premature dreams for them, when I nearly bump into Ginger. 'How's it going?' I say. 'Still like the job?' I was able to help her find work last year when she was desperate. One of the great things about being a postie is learning about who needs what and somehow being able to put them together.

'Love it,' she smiles and her whole face, sad in repose, looks suddenly animated. 'It's going really well. I'm doing less days now, which suits me fine.'

We talk about this and that, and I admire her new haircut. Ginger's hair is dark brown, no ginger in it at all. She explained to me once that her mother was a big fan of Ginger Rogers, hence the name. She's easy-going, pleasant, but today she seems slightly troubled. The smile has faded and there's a frown on her face.

'Is anything wrong?'

'Wrong? Um, no, nothing,' she hesitates, as if about to say more, but then changes her mind. 'Nothing's wrong, gotta go. Any post for me today?'

She's off as soon as I tell her there's nothing for her, waving a friendly goodbye. She's still uneasy, though and I wonder what's up, hope it's nothing major.

My last stop in Poldowe is at Delia's house. I'm increasingly worried about what I'm afraid is dementia. Since that first day last January when I began to really notice her forgetfulness, she's got worse, I'm sure. Her neighbours, like Clara and Ginger, are concerned, too, but don't know what to do about it. They've been helping her out for years as she's always been a bit helpless and fragile, but this is getting too much for them.

Today I get a shock. Delia, who usually dresses meticulously despite her forgetfulness, is sitting in her usual armchair with her soft brushed cotton nightdress on. It's pulled up to her thighs, which are naked and thickly veined. Her feet are bare, scarred with corns. I've never seen Delia without a pair of sturdy beige shoes on her feet; she never even wears slippers, usually.

'Oh good morning, Tessa,' she says, as if she's fully dressed and greeting me as she used to, when she was well. 'Lovely morning, isn't it? I opened all the windows this morning.' She makes no move to pull down her clothes or cover her bare thighs.

I agree it's a beautiful day and don't mention the fact that the windows haven't been open for ages; it smells stale and musty in here. 'Are you all right, Delia?'

She looks puzzled. 'Of course, thank you, dear. Why do you ask?'

'It's just that . . . that you're still in your night clothes,' I say gently.

She looks down then up again at me. 'Why, so I am, dear. I must have forgotten to get dressed this morning.' Her face takes on a panicky look as she says this. 'I'd better go now, shall I?'

She stands up, wobbly and uncertain. From outside I can hear her cat meowing, yowling even. She must not have even let him in yet from his night prowling. Delia doesn't seem to notice the sound, which is worrying. She loves that cat. I don't trust her to go upstairs on her own so I offer to go with her. She accepts gratefully. When we get to the bedroom I wonder whether to stay or to go. I want to give her privacy, but on the other hand she's looking bewildered, standing by the bed with a confused expression on her face.

I say, 'Do you want me to help?'

'Oh yes. Please. If you don't mind. I feel . . . I feel not quite myself today. Perhaps I'm not quite well after all.'

I'm almost relieved by this. Perhaps she has a touch of the flu, some kind of virus. Something she'll get over. I say, 'Why don't I help you back to bed then, if you're feeling ill? Best place for you. I'll help you get comfortable if you like.'

She seems to visibly pull herself together, taking a deep breath and facing me again, this time more certainly. 'I feel better now. Much better, thank you Tessa. I'd like to go downstairs. If you could just help with some zips, perhaps? It won't take a moment.'

She goes to her old-fashioned, heavy oak dresser, takes out underwear, and vanishes into the bathroom with them. I stand awkwardly in her bedroom, feeling intrusive but not wanting to leave her alone. I look around at the ancient brass bed, a dark oak wardrobe, old-fashioned velvet curtains. These haven't been opened yet and the room looks gloomy and forbidding. 'Shall I open the curtains for you, Delia? Let the sun in?'

She comes in, modestly covered with a long satin slip, old and not as clean as I'd have expected from Delia, who has been meticulous in her dressing in the past. 'Do open them, thank you. And the window, please?' She seems to have forgotten that she'd told me she'd already done this. It's worth the struggle to open it. The air coming in is fresh and sweet, taking away the musty stale smell that I'd noticed when I came in.

Delia finds a dress and I help her put it on, pull up the zip. She seems to be coping all right with thick beige cotton tights and her usual shoes, and by the time we get downstairs she seems quite herself again, even remembering the cat. When I finally leave, she's feeding it some dried cat food, forgetting I'm there while she coos over it.

I worry about her as I finish delivering the post, though the sight of Guy's van still parked on the street outside Clara's house lightens my mood. Before I get back into my own van, I check in at the local shop. The shop is empty, so I get a chance to talk to Melanie about Delia, as I know the shopkeeper is one of the villagers who looks after her.

Melanie is very concerned. 'I've noticed she's getting worse, and so have the others who check on her.' She sighs. 'It's hard, her not having any blood kin to call on. Still, we're like family, round here, so we'll keep an eye on her, don't you worry, Tessa. You got enough on your plate as it is, what with working full-time, trying to get your house fit to rent, looking after the family, scraping and making do.' She gives me a motherly smile and pats my hand. I feel like a twenty-year-old just starting out in the world, the way she's trying to reassure me. Melanie makes people feel like that, I've realised: that you're a little chick and she's the mother hen looking after you, even though you're more or less the same age.

It's not until I've left the shop, munching on some amazing chocolate chip cookies the bakery man has just delivered, that I wonder how she knew all that about me. This isn't even my village; Treverny is several miles away from Poldowe. I've never confided in Melanie; we've exchanged pleasantries when I've gone in, but that's all. Typical Cornwall, I think as I brush biscuit crumbs from my uniform. Or this part of it, anyway. Everyone knows everyone else's business, though I suppose that's village life anywhere. Not that I mind. Not when they use the information like Melanie does, to reassure, console, and help. I've seen her do it to others, sympathising with someone she's heard lost his job, or his dog, or whatever. The grapevine here is strong, but it's used to send news along so that people can do something to help if need be.

I trot back to my post van feeling quite light-hearted. Delia will be cared for, and young, or not-so-young, love seems to be doing just fine as Guy's van is still parked at Clara's and he is nowhere to be seen. The only person that slightly worries me is Ginger. She really did act oddly, though I'm sure I'll find out what is bothering her soon enough. In the meantime it's a fabulous day, and I can't wait to get out of uniform and walk Jake on the beach.

A couple of hours later, we're at Penwarren beach, smelling the sea air, romping along. The neap tide is right out, as I knew it would be, and Jake and I leap over rocks, inspect the pools, and examine the mass of seaweed on the shore. Several people are out walking, and we wave or shout greetings as our dogs rush up to each other, sniff, play, or run for a while before following their owners along the shore.

On the way back I notice a familiar couple coming towards me. It's Leon and Kate, strolling along barefoot, dressed in shorts and brightly coloured T-shirts that look brand new, the colours not yet faded from weeks in the sun. 'Great to be retired,' Leon says. I nod, thinking how ludicrous it is that a man of his age, looking years younger as well, is already retired.

We stand for a few moments admiring the way the waves are splashing against some nearby rocks, sending a delicate spray of iridescent seawater up into the air where it glistens in the sunlight. The light plays upon the mounds of seaweed on the shoreline, turning it luminous green, gold, and fiery red. 'Beautiful, isn't it,' I murmur.

Leon and Kate follow my eyes, stare at the seaweed, then

glance at each other. Leon says, 'Seaweed? If you ask me, it's the one thing wrong with this beach. Awful stuff.'

Kate is agreeing with him. 'You can't walk in it, can't swim in it. Quite honestly, I think it's disgraceful, that the local council, or whoever is in charge of the beach, hasn't done anything about it.'

I can't let this go. Figuring they're still city folk, still naïve about rural living, I cheerily explain to them what I learned about the ecology of seaweed, its necessity. 'I felt like you did, before we moved here. But now that I know how important the stuff is, how many sea creatures live or feed on it, I think differently about it.' I pick up a strand of red-green seaweed, holding it out to show them. 'There are so many varieties! The Cornish Wildlife Trust did a survey of them all recently, and would you believe there are at least 180 species of red, brown and green seaweed. I've been reading about it on the website; I can give you the link.' I lay down the seaweed carefully. Jake sniffs and then dismisses it, racing after a seabird. 'The divers found all sorts of fantastic things along the Cornish coast – sea fans, anemones, wonderful things like giant brown forest kelp, and something called mermaid's ear, a delicate pink sea plant. There's such a wealth of marine life living on seaweed and sea sponges, even seahorses!'

Finishing my spiel, I beam at Kate and Leon, feeling like a benevolent schoolteacher, having clearly and kindly explained a difficult subject. But they're not beaming back. In fact they're both frowning. Finally Leon says, 'To each his own viewpoint. Quite honestly, I don't think messing up a good beach with that stuff does any good to anyone.'

I'm taken aback by this and don't know how to respond,

but it doesn't matter as the couple are already talking about other things. Soon Leon is making me laugh with an anecdote about some business colleagues in London. They're both so entertaining, and so personable, but I can't help feeling uneasy as finally they carry on with their walk and I head homewards. Life in Cornwall hardly seems to be giving them the peace and tranquillity they are searching for. Kate remains determined to have the peacock removed from the Humphreys' home, and she hasn't made herself many friends by employing the furniture maker from Bristol. The whole village has seen his very smart, brand-new Renault van, and feel it's a terrible slight not only on Guy, but on them all.

Still, it is not my problem. I've been keeping my head down, trying not to get involved. I'm still optimistically hoping the Wintersons will settle in to village life.

Annie and Pete come over for dinner the first weekend in May, just before they leave for Devon. We're all trying very hard to make it a festive occasion, but it's an emotional evening for everyone. Even Pete, thrilled as he is to be taking over the farm, admits to feeling a bit shaky. 'I've never lived outside of Cornwall. Never farmed, either,' he confesses. 'I've been to agricultural college, worked with farmers all my life, and spent weeks on farms, but not like this. Not with the entire responsibility of running a farm on my shoulders.'

Tonight, over chilled white wine and a prawn risotto, we're making plans, looking to the future. Annie has found us two one-week rentals for our house and wants us to spend both weeks on Dartmoor at the farm. Ben and I agree to stay for one of the weeks but no longer. 'We don't want to overstay our welcome,' I tell the couple. 'You know the old saying about fish and houseguests – after a few days they start to go off. We call it our Three-Day-Fish rule!'

Annie makes a face, 'You're not houseguests, you're our family practically. We've known each other for ever.'

'Let's see how it goes, OK? We'll stay for a bit, and if we can help on the farm, we'll extend our stay. But we've got our tents, our camping gear, so we won't be homeless when our house is rented.'

The evening goes on longer than usual, as if the four of us are all reluctant to call it a night, knowing that this is the end of a short but rich period in our lives. But we'll have more evenings I'm sure, just as Annie and I will have our girlie days out. We'll be older, though probably no wiser, and the venue could be anywhere, but that's not important. What matters is our friendship, which will endure, as Annie says, even on deepest darkest Dartmoor.

'And if it can survive there, it'll survive anywhere,' she adds as we finally say goodnight. We hug each other tightly and then they're gone.

Though we've said our goodbyes, I decide I have to see Pete and Annie off a few days later. I'm working, but I manage to jiggle things about so that I'm delivering to Pete's village at the time I know they're leaving. I've brought along a mass of flowers – daisies and marigolds from the garden – and a small collection of tiny seashells, ones I've found over the past few weeks that I want to give Annie as a reminder of her Cornish roots. After all, she married a Cornishman, didn't she? She's one of us now, wherever she ends up.

There are a few other houses scattered around the outskirts of Pete's village where I deliver first, since I know I'm too early for Annie and Pete. I want to get the timing exactly right.

I've brought along some rice confetti, too, the same as we had at their wedding, to wish them Godspeed and good luck. I've also got a straw basket, tied with a pretty embroidered ribbon, and filled with Cornish clotted cream, scones, and pastries baked only that morning in Morranport. I'm determined they'll take a piece of Cornwall with them when they leave.

I've got a card from Canada for a farmhouse nearby, and I know it's from the farmer's son. It is obviously a birthday card as he's had several this week. He told me proudly that no one could believe he was sixty-five, retirement age, not that he had any intention of retiring. I agreed, and was suitably complimentary, although I'd have sworn the man looked seventy-five and not a day younger. It is a hard life, farming. Looking at my watch, I decide I have time to make one or two more deliveries before heading to Pete's cottage, if I hurry. I roar into the farmyard and leap out, birthday card in hand, ready to throw it onto the shelf in the open front porch where all the farmer's post goes. I'm in such a hurry that I forget about Nips, the six-month-old Labrador.

Now, I adore this puppy. She's gorgeous and golden and sweet, with huge brown doggie eyes that look at you as if she's just discovered love. I always take the time to play with her, even throwing her the ball I keep in my postbag for friendly playful dogs. But today I don't have time to play. 'Down, Nippy Nips,' I shout, as she leaps up, tries to kiss me. 'Down, girl.'

She's well trained, and obediently lets her bottom alight briefly on the ground before leaping up again. Nips is bright and intelligent, but totally manic. She wriggles and waggles, squirms and squeals, and absolutely cannot stay still for a moment. Up she leaps again, and before I can stop her, she's grabbed the card I've been holding, thinking it's a toy for her to play with. Off she runs with it, tail proudly high and wagging, out into the grassy field by the house.

As I'm screaming at her to come back, running after her, I'm joined by the farmer and his wife. 'The post,' I gasp. 'I've got to get it back.'

The three of us leap about trying to head off the dog. Nips is loving the game, dodging us with artful cunning. The farmer is getting more and more furious. All of a sudden he rushes to his Land Rover, parked near the postal van, and comes out brandishing a shotgun. 'Oh God,' I cry. 'Don't shoot!' As I shriek, a shot rings out. My knees go weak and I fall to the ground. 'Nips,' I cry to the farmer's wife who is standing nearby. 'He's shot Nips!'

She's looking at me as if I am the crazy one. 'Don't be so daft, maid, he be soft as shit over that puppy. Wouldn't harm a whisker on her face. He done shot in the air. Nips is a gun dog, one shot and she goes right to her master's side awaiting orders to fetch.'

I look around cautiously and sure enough, there is Nips sitting happily alert at the farmer's feet, while the man is tearing open his card and smiling widely as he reads it.

I walk shakily back to my van, refusing the cup of tea offered by the farmer's wife. 'Pete and Annie are moving to Devon today, and I want to see them go, give them a good send-off.'

The farmer's wife says, 'Well now, they be off today? I'll be darned, I thought 'twas the end of the week.' She starts to rush towards the house.

Her husband shouts after her, 'Where you be off to?'

'T'grab the scones cooling on the kitchen table. Get the

Land Rover going while I collect them. Leave that bloody gun behind, you're not shooting rabbits now.'

I tear off in a hurry; I've got one more delivery to make but it's on the way to Pete and Annie's and I think I have time, despite the Nips drama. To be sure, I text Annie and find out they're running a bit late but should be off in about fifteen minutes. Driving up to the next house, an isolated bungalow on the edge of the village, I rush up with a batch of packages, smaller stuff ordered from eBay no doubt. Over the last couple of years, we posties have noticed how many more packages we're delivering, as Internet shopping gets increasingly popular. These middle-aged parents, and their two teenagers, are great customers of the web, always telling me of the wonderful buys they've made. It's almost like a hobby for them, buying and selling, too. They've only got one car between them, which the father drives to his work as a mechanic in a garage near St Geraint, so the Internet has opened all sorts of doors to them. Recently the mother found a stack of LPs in the attic, early ones of '50s and '60s pop groups, in brilliant condition. They used to belong to her own parents, and she sold them all on eBay, making a tidy sum.

Everyone's at home today, and all want to chat, ripping open their packages to show me what they've purchased. I say, 'Sorry, not today, show me next time, OK? I've got to get over to Pete and Annie's to say goodbye.'

'Oh. Right you be, they're off Up Country today, if I remember rightly,' the mother says.

'Well, yes.' Everything north of the Tamar is Up Country to the Cornish. 'Not far, just to Devon.'

The husband rolls his eyes, sucks in his cheeks as if I've said they're off to planet Jupiter. His wife says, 'Lordie, I was wanting to give them a stack of *Cornish Life* magazines I got. That Annie has taken so well to our way of life down here, she's gonna miss us like mad.'

The husband says, 'I ain't properly said goodbye to Pete, the time's gone so quickly, didn't realise he'd be off so soon. C'mon, let's see if we can catch'em before they go.'

In moments the whole family are in their car, hurtling down the lane and up the road towards Pete's house. I'm right behind them, and when we arrive, I see the farmer, his wife, and Nips the Labrador, all crowded around Pete's pick-up truck. The eBay family rush up to join them, and I see that there are other locals, too, a whole crowd of people seeing Annie and Pete off to their new home.

Annie gives a cry of delight when she sees me. Luckily Pete hasn't started his old pick-up yet for she leaps out to give me a big hug. Pete gets out as well, and he's warmly embraced by all his friends and neighbours. Annie is, too, and I can see that in the short time she's been here, she's already become a well-loved fixture of the village. Pete was already known and liked, but the trouble was, he was so very much liked that at first the locals were suspicious of Annie, this London girl who'd stolen their boy's heart. I can tell by their faces how she's fitted in, how they've accepted her.

I get out my basket of goodies, thrust it into their truck. Others are also giving the couple going-away gifts, mostly food: homemade chutneys and jams, fresh farm eggs, early vegetables from local gardens. I get out the confetti, and luckily I brought stacks of it, for everyone to throw some. The couple climb back into the pick-up in a flurry of confetti and well wishes, and I give Annie one last hug. She's tearful, as I am. 'I'll miss you, Tessa. I'll miss everyone. Cornwall, too.'

'I'll miss you. But hey, look how you've settled in here. You'll charm the Devonians as quickly as you charmed the Cornish, and by the time we get up to see you, you'll be a proper Dartmoor farmer's wife.'

She smiles, and Pete waves, and off they go, to cheers and good wishes. A few of the local boys follow the pick-up along the quiet road, and car horns honk. Other villagers leave their houses and wave, and by the time the pick-up is out of sight, it's like a street party.

'She's a good maid,' an older woman says to me. 'Well worthy of our Pete. He's a good'un, too.'

A bearded man standing next to her adds, 'More's the pity they be gone, now. Ain't right, they leaving us. They belong here.'

There are staunch murmurs of agreement for this. I nod, blow my nose, and go back to my van, where I sit for some time before finally pulling myself together and getting on with delivering the post.

CHAPTER NINE

Home to Roost

The days and weeks fly by and Cornwall is filling up as the holiday season gears up towards full summer. We've had some long days of monsoon-type rain which flattened the bluebells and the white flowers of the wild garlic, but now the weather is fine again. I'm walking along the cliff path at Morranport with my friend Daphne, enjoying the heatwave we're having. It's still May but it is better than summer, with temperatures in the high twenties. Next week the place will be bustling with visitors as it's half term and the forecast predicts more of the same.

Today we have it nearly to ourselves, perhaps because we've left Morranport at least two miles behind us. It's also late afternoon, and the second homers and cottage renters are setting up barbecues, feeding the family, deserting the beaches. Later on, when the season really gets going, the place will be buzzing at all hours.

Daphne and Joe have been exceptionally busy with the farm

for the last month and more, hard at work after the frozen winter. So we've not seen each other as much as usual. We became close friends during our first year in Treverny, when Ben became ill and was hospitalised for a time. Daphne and her husband Joe were fantastic, helped with the children, the dog, even the cooking. Their two children are more or less the same ages as Will and Amy, and they're all firm friends. Joe and Daphne have a lamb of ours, Patch, that we tried to raise for food, but the children – and I – became so fond of him we couldn't have him killed. I learned to my cost that neither I nor my family could kill a creature we'd named.

Luckily, their children wanted a pet lamb so Patch is theirs now, cropping the grass contentedly with the other sheep in one of their many fields. Or I should say, the four children share him. Patch has become quite fat, cheerfully waddling towards any human he sees, hoping for titbits. He'll never know how lucky he is, how close he came to being lamb chops.

As Daphne and I walk along, watching the flat tranquil sea, the gulls sitting like ducks lazing on the water, we catch up with each other's news. After a time Daphne says, 'Your new neighbours. I'm not sure about them.'

'Kate and Leon? They're OK,' I hesitate, not knowing how to go on, for I see the sceptical look in Daphne's eyes.

'I don't know, Tessa. I met her in the village shop a while ago, tried to chat with her, and she pushed this petition at me. I couldn't believe it when I read it. You won't either.'

'About the Humphreys' peacock, Emmanuel, isn't it?'

'You know about it? You haven't signed it, have you? I didn't bother to read the names. Well, to be honest, there were hardly any. Maybe two or three, and I could see at a glance that they were all people renting around here.'

'Of course I didn't sign it. You know me better than that.'

Daphne looks at me almost accusingly. 'You and Ben have been friendly with them, haven't you? I know you said you've been over there to dinner a few times, and they've come to you. Why didn't you advise Kate against doing such a stupid thing?'

I'm a bit taken aback by her tone. 'Daphne, come on, this is me you're talking to. Of course I tried to talk her out of it. It didn't work, as you can see. She says it really causes her stress, that noise.'

Daphne shakes her head. 'If the noise of a bird causes her stress, she shouldn't have moved to the country. Next thing she'll be complaining about the noise of the sea.'

I try to stick up for my new friend, but it's hard, as I agree with Daphne. All of us who live here have put up with incomers who complain about the smell of dung, the darkness of the village streets, or the sound of tractors running day and night, as happens sometimes when a couple of good days come after a spell of bad weather. Who can blame the farmers for working all day and night when they can? They've been doing it for centuries. It's the same old story – some people want to start a new life in a rural community but they also want to change that life to be more like their old one in the city.

I didn't think that the Wintersons were going to be like that, but lately every time I see them, there seems to be something bothering them. Daphne is now talking about the way they've brought in a craftsman from Up Country to make their shelves, when there are perfectly good ones, if not better, locally. 'As for that concreted front garden . . .' she can't go on; she merely shakes her head.

I say half-heartedly, 'You've got to admit it looks quite stylish. Those tiles, the garden furniture – all very elegant.'

'Don't give me that, Tessa. You dislike it as much as all us villagers do. Yes it's stylish and sophisticated and tasteful and all that, but it doesn't belong in Treverny. Or any other village I know of down here.'

I don't answer – I still keep hoping that Kate and Leon will settle in – but Daphne knows I'm uneasy, so she changes the subject. 'Look, on the cliffs over there. A couple of guillemots.'

We stop to watch the birds, standing like statues looking out to sea. Their beaks are sharp, very dark, razor-like. As we walk on we spot gannets, recognisable by their white body and black wing tips, and the way they dive from great heights into the sea. We pause again, admiring their graceful high swooping dives.

And then, about a half mile further on, Daphne cries, 'There, look! In the cove, there! Seals, masses of them.'

It's one of the great joys of spring and summer, when the day is warm and the seals come out to bask on the rocky islands near the sand. I've seen them here before, many times, but it always fills me with delight. There are at least a dozen of them, lazily washed up on the tide and clinging to the rocks, holding on as the water recedes, giving them a perfect spot to sunbathe. Once they make their way up onto the rocks, it's a wonderful sight to see them flapping about making themselves comfortable, juggling others with their flippers to make room. Now, they're motionless, dozing, their skins glistening, not quite dry yet. There are hours of daylight left so I guess they'll stay put until the next tide and let the water float them back out to sea again.

The seals we have here are the Atlantic Grey Seals, and I've seen them in more than one place around the Cornish coast. There is something very human about the way they empty their lungs before plunging into the sea to find food, for like us, they can't breathe underwater. Although unlike us, they can hold their breath for about eight minutes, and up to thirteen if they are resting rather than hunting. We stand and watch them for some time, not in a hurry, just enjoying the sun, the seals, and each other's company.

For the rest of the walk, Daphne and I forget about peacocks and petitions, about incomers and locals, and their occasional frictions, and just enjoy the sea life around us. The plant life, too along the verges, the white flowers of garlic mustard crop up everywhere and fill the air with their pungent garlicky scent that mingles delightfully with the sea air. A colony of herring gulls has made its home in the cliff tops, and the gulls are calling loudly to each other as they search the sea for food.

On the walk back Daphne says, 'This has been so good. Joe and I have been so busy on the farm lately I've forgotten what it's like to take a couple of hours off and just walk by the sea. Thanks for suggesting it, Tessa. I needed that.'

'Well, with Joe suddenly deciding to take time off and do a barbecue this evening, I thought it'd be a great time to let the men get on with it and we'd have a chance to catch up.'

'Good that Ben's there helping him, though,' Daphne smiles. 'Joe likes to concentrate on the spare ribs when he barbecues. At least Ben can keep an eye on the kids, make sure they don't get up to something outlandish.'

We quicken our steps, hungry now, and looking forward to a beer or cider, a glass of wine, some food. We get into Daphne's car, parked at Morranport, and head home. As we drive through Treverny on the way to the farm, we pass the Wintersons' house. Kate and Leon are sitting on their smart terrace drinking what look like gin and tonics. We wave as we pass, as they do. I'm hoping that maybe Daphne will stop, invite them to her place for a drink or even food; I know Joe always cooks enough for ten when he barbecues. Maybe if Daphne could see them relaxed, at ease, she'd warm to them more.

She doesn't even slow down. And I have to say, I can't blame her. Daphne's a kind woman but she grew up around here; she, and others like her, do not take to criticism of the way they've lived for generations.

I try to push all uneasy thoughts about my neighbours out of my head as we reach the farm, and the shouts of happy children greet us as we join the others. That night we stay late, watching the moon and stars come out, and then some bats gliding from under the eaves of the barn where they have their home. From somewhere in a meadow comes the cry of an owl, then another. It's so warm that we stay in shorts and T-shirts, even when we stroll through the fields to the place on the farm where you can see the sea, there's not a breeze on the higher hillside. We watch the black night water glittering in the moonlight, hear the owl hooting again.

It's much later when Ben and I walk home through the silent village arm in arm, Amy and Will running happily ahead with Jake, who is such a frequent visitor to the farm now that he's learned not to chase sheep.

'I'm sleepy,' I murmur as we stumble into the dark house, turn on some lights, shoo the children upstairs. 'Great evening, but good to be home.'

And it is. Not just home for tonight, but home for good,

here in this village, in this part of Cornwall. I feel a sense of belonging so strong that it almost overwhelms me. In bed, I lie awake long after Ben has gone to sleep, watching high clouds move across a full moon, hearing owls again, imagining bats and other night creatures, flying and scurrying about the countryside. Even when I drift off at last, the sounds linger on in my dreams.

Emmanuel cocks his head and eyeballs me as I walk into the Humphreys' garden. He's calculating the odds of my having a cheese sandwich on me. The Duchess, smarter, ignores me, knowing I've given up feeding the peafowls. When they first arrived, I always had a titbit to give them but they followed me around so persistently, and after a time, so annoyingly, that I soon stopped.

Emmanuel is quiet, anyway. In fact I haven't heard his cry for a few days, though that doesn't mean to say he doesn't carry on in the mornings when I'm at work. He is a beautiful bird, though, all that luminescent blue and turquoise. I wish Kate and Leon would come over to Poet's Tenement with me, meet Edna and Hector, but they hesitate and always make some excuse if I mention it. I think Kate's a bit wary of them, and it's not just the peacock. She's used to eccentrics in the city, takes them in her stride from what I've heard her say about her old neighbours, but in rural areas she's uncertain. I'm sure she thinks the Humphreys are barmy, from having seen them in their strange clothes, and heard tales about them from the locals.

Before I reach the house, a loud voice stops me. It's Doug, in the nearby field, carting dead branches away in a wheelbarrow which he leaves unceremoniously in the middle of the meadow to chat. As usual, Doug's chats are peppered with dire warnings, accompanied by rolling eyes, puckered lips through which a soft doom-ridden whistle sounds as he finishes a sentence. 'Hey m'maid, glad you be here. You got to talk sense into them two indoors.'

'About Emmanuel, you mean? Goodness, Doug, what can Hector and Edna do about their peacock? They can't stop the bird from screeching now and again.'

This sends Doug into a tizzy of rage. 'Shite, maid, I ain't got no problem with that bird of theirs. I like the daft thing, tame as anything, never tries to go for me like a goose or something, nor does his mate, that little peahen. It's that woman up at the house near yours that don't like Emmanuel, that Up Country maid, what's her name?'

'Do you mean Kate Winterson?'

'That's the one. D'you know what she did? She stopped me right on the road, right on me way to the farm to do an honest day's work, started on gibbering something about noise, can you believe? The bloody peacock! She then shoves this paper under me nose, asks me to sign. A bloody petition to get rid of Emmanuel!' He's so indignant he's turned bright red. After a few head shakes and incredulous whistles, he goes on, 'I ain't particularly partial to peacocks, but there's nowt wrong with that bird. Why, his cry ain't no worse than your bloody cockerel, maid, now is it?'

Oh dear. I wonder if Kate will start going on about Pavarotti. He does crow rather loudly now and again. 'Doug, you didn't say that to Kate, did you? About my cockerel?'

'Course I did! I told'er, maid, if you want to complain about noise, how about that noisy chicken of Tessa's?'

'You never complained about it before. I didn't know his crowing bothered you.'

He gives me a look he's often given me before, that of an exasperated Cornishman trying to impart local logic to someone from Up Country. 'Course it don't bother me, what the bloody hell d'you think I be? Some city bloke? Why would a cockerel crowing his bloody fool head off bother me?'

'But – you told Kate . . .'

He cuts me off. 'I told her some home truths, maid. If you do be buying a house in the country, you bloody put up with bird noise, be it cockerel or peacock, what's the difference.'

I think actually there is a bit of difference between the sounds, but Doug's right. And I have to admit, sometimes Pavarotti does go on all day off and on, when he's in an exuberant mood. 'Well, Doug, who knows, maybe Kate will take out a petition against my bird next.'

He shakes his head. 'No, maid, no fear of that. You be a friend, the only one she got in Treverny. No fear of her spoiling that, maid. You be the only one on her side.'

I have an uneasy feeling that Doug is right. I don't like it, don't like being on someone's 'side' especially here in this village that I feel is truly mine, truly home at last. 'I'm just a neighbour, a friend, Doug. Not on her side as you put it.'

He doesn't think this worth answering but shakes his head mournfully, then livens up as he remembers why he called over to me in the first place. 'You got to talk to Hector and Edna, about that tree, the old holm oak. It's on its way out for sure.'

I sigh. 'I know that, Doug, and so do they. A proper tree surgeon has even had a look at it and agrees it's got to come down. Only they won't have it.'

He makes his exasperated face again, with the whistle, 'Because of them bloody rooks.'

'Exactly. The rookery's been there for years.'

'But that's the point, maid. Don't you see, it be so over-crowded now the new rooks are nesting in t'other trees around the place. So t'will allus be rooks here, if that's the worry.'

I hadn't thought of that. Doug goes on, 'Talk some sense in to them, maid. I like them two. They be good old-fashioned sorts.'

I'm not sure Doug would say that if he'd witnessed Hector's display of Tai Chi in the kitchen last January, but I keep quiet. Again, I know what he means. They're from a bygone era, without computers, mobile phones and all the other parapher-nalia of modern life. Despite their travels, their vast knowledge of so many different things, there's a real old-fashioned inno-cence about the couple which makes the locals very protective of them.

'I'll try, Doug.'

He nods and goes back to his wheelbarrow and his work while I seek out the Humphreys. I've got my usual supply of eggs for them from my hens. I find Edna and Hector in the back garden, sitting in rickety ancient deck chairs apparently asleep, their faces turned to the sun, arms spread out on the wooden struts of the chairs, palms facing upward. They are so still that for a moment I fear the worse, especially when a discreet cough or two doesn't rouse them. I call out their names and when there's no response, I start quickly towards them, my heart beating fast. Before I reach them, Hector's low voice, murmurs, 'Hello Tessa, my dear. Lovely to see you.'

I wonder how he can, when he hasn't opened his eyes, but his voice sounds normal and reassuring. Edna, though, has opened hers, and smiles at me, 'How nice to see you.' She beckons me to sit down on the old moss-covered tree stump which has been there for years. There is no other place to sit in this ramshackle back garden, which is no more than a wilderness with a space cleared outside the back door where granite slabs have been laid to make a kind of rough patio. Doug has made some attempt to keep down the weeds and excess foliage and, though it's often a losing battle, right now the land is at its best here. It's a sea of bluebells, some of the biggest, bluest, I've ever seen. The bluebells here always seem to come out slightly later than others on the south coast, and now they're glorious, the scent amazing.

I say, 'Sorry if I've disturbed your afternoon sleep. Great idea, a nap after lunch, especially in this weather.'

Hector opens his eyes and sits up, 'Oh, we weren't napping. We were practising our deep breathing.'

Edna beams, 'An old sage in India told us once that when a person is born, they are given a certain number of breaths to use in their lifetime. So, of course, the secret of longevity is breathing slowly, deeply, to eke out those breaths.'

Hector is nodding in agreement, 'The worst possible thing to do is to breathe fast, shallowly. You use up your lifetime's breaths too soon, you see.'

They look at each other, smiling. Edna says, 'Well, we shall see whether it works or not. I suppose we won't be sure until we reach a hundred.'

They are both out of their deck chairs now and before we can talk about anything else, or even have a cup of the tea which Edna promises is forthcoming, they give me a little lesson in deep breathing. 'In through the nostrils, that's right, Tessa, slowly, deeply, first feel your belly expand as your diaphragm sucks the air in, then feel your chest expand as you breathe deeply into your lungs, hold it there for a second or two before slowly – with control, Tessa! – breathing out. That's right, slowly, in, in, in, then out, out, out.'

When they're satisfied I know how to breathe properly, they bustle me into the kitchen where we have a good cup of English breakfast. I must say I feel very relaxed after my session of deep breathing. If that's what got these two to such a fit old age, I'm all for it. But then it could be their Spartan diet, or the concoction of strange herbs Edna uses for her various teas, or the meditative walks they do up and down their garden path winter or summer, or the Tai Chi – or any one of the other things they must do that I don't know anything about yet. That's the delight of these two, I'm always finding out new things about them.

Or it could be luck that the two of them happen to have great genes.

And thinking of longevity, I finish my tea quickly and mention the tree again. 'Doug is worried about you. So is everyone. I know you like your independence, and it's your life, but if that tree crashes into your house, with you inside . . .'

'We'd be crushed to death,' Edna says, cheerily.

'We know that, dear maid,' Hector adds, also quite cheerful. 'So we will take the precaution of making sure nice people like you, and others who visit us, don't come during a storm, or any kind of fierce wind.'

We're wandering out to the front of the house as we speak, to look again at the tree which is causing all this trouble. It looks even more staggy headed, as Woody put it, than it did a few months ago. Behind it the other trees, English oaks and magnificent beech trees, look positively brimming with health, at least to an untrained eye, although Woody did say they were quite ancient, too, and needed to be watched carefully. But they're not a probem at present, and it is the holm oak, home to the huge rookery, that's the worry.

Doug is right, though, the younger rooks are starting new nests in the other trees. I mention this fact to the Humphreys, but of course they've already noted this. I say, 'So if you have the dying tree down, the rooks will all simply move next door. No problem.'

Both the Humphreys look at me as if I haven't understood a thing, but Hector answers kindly, 'Would you like to be forced out of your house?'

'And made to move on, against your will, even if it was only next door?'

'You see, maid, we choose our homes, fill them with loving care and they become part of us. It's the same for the rooks.'

I give up. Edna and Hector have settled down on the bench in front of their house to watch their beloved birds. I perch on a wooden stool next to it, since they've asked me to stay and watch with them. Edna smiles. 'Hector and I sit here looking at them for hours.'

I can see why. Rooks are fascinating birds. I look up at the ones nesting in the trees. Once I thought they were all jet black, but now, with the sun slanting through the branches and shining on the rooks, I can see that they have all sorts of glistening colours in their plumage, blues and purples and burnished copper. They are such sociable birds, too, always chattering amongst themselves, or so it sounds. The cacophony of noise now as they feed their young, flying to and fro, busying themselves in the tree, is so loud that it's a wonder Kate hasn't also started a petition about the rooks. Neither Edna nor Hector has mentioned the peacock one, so I gather they don't know about it, and I'm certainly not going to tell them.

As I sit watching the activity in the rookery, stealing a glance now and again at the old couple sitting on the bench, a great sense of peace and calm settles on me. It's a windless day, with a few clouds but enough sun to cast patterns and shadows in the tree and along the ground, and enough blue sky to contrast brightly against the glossy feathers of the rooks. Other birds are also around: five or six swallows perch on a telephone wire, and a few sparrows are flying in and out of the eaves of the house. A faint scent of some kind of flower or blossom I can't identify is wafting through the front garden. I could ask Edna, she'd know, but she's in another world, entranced, watching the rooks. She and Hector look so utterly still, so completely contented and at peace, that I don't want to disturb them. So I turn my eyes back to the rookery and see the most amazing sight. A kestrel flies down towards the holm oak and suddenly four or five rooks are chasing it away. The bird of prey retreats and the rooks return.

'That was incredible,' I say, when they've all settled again.

'Yes, it's quite a sight, isn't it,' Hector agrees. 'We've seen the rooks chase buzzards before. One only has to glide too near the rookery and they work as a team, two, three or more chasing the buzzard away. They never go far after it; the rooks come back as soon as they've chased it off.'

As we watch, a great number of the birds fly up out of the tree and circle around high up, before flying into the distance. 'Good weather,' Edna says. 'When they make those sweeping circles low in the sky, bad weather is on its way. They're much more reliable than the weather forecasts we hear on the radio.'

I finally tear myself away. I can understand why Edna and Hector do not want to cut down the holm oak. And yet all things die, everything has to end. Perhaps by next autumn, when the westerly gales hit Cornwall, they'll have second thoughts about the tree. I hope so, for their sakes.

A week or so later, I'm outside trying to tidy up the back garden when I get a wonderful surprise. We have swifts nesting in the roof of our house. They've declined so much, become so uncommon in Cornwall, that the Wildlife Trust has asked people to contact them if we see them nesting anywhere.

The person on the phone at the Trust told me that the reason for the dramatic decline in numbers seems to be modern building techniques which block up their nesting sites. Most of them nest under broken roof tiles, in open eaves, or holes in walls, but now the old properties have been repaired, holes concreted up and eaves fitted with grills. Roof tiles that were put on decades ago have been repaired or, more usually, new ones are fitted closely together. Because of all this home improvement, in the last forty years swift numbers have dropped by forty per cent.

I want to mention this to the Wintersons, for they've got Guy back making repairs to Treetops. There won't be a single place for a swift family to nest on that property. Maybe Kate and Leon haven't a clue about swifts. I didn't, until I read about their decline in the local newspaper. At least I know that, unlike seaweed, the Wintersons do like birds; both of them have mentioned how wonderful the bird life is in Cornwall, except for peacocks, of course.

I decide to go over then and there. I haven't seen Kate for a couple of weeks as she's been up and down to London catching up with friends, the theatre, new restaurants. Leon is busy there this month with consulting work, so Kate likes joining him. They use a friend's apartment, some film maker who is abroad half the time.

On my way I stop to watch the swifts. It's evening and they're swooping around the sky, making their peculiar screaming sound, looking so graceful with their long stream-lined black wings, slender bodies and tails. It's such a wonderful sight, and such a short time we have the chance to see them, for they'll be gone again in August.

When I arrive at Treetops, only Guy is there, working on some guttering. After we've chatted, mostly about Clara – the relationship is going a storm now, after his initial agonising shyness – I ask if my neighbours are home, for no one has come out. Guy says, 'Nah, they've gone somewhere with some London friends they've got visiting.' There's a distasteful look on his face. 'Probably talking about that posh furniture maker from Up Country.'

There's not much I can say but I try, 'I don't blame you for being cross about all that, Guy, but I'm sure if they knew your work, how professional it is, they'd have kept you on.'

'They didn't even ask to see my stuff. I could've taken them to homes that have shelves, even furniture I've made. But those two didn't want to know.'

I change the subject. It's done now, no point talking about it. 'Well, I'm sorry they're not in. I was going to mention the swifts, you know we've got a nest in our eaves? Treetops has a couple of loose roof tiles that would be perfect for swifts, wouldn't that be exciting if one nested there? Thought I'd warn Kate and Leon not to repair it. I know they're interested in the birds around here.'

Guy has stopped work and sat himself down on the new hardwood picnic table in the Wintersons' garden. 'Think I don't know about the swifts, Tessa? I told them I didn't want to patch up the places where they might have a chance to nest, but Leon told me the birds had plenty of places to make their homes and they didn't want a leaky roof all summer, so I should get on with it.'

I'm shocked. 'Surely he wasn't that rude, Guy. That doesn't sound like Leon.'

Guy gives me a sheepish smile. 'OK, those weren't his exact words. And no he wasn't rude, in fact he couldn't be more polite. He used different words, is all, but the meaning, that were the same. He wants his house perfect, and if that means covering up the eaves, so be it.' His smile is replaced by a frown. 'I wanted to tell him to stuff it, do his own eaves, especially as he's happy enough to have me as an odd-job man but not a skilled carpenter. But I need the dosh, Tessa,' he looks down quickly, but not before I see a blush on his face. 'For, um, me and Clara, y'know? She wants me to move in to her place, move out of the digs I got. And I want to pay my way, not live off her.'

I totally embarrass him with a huge hug and great kisses on both cheeks. 'Steady on, Tessa maid,' he mumbles, face bright red, as I congratulate him and wish them both well.

I leave, sad about the birds, but happy for Guy and Clara. Before I go into my own home, I stand for a long time, watching the swifts, hoping they'll be around for many more years despite the odds against them.

CHAPTER TEN

Lost in the Storm

It is June and the weather has turned grey and drizzly; the holiday crowds now appearing are not well pleased. There are droves of them, and it's not even official summer holiday time, but lots of families, some with pre-school age children, others who have taken theirs out of school during term time, are holidaying early to save on the sky-rocketing expense of accommodation and so on during July and August. I've had a few phone calls from the rental agency wanting to know how I've got on with my 'home improvements'. We've completed some repairs, slowly but surely, and are starting to check off their exacting requirements, but I've told them the property won't be one hundred per cent ready until next spring. It's a relief not to do it all at once; we'd never have managed it in such a short time, either physically or financially. And we have those two weeks already booked in the summer, with people who like the sound of our house exactly how it is. It's a start, to condition us slowly to this renting lark, and will earn us a bit of money in the meantime.

I talked to Annie the other night, and asked how she was settling in on Dartmoor. 'I absolutely love it,' she surprised me by saying. I knew she'd adjust to being a farmer's wife eventually, as she adjusted to life as an agriculturist's wife in rural Cornwall, but this seemed quick. 'I must have lived on an isolated moor in another life; I feel so at home here,' she went on. 'I'm getting fond of all the animals. The locals, too, are really nice, friendly and helpful.' She paused. 'And then there's Timothy.' Her voice was soft and soppy.

'Who's he?' I asked, slightly alarmed. Newly married and sounding dreamy over another man? What's going on?

'He's a darling. I'm crazy about him.'

Now I was totally alarmed. 'Annie, what are you on about? Who is Timothy? What about Pete?'

'Oh, he likes Pete, but it's me he's really fond of. He ignores Pete when I'm around,' she laughed, a giggly, girlie laugh. 'I have to be careful that my husband doesn't get too jealous. He might ban Timothy from the house.'

Oh God. As she talked, I started envisaging a gorgeous younger man, a toy boy, some rustic Dartmoor yeoman with healthy outdoor bronzed skin and body to match. Annie definitely sounded flirty, talking about this Timothy. Was she getting lonely out on that isolated farm, and looking for a mild flirtation to liven things up? Silly woman, I thought, this wasn't on at all.

I said firmly, 'Look, you listen to me. This doesn't sound good. It's OK, I'm your friend, I know you probably had a brainstorm when you were wrenched away from Cornwall and thrust up on a wild granite-covered moor, but you mustn't throw it all away.'

'Throw what away? What are you on about, Tessa?'

'Your marriage. Pete. I know you probably think it's only a flirtation, but it's still dangerous. Especially if Pete is jealous. You've got to give him up.'

'Who, Pete? Are you crazy?'

'It's you who's crazy. Not Pete, this Timothy.'

There was a long silence on the phone. Then Annie began to laugh. 'Annie, this isn't funny. If you only heard how soft and dreamy your voice became when you talked about this Timothy, you'd understand why Pete gets jealous. That's the way you used to talk about him.'

Annie was laughing so hard by then she couldn't talk. Convinced she was having some sort of breakdown, I said, 'Annie, I'm coming up there to see you. Tomorrow.'

In between gulps and convulsive sobs as she struggled to stop laughing, Annie managed to say, 'You think Timothy is a man. Tessa, he's a sheep. A twelve-year-old pet sheep.'

I kept quiet for so long that Annie thought I'd hung up. I said, not exactly intelligently, 'A . . . a sheep?'

'Honestly, Tessa, as if I could ever fancy another man when I've got Pete!'

'Um, maybe I did overreact a bit.'

'A bit? It was hilarious. Wait till I tell Pete, he'll roar.'

I clutched the phone. 'Annie, don't you dare tell Pete, it's too embarrassing. Just tell me about this sheep you're so soft on.'

'Well, Pete's uncle got him as an orphan lamb twelve years ago, bottle fed him and all that. He had a farm worker at the time and the worker's child got so fond of the lamb that Pete's uncle let him have it to keep at the farm. When the family left and moved away, he didn't have the heart to get rid of Timothy. He's as soft-hearted as Pete, they're very alike.'

'Who, Pete and the sheep?'

'No, you dodo, Pete and his uncle. Timothy is now a beautiful sheep despite his old age, and so sweet. A bit arthritic, unfortunately, but he's on medication. I tried all sorts of herbal and homeopathic stuff but it didn't work, so the vet put him on horse tablets.' She giggles, 'They have no drugs for arthritis in sheep, apparently – the poor things get eaten before they live long enough to develop it, I suppose. Timothy gets the same dosage as a small pony. I give it to him in half a banana.'

'A banana?'

'He loves them. Apparently dear old Timothy once got into a wheelbarrow full of rotten bananas Pete's uncle had for the pigs, and he ate so many he blew up like a balloon. Lay there all swollen, nobody thought he'd survive. But he did and he's loved bananas ever since, can't get enough of them, though he's only allowed half a day. He's such a character, Tessa, I'm quite in love with the daft animal. Wait until you meet him.'

Before we hung up, we made plans for our visit to Dartmoor for one of the weeks when our house is being rented. Annie said again we were more than welcome to stay with them for both weeks, but I don't want to overstay. A week will be lovely, and then we'll camp as planned.

There's a blustery gale coming from the sea that is so fierce it's hard to open the door at the Morranport post office. I say hello to Holly and ask her how the part-time job there is going. 'Fine, I love it,' she tells me.

'I'm sure you're a great help to Nell.'

She grins and nods her head, making the dozen or so tiny plaits around her head bob up and down. She's wearing a short denim skirt, flowery leggings, and sequinned flip-flops, despite the torrential rain. There are enough bracelets on her wrists, and beads and baubles around her neck, to start a shop. She's like a colourful exotic bird, and I must say, brightens up the place on a stormy grey day like today wonderfully. She says, 'Yeah, I've been an amazing help, me.' She winks at me mischievously. 'Though mebbe not that much in the shop.'

'What do you mean?'

'Matchmaking, more like. The two old dears, Woody's granddad and Nell.'

'Holly, keep your voice down! Nell will kill you if she hears you calling her an old dear.'

Holly rolls her eyes, 'Don't worry, she's out.'

'Out? I've never known Nell out of the shop when it's open.'

'Ah, now, that was before I got here. She's out sure enough.'

The place is empty, the weather keeping the holiday makers well away from the sea, but I roam around the shop anyway, looking behind the post office counter and inside Nell's tiny office space to make sure she's not lurking somewhere about to jump out chiding us for talking about her. Holly says, 'I tell you, she's out. With Sydney. Left ages ago, said she'd be back in half an hour.'

'Where are they going in this weather? Look at the rain coming down now, it's horizontal. It's a full-blown gale out there.'

We look through the window at the storm. The sea is foaming and churning on the surface, black underneath, and the sky is bruised purple and charcoal. Heavy raindrops splatter against the windowpane. Holly says, with a smirk, 'They've gone for a walk.'

'What? They can't be, not in this.'

'That's what Nell said. Said they'd go take a look at the storm. They got on waterproofs and wellies.'

I'm suddenly concerned. Neither of them is young after all, and this wind could blow them right over. Or what if a freak wave washes them out to sea? It can happen so quickly. 'Holly, are you sure she said she'd be back in half an hour?'

'Yeah, I'm sure,' she looks at her watch, which seems to be a huge face of Mickey Mouse and looks far too large for her thin wrist, and frowns. 'Should of been back by now. Been gone nearly an hour.'

I'm already zipping up my waterproof, pulling up the hood. 'I'm going to look for them. It's dangerous to be walking by the sea in this. I can't believe they're crazy enough to be out there this long.'

I go out into the fiercest storm we've had since last winter. The waves are crashing over the sea wall, soaking the footpath, and even the road. I look down the length of it and don't see a single soul.

I'm starting to seriously worry. Where are they? I walk along the road, well away from the spray. The wind is lashing me, as is the rain. I start to run, calling out, 'Nell! Sydney!' The only reply is the howl of the gale. My heart starts to pound as I run faster, call louder, until at last I reach the end of the sea wall where there's a lone cottage before the path veers up to the cliff top. This is the home of two of my well-loved customers, Archie and Jennifer, retired teachers, both Cornish, who have lived in this house all their married lives. Archie's family were all fishermen, and this was his father's cottage. I love the fact that it's still a home to a fisherman's family, and not a second home as no doubt it will be one day, as the couple have no children to pass it on to.

I look up onto the cliff top. If Nell and Sydney have gone up there, on that narrow path right at the edge, the wind would have blown them off in moments. I'm sure they're sensible enough not to have attempted the cliff. The more likely scenario is that they stopped by the sea wall to watch the thunderous waves and were knocked down, pulled in. My heart is beating so hard at this thought that instead of running all the way back to the post office to raise the alarm, I bang on the door of the cottage in front of me.

After a moment Archie appears, his mouth open in surprise as I say breathlessly, 'Quick, we need to phone. The coast guard, the lifeboat, somebody.'

'Tessa, come in, the phone's in the kitchen. What's happened?'

As we rush towards the kitchen I say, 'It's Nell and Sydney, they've disappeared, went for a walk along the sea front and there's no sign of them. I think they've been swept out.'

Like some whacky film, I stop short, do a double take, and stare at the kitchen table. Sitting there serenely drinking tea is Nell, with Jennifer on one side of her and Sydney on the other.

For a few moments I freeze, not quite believing my eyes. Then as relief washes over me, making me weak at the knees, Archie says, 'You don't need to make that phone call, so why don't you have a cup of tea instead?'

Nell is glaring at me. 'Maid, did you be thinking that I cannot look after meself in a storm?'

I make myself look contrite. 'Nell, I'm afraid I did think that for a moment. I should have known better.'

Sydney says, his eyes twinkling, 'And d'you think for one minute I'd have risked dear Nell's life in a storm like this'un?'

'Um, no. Of course you wouldn't.'

Everyone has a huge smile on their face as the teapot is brought around, a cup placed in front of me. Nell refuses a second cup, stands up and says, 'I'd best be off. Don't want anyone thinking I do be neglecting the shop, just because I take a breather every now and again for a spot of fresh air.' She stares at me with her best haughty look, as if daring me to mention again that the fresh air is a Force seven or eight gale.

I look her straight in the eye. 'We all need a walk in the fresh air to clear our heads sometimes, Nell. But you don't need to hurry back. Holly is minding the shop and post office just fine. The storm's kept all the customers away, anyway.'

But Nell insists on leaving, and Sydney insists on accompanying her, and I'm left with Archie and Jennifer, drying out in front of their Aga, kept on low even in the summertime. I spend a lovely half hour catching up with them, looking at Jennifer's latest watercolours (she sells quite a few of her wonderful paintings in the summer) and talking to Archie about the progress of his book on Cornish history.

On the way home the storm breaks at last, and the sky is arced with rainbows, not just one or two, but at least three, and a hint of a fourth. I pull into a hillside layby where I can look out over the fields and cliffs to the sea. One rainbow is all one colour, or so it seems from here – a streak of crimson going straight up from the sea to the sky. I've never seen that before, and I watch for quite some time, until the light changes and it fades from view. There are so many things I'm seeing in Cornwall for the first time, I feel like a baby in a bright new world.

The phone is ringing when I walk through the front door a week or two later and I grab it, still wearing my postie uniform. I wonder if it's Ben, who is Up Country doing a voice-over. There have been a spate of these recently, which is great for our income but I miss him when he's not around. At least he's not on a six-week theatre tour as he was this time last year.

But it's Annie, and I'm immediately alert as I only talked to her the night before. 'What's wrong?' I blurt, before she has time to say more than hello.

'Nothing. Everything's fine. But look, I've got a friend who has a problem and I suddenly thought you'd be just the one to help.'

I sit down to listen, as Annie explains. 'This friend, Dominic, I've known him for ages; he was at our wedding, remember?'

'Yes, I remember Dominic. And?'

'His parents pulled up their London roots and moved to Cornwall, up on the north coast. St Petroc, the village is, you know it.'

St Petroc is a seaside village, a fabulous harbour town with a couple of beautiful beaches, great cafés, art galleries, and shops. The harbour is filled with fishing boats instead of yachts as this is still a working harbour, and the pier is stacked with nets and the paraphernalia of the fishermen. The village is a family favourite and we've visited it often.

Annie continues, 'This was six or seven years ago. Dominic's parents started a B&B right on the seafront, opposite the pier and harbour. Great little place, I stayed there once long before you even moved to Cornwall.' She sighs deeply. 'In my wayward youth,' she reminisces, 'so long ago. I was with that . . .'

'I know all about your lurid past, Annie, now forget it and get on with what the problem is.'

'The B&B is called The Blue Seashell. It's got a great blue seashell over the door.'

'Duh. Really? Not a green one?'

'Don't be facetious, Tessa. I just mentioned it as you might have seen it.'

'I think I have. It's a darling house, an old fisherman's cottage.'

'They're all darling fishermen's cottages in St Petroc. Anyway, the couple, Dominic's parents, made a real go of it, are doing terribly well, booked up almost all year. Well, except for the winter months when they go off to the Maldives or something and shut the place up.'

'Goodness, they must be doing extremely well.'

'Well, they are. They work hard, too. They must both be around sixty now, though they look years younger. They've got such energy, but now here's the problem. Dominic's mother is due to have an operation in a week's time, nothing critical but not something she can postpone. His dad's sister was coming to help run the B&B but now their father – Dominic's grandfather – who has a birthday soon, eighty-eight or eighty-nine, has just been told he's terminally ill and has only another six months to live. He's in Canada and now, of course, both Dominic's father and aunt want to be there with their father for his last birthday. They've frantically tried to get cover for the B&B for the week after next but can't find anyone at this late stage. Today's the first of July as you know.'

I'm beginning to get her drift. 'And in a week's time, our house will be rented.'

'Exactly. You need to vacate your house and they need someone to live in and run the B&B for that one week. I believe they've got someone lined up afterwards, but no one when they first go. What do you think, Tessa? Think you and Ben could run a B&B? It'll be better than camping anyway – that's the week you were going to, isn't it? There's a family apartment in the B&B where all four of you can stay; think of the fun Amy and Will can have, the beach practically outside their door. And you'll get paid for it, as well, how about that?'

I'm nearly delirious with excitement. A proper place for us

to live instead of camping out, and getting paid, too. I've never run a B&B before but I can learn, and so can Ben. Loads of people come down to Cornwall and start one from scratch. I've got ex-farmers on my round who have done just that, when they couldn't make a living from the land any more. I'll get lots of advice from my customers.

'We'll do it!' I shout. 'Tell Dominic we're on.'

'You don't need to holler, I can hear you. I'll tell him at once.'

Later, talking about it to the family, I'm pleased to hear that they are as excited as I am. 'It'll be such fun,' I say. 'I know we don't know much about running a B&B, but we're willing to learn, and we're friendly people, aren't we? I'm sure the guests will forgive us if some things don't go exactly right once or twice.'

The next day I take a good look around the house to see if we're ready for the family that's coming down from London to stay. It looks gleaming. We've replaced the cracked window-panes, bought a barbecue for the garden and a microwave for the kitchen. I hated buying the microwave especially. We have to think carefully about the cost of whatever we buy, and to waste money on something we don't want is painful. Annie's London friends have been down and seen the house, insisted they loved it 'just the way it is', which gladdened my heart. Once we're with the rental agency next year, we'll have to take down many of our personal things, the photographs, books and paintings we've acquired over the years. Everything has to look impersonal, with everything of character taken away, but for now they can stay.

I've not replaced our old washing machine, for I really do loathe throwing out something that is perfectly serviceable.

Next year, when we're with the agency, will be time enough for a new one. There is a load of clothes in the washer now, and I go to see if they're done. To my horror, there is water everywhere, all over the floor, pouring from my trusty washing machine. It's stopped and I open the door gingerly. More water cascades out and I shut it quickly.

This is just what I don't need. Ben's away; he knows the machine's funny ways and can get it going sometimes when there's a blip, but he won't be home until late tonight. My spare uniform shorts are in there and I need them for tomorrow; I got a bit carried away rummaging in some brambles trying to find a ball for the toddler son of one of my customers and I ripped my other pair earlier. The weather's hot and humid, with temperatures tomorrow predicted for the high twenties; I don't want to wear the heavy Royal Mail trousers, that's for sure.

I pull on shorts and a loose T-shirt, fasten my hair into a ponytail and mop the water on the floor, drain the washing machine. I then do all the things Ben does – like examining the filter for a blockage and checking the door. But it won't start. It seems stone dead.

I have to get it going so I phone Al, the young man who has done numerous repairs on various electrical appliances in our place. I get him on his mobile and he tells me he's in Treverny anyway, next door with my neighbours, Kate and Leon, and will be right over.

He's here in fifteen minutes. 'Good timing,' he says as he bounces in. 'Those neighbours of yours, they bought this fancy telly down from London, along with other electronic stuff, and I had to wire it all up. They got some cash, don't they?'

I shrug. I'm not about to be drawn into talking about them

with Al. He goes on, 'I had some raffle tickets for the village footie club, some great prizes. I asked your neighbour if he'd like a ticket and he said no, but he gave me a tenner anyway. I tried to get him to take the tickets but he said he didn't want'em.'

Instead of looking happy about this perk, Al looks positively glum. I say, 'Well, that's OK, isn't it? It was generous of Leon, giving you ten pounds.' Even as I say this, I'm beginning to realise I spend a great deal of time trying to justify or explain our neighbours' actions to the locals.

Al says, 'The cash is fine, yeah, we can be doing with it all right, but man, what's wrong with taking a raffle ticket? Aren't our prizes good enough for him?' He shakes his head, scratching it as if searching there for words. Finally he says, 'Some folk just don't get it, do they.' It's a statement, not a question. 'They just don't get that money's not everything. We all want it, and need it, but hell, it's not all there is.' He finally looks up at me. 'And it sure as hell's not a substitute for other things. D'ya know what I'm saying?'

I nod. Actually, I do. It's something that the Wintersons haven't learned yet, and I'm beginning to wonder if they ever will. The other day I was talking to them both about a fund-raising event some of the villagers want to hold to raise money for repairs on the hall. We plan on having cake stalls, second-hand clothes stands, games with prizes for the children – the usual stuff of village fetes all over England. I was in Kate and Leon's house, drinking coffee, enjoying the breeze blowing through the open windows. All their new kitchen units gleamed, and the Italian tiles on the floor glowed rustically in the sunbeams. I thought how the rental agency would love this house, everything new, in perfect condition.

'Would you like to take part in the fundraiser?' I asked them, thinking it would be a great way for them to get to know some of the villagers. Apart from us, they haven't seemed to make any friends.

Leon and Kate looked at each other. I went on, 'You could run the cake stall. That's great fun. There's always loads of the most delicious baked goodies on sale, all made by the locals. I always get some for the freezer; you can't make them for the price.' Kate looked doubtful so I babbled on, 'Or you could both run one of the games stalls. Like throw a ball at a teddy, or guess how many buttons are in a bottle.'

They still looked doubtful, but then Kate said, 'I'd like to help, and I know Leon would, too.' She looked at him and he nodded at her to go on. 'But – I'm not much good at that kind of stuff.'

Leon broke in then. 'It's hard for either of us to commit right now, Tessa. But look, it's a great idea, and like Kate said, we'd love to help. After all, Treverny is our village, too. I'll tell you what we'll do – we'll make a donation to the village hall fund.' He smiled broadly, pleased at his solution.

Kate looked relieved. 'That's what we'll do, yes. In fact, wouldn't it be easier if everyone did that? I mean, I know money is tight everywhere these days, but let's face it, if most of the locals go to the fete – and they'll support it, as they always do – they'll probably each spend, say, ten pounds, or so. Well, wouldn't it save a lot of time and energy if everyone just gave that amount to the village hall fund?'

They both looked at me with such an expectant look that for a moment I didn't know what to say. Like Al said, they just don't get it. The fundraising fete is not only about money, it's about people getting together, doing things together, keeping their community alive.

Tactfully, I tried to explain some of this to Leon and Kate, stressing the fun we villagers get from these efforts, and they listened politely but it was obviously not their thing. So I asked them about the play they saw at the Old Vic in London last weekend, and they asked me how the filming was going – Ben's in another episode of *Doc Martin* – and we spent another twenty minutes amiably chatting. When I left, they walked me outside and as we were saying goodbye, we heard the dreadful screech of Emmanuel again.

Kate overreacted theatrically, making a face and holding her hands over her ears. Leon frowned. 'Damn bird,' he muttered. 'Really, it shouldn't be allowed. It really shouldn't. Poor Kate gets headaches from that noise, and I must say it drives me up the wall every time I hear it. It sounds like fingernails scraping a blackboard, only ten times as loud.'

I murmured something about not noticing it so much but Kate cut in, saying, 'I tried to stop it, but do you know, no one signed my petition. Well, none of the locals. Two or three who own homes here but live in London did, but that's all. No point taking it further if no one backs us up.'

It seemed they had forgotten that I didn't sign it either, nor did Ben, for they looked at me as if expecting a sympathetic glance. I nodded non-committedly, relieved that Edna and Hector weren't going to be hassled, and rushed back home.

I stop thinking about Leon and Kate as Al inspects the washing machine. I bring him tea and a large piece of carrot cake – he requires mounds of food when he comes to repair something – and wait for the verdict. Finally, he finds some part that's faulty, says it can be repaired easily, then tells me the astronomical cost. 'That's settled it,' I say. 'We'll have to have a new one.'

He's horrified. 'No, no, no! Of course you don't. That's what a new part would cost, but hey, I'm sure I can find you a second-hand one. Leave it to me.'

'It's fine. We'll have to have a new machine when we start proper rentals, so no point wasting money repairing this.'

'It won't cost much, honest. A second-hand one is cheap, I know just where to look, too.'

We squabble about this for a bit, me insisting on a new machine, Al insisting it can be mended inexpensively. Suddenly I stop, seeing the ludicrousness of the situation. He should be convincing me to spend the money on a new appliance – his parents own the shop we'd buy it from – not the other way around. Then I remember yet again that this is Cornwall. They do things differently here. It's such a sensible way to live – instead of chucking things out as they get worn and immediately buying new, this frugality saves resources.

So in the end I let Al have his way and tell him to find the part, to mend the machine. Eventually we'll have to get that new one, but if he fixes it, as he says he can, then it'll do for a few more months at least.

When Al leaves, I take Jake off to another of my favourite woodlands for a walk. The storms at the end of June have subsided and July is, though cooler, sunny and pleasant, with only the occasional shower to keep us on our toes. Today it rained briefly in the morning and the foliage shines in the sunlight, not quite dry yet. Patterns of shade and light mottle the woodland floor, and create shapes between the leafy trees.

I breathe the peculiar woodland scent, a wonderful heady mix of damp earth, old wood, past rainfall combined with hot sunlight. Because we're so close to the sea, there is a faint tang of salt and ozone, though barely perceptible – more like a hint of some faraway scent that you can only just make out.

Jake is rummaging in mounds of dead leaves not yet fully composted back into the earth, and occasionally gives an excited yelp when he discovers the scent of a rabbit, a squirrel, or mouse. The trees and stones are covered with lichen. It seems to be all colours, green, grey, yellow, and white.

I finish my long amble on one of the many wetlands that abound in Cornwall. I wander across the tidal estuary watching the waders pecking the mudflats. The river water is churning now; a hefty breeze has sneaked up on us. Sandpipers scurry along, watched by an egret standing motionless on a rock. The smell of water and wet earth is quite strong here, exhilarating. Gulls skim and swoop over the waves.

Jake and I head back just as the rain starts. It's only a shower, and a warm one at that, so I don't mind not having a water-proof. The rain on my face is as life-affirming as the sunshine. You can't have one without the other, I tell Jake, as we both quicken our pace towards home.

CHAPTER ELEVEN

Summer Days

The week before we leave for the B&B is a busy one. I've taken a week's holiday from the Royal Mail, and will take my second one when the next group of Londoners come to rent our house. Ben has taken the same time off from the café where he only works sporadically anyway, when there are no acting jobs around. We'll spend a week at St Petroc manning the B&B then a week back at work. Later we'll have a proper holiday with Annie and Pete on Dartmoor.

Work is, as usual, time-consuming during the summer months. The houses that were empty all winter are suddenly lived in again and I have to deliver to them, mostly junk mail, but it has to be done. People are also more chatty in the warm weather, which is fine with me but it makes my deliveries longer.

Doing my round at St Geraint, I'm more aware than usual about how noisy, how loud, the visitors from Up Country are. Not just the day tourists, or the campers and cottage renters, but also the second homers who come year after year. I didn't notice it so much at first though I heard some of the locals mention it, complaining that no one knew how to talk softly these days. Now I've heard it, too, hear it this morning as I'm walking along the main street of the town, the sea on my left and the little shops and cafés on my right. It's a perfect holiday scene, the day tranquil, still, and sunny. A couple of terns sit on the harbour wall, herring gulls cry to each other overhead, and people are strolling, eating ice cream, admiring the clear emerald and blue sea glassy as a mirror under the perfect sky – and talking. Loudly. A couple nearby are admonishing their children, two docile little girls, for letting ice cream drip down their arms and onto their pretty summer frocks. They chide kindly, without rancour, but loudly, as if they want the whole street to know what pride they take in teaching their daughters the proper way to eat ice cream. On the other side of the road, staring at the sea, a middle-aged couple are discussing where to go for lunch. They can't both be deaf, surely? Their voices are raised so high they must reach the ferry about to leave the harbour. And now another man and woman, holiday dressed in shorts and flip-flops, stop me to ask directions to the Roswinnick Hotel. Although they are standing right next to me, they seem to be talking to someone at the end of the street. They are certainly not deaf, for I direct them in a soft voice, but their thanks and comments on the hotel nearly blast me off the pavement.

I've come to the conclusion that this is the kind of persona a person has to adapt to get ahead in a large city. You have to be more vocal, brasher, more noticeable. Your voice no doubt becomes louder without you realising, as you struggle against all the zillions of others trying to make their mark, to be recognised, to get somewhere.

Passing the posh Roswinnick Hotel, I remember chatting with the valet there, before he moved on to other work. He used to have great fun parking all the guests' cars. His favourite was Rowan Atkinson's Austin Martin DB7 Vantage, the same car Rowan used in the film *Johnny English*. The valet was overwhelmed at the thought that he'd be parking this amazing car. Brimming with excitement, he phoned his mates, told them to come outside and they'd see a fine sight. Full of curiosity, they came out of their homes, wondering what was up. They didn't have long to wait for there was their friend the valet, taking the long scenic route around the village to the car park, grandly waving to his mates from the wheel of that fabulous car.

I was in my postie van that day and saw it all, the fabulous car, the valet waving, his friends cheering as he drove by. I gave a cheer, too, as he passed, though it wasn't until later that I learned who owned the car.

Mickey at the boat yard is busy, mending and maintaining the many yachts moored here. They all seem to be out today, the placid sea is full of them, shining white and silver in the sunlight. I exchange a few words with him, mostly commiserating as he berates some of the yacht owners who want a repair or a paint job done immediately. 'I tell'ee, maid, them boat owners can be sumptin' else,' he moans. 'All puffed up with importance, like a feisty gull. Not all, mind, but more'n some. Drives me wild.'

'I know how you feel, Mickey. But they pay good money. You work hard in the summer but you make enough to take it easier in winter.'

He looks up from under an upside down hull, 'Be that as it may, maid, money ain't everything, y'know.'

I nod and agree as I throw the post into the van and head

off on my rounds. I've been hearing a lot of that lately. It seems a contradiction, too. On the one hand, people in Cornwall are really struggling to make a living. Jobs are scarcer than ever, wages lower, inflation higher. So money, and making it, is vitally important. And yet, as Mickey, Guy, Al and others have said to me, it isn't everything. It's ironic, I think as I drive along, sunglasses in place to reflect the glare on the bright summer's day, that those who have least, know the importance of other things: time, leisure, respect, quality of life. They might not put it in so many words, but that's what they mean when they say, 'Money ain't everything, y'know.'

When I get to Poldowe, Clara stops me in the street before I get to her house. 'Nothing for you today,' I say cheerily. 'Not even the junk.'

'I wasn't after the post. Tessa, I'm upset.'

'Oh goodness, are the cats all right?'

'Yes, fine,' she brightens for a moment. 'Guy and I have managed to find homes for every one of the latest four strays brought in.' Her brightness fades and her face darkens. Oh no, I think, it's not Guy, is it? She must sense what I'm thinking for she smiles and looks years younger. 'Guy is so terrific. He's moving in with me, y'know. When summer is over. Right now he's got so many jobs on, repair work for the second homers and stuff, that he's out till late, getting it done. So we'll wait till September.'

'I'm so glad for you both. You're lucky to have each other.'

She looks dreamily out over the church and the sea beyond. I tell her I'd better get on, and that brings her back to earth. 'Oh Tessa, it's Delia I'm worrying about. She seems so, I don't know, confused most of the time. We're all keeping an eye on her, but we wanted your opinion. That is, Ginger and I did.

She was going to talk to you weeks ago about it then changed her mind. But since then things have got so much worse.'

I remember that time when Ginger confronted me in Poldowe, troubled about something but not saying what it was. Clara goes on, 'Ginger decided we could handle Delia ourselves. She's one of us, born and grew up around here. Ginger thought it over and decided it wasn't right to call on someone else.'

I can understand this. 'Look, Clara, if there's anything I can do, let me know. I've also been worried about Delia.'

Clara looks relieved. 'The thing is, you see loads of old people on your rounds, are any of them as odd as she's getting? Ginger and me, and Melanie, too, from the shop – well, we're getting so we don't know what's normal for folk Delia's age and what's not. Maybe we're all too close to her.'

I'm on my way there anyway so we go to Delia's house together. But Ginger is already there, making tea for the older woman. So is Melanie, who is fussing around Delia trying to get her to eat a tea cake she's just brought over.

We all greet each other and then I try to talk to Delia. She's worse since I last saw her, over a fortnight ago as my round was changed for a short time because another postie was ill. I'm shocked at how bad she looks, thin and worn, her eyes wide and frightened in a pale face.

But she sees me, smiles and knows who I am, calls me by name and asks if there is any post for her. I'm relieved, for it seems like the old Delia. Then in a few moments she seems to have forgotten. 'Clara, who is this woman? Why is she here?' Delia grows agitated. Clara soothes her, holds her hand, until she calms down. I go into the kitchen to talk to Ginger who says, 'She's like this all the time. She didn't know me when I first came in today. Then something clicked into place and she remembered, seemed perfectly normal for a time, then suddenly off she went again, acting strangely.'

'Is she eating?' This has been our worry all along.

'Oh, between Clara and Melanie and me, we make sure. And the other villagers, too. We have a rota, bringing in food for her. And she still gets her Meals on Wheels.'

'But does she eat it?'

'We always sit with her, make sure she eats at least enough to keep going.' She finishes washing up some plates, pours tea into several cups. 'That's the hard part, making her eat.'

I help her bring the tea out to the sitting room. Melanie says, 'I'd better get back to the shop, relieve Tufty.' I've also got to get on, so I walk out with her. Clara comes with us, leaving Delia with Ginger who says she'll sit there a while, to make sure Delia drinks some tea and eats something. 'Will you change her bed, or should I come back?' I hear Melanie say quietly to Ginger who answers, 'That's OK, I'll do it, you did it yesterday, and Clara the day before. My turn. I'll wash the sheets, too.'

Just as we are going, Delia tries to leave the house, hysterically repeating that she must find her father. The village women calm her soon enough but it is a worrying sight.

Outside, Melanie goes off to the shop and I stand talking to Clara who asks, 'What d'you think, Tessa? What we were wondering really was, is there anything to be done? You know, like medication, or something.'

'She needs special care, Clara,' I try to soften it but I'm horrified at what I saw and heard. Delia is definitely far worse than she was even a few weeks ago.

Clara says, 'What do you mean, special care?'

'The social services. You need to call them. They'll know what to do.'

Her face hardens into stubbornness. I've seen her like this before, when someone has been cruel to a cat. Fierce and determined. 'Can't do that, Tessa. We look after her. Me and the others. We be doing it since her husband died. First t'was our mums bringing her food, helping her out when her husband first died and she didn't go out no more, then us'n took over. She don't need care, she got us.' Her speech has gone into dialect, the first time I've ever heard Clara talk with a Cornish twang. Though I've noticed this with some of the other locals, how they can lapse back and forth, I've never heard Clara doing it before. It's as if she's closing in, keeping out outsiders, especially social services.

This kind of protectiveness is something I've often witnessed, the way the locals band together to look after their own. 'Clara, I'm sure you and the others know what you're doing, and I know you look after her, but if you ring the social services, they might give you some advice, some help, too, if need be.'

She's shaking her head, not looking at me, as she says, 'They'll take her away. Put her in a smelly home somewhere. It'll kill 'er. She needs her own home.'

I leave it there. It's very admirable, what they are doing, but I'm afraid Delia will only get worse. They can't be there all the time. And all of them, Clara, Ginger, Melanie, have jobs, lives, of their own. They'll never be able to look after her twenty-four hours a day.

I can't linger any more but carry on with my deliveries, hoping against reason that I'm wrong, that this is a blip, that Delia doesn't have dementia as I fear and that she'll return to her old self before long.

After Poldowe I'm in my van again and off to Trescatho, an isolated village on a road leading nowhere. It's high on a woody hill overlooking the sea, and in the past few years this sleepy village has been converted to a ghost town with a handful of permanent incomers, and a heap of second homeowners.

Two of the permanent residents are the Armstrongs, who moved in a couple of years ago and have settled perfectly, endearing themselves to the locals in other villages by their good-natured spirits and love of all things Cornish. I deliver to them last, as they're pleasant to chat to and I welcome the cold drink they have waiting for me in this hot spell. Before I get there, I'm stopped by someone called Donald Wilkins and his wife, Maddie. They've bought one of the old thatched houses in the area as their 'summer cottage' and have been trying to get it repaired, and in places newly thatched. They're both in the garden, sniffing the air like a couple of terriers, trying to get a whiff of the sea a couple of kilometres away. At the very end of the long garden is a cedar tree, quite an old one, and I can see Woody on a ladder, sawing through one of the branches.

He breaks off when he sees me, coming down the ladder to say hello. Donald and Maddie frown a little at this, and I can tell they don't like him chatting when they're paying him by the hour. I feel like saying, 'Money isn't everything, you two,' but I refrain. Woody is a hard worker, always conscientious, and the Wilkins will get their money's worth of work. They obviously know this, for they don't say a word and even force a smile as he greets me and goes off to his van to grab his rollies, for a smoke and a chat.

While he's gone Donald says, 'Well, at least he shows up when he says.'

'And does the work,' Maddie admits.

'They all do, in the end. The locals. Sometimes it's in their own good time, but they get there in the end.'

'Hah, do they?' Maddie is indignant. 'We're still waiting for our thatcher.'

'He's the best in the West Country, we were told,' Donald goes on with the story. 'So we phoned him two years ago. He came, looked at the thatch, said he'd take on the job, and then we didn't see him for a year.'

'We would have got someone else but everyone warned us not to, that this chap was the very best.'

I say, 'But he came in the end, didn't he? I'm sure I saw him here in spring.'

Donald looks grim. 'Oh, he came all right. He got all his equipment, got the new thatch, his ladders, scaffolding and whatnot. Up he climbed and within minutes he was down again, packing up his stuff.'

'Why?'

'Because he'd found some birds nesting in the thatch. Sparrows. He said he couldn't disturb them, and would be back when they'd flown. Can you believe it?'

I can, but I don't say anything. Maddie says, 'I asked him why there isn't netting covering the thatch here, like there is in Surrey. To keep the birds out.'

'What did he say?'

They look at each other, a hopeless look, as if they'll never understand the way of the world down here.

'He said, "We don't be holding with that kind'a thing in these parts."'

I start to laugh, but when I notice neither of them is even smiling, I try to look solemn. Luckily Woody has joined us, a rolled cigarette lit between his fingers. He plops down on the warm grass and stretches out, propping his head up with his hand, elbow on the ground. 'So how're things, Tessa?'

'OK. We're off next week, to St Petroc, to do our B&B stint.'

'That'll be a right laugh.'

'I hope so.'

He takes a long drag on his rollie. The smoke floats in the direction of the Wilkins, hovering nearby, and drives them away back into the house. I wonder if they're at the window, timing Woody's break. 'Holly's loving the shop job,' he says on an exhalation. 'It's great for her to be getting out, seeing people. She was getting lonely in the caravan, gardening on her own all day. No one but my old granddad up the road to keep her company.'

'How is Sydney anyway?'

He grins. 'Never see'im these days. He's over't Nell's quite a bit.'

'It's that serious?'

'Don't know about that. All I know is, the two are together more'n they be apart.'

'How do you feel about that?'

'Me? I'm glad as hell. Me and Holly been worried about the old man, all alone, fussing over the two of us in the caravan like we was babies. Hardly notices us now. First the cats to take his mind off of us, now Nell. 'Tis great, we love it.'

When I leave and toddle off to the Armstrongs' house, I feel quite cheery about Nell and Sydney. And, I have to admit, about the thatcher who refuses to work where birds are nesting.

Mr Armstrong and his wife are keen bird lovers, and I find them both putting seed in a bird feeder. 'Ah, hello,' they call out. 'You've just missed the cirl bunting. She was here again earlier this morning, on our bird table.'

The couple have kept me informed about cirl buntings over the last few weeks, for they are passionate about the birds. 'They used to be common in southern England and Wales,' Mr Armstrong told me. 'They were known as the village bunting, a hundred years ago. They're from the same family as our yellowhammers.'

Mrs Armstrong sighed. 'And then like so many of our beloved birds, they started to decline.'

'And actually became one of England's rarest farmland birds.'

'What was the reason?' I asked

The Armstrongs looked mournful. 'Changing farm methods. Fewer small fields, fewer mixed farms.'

'So when did they start to come back?

'About seven or eight years ago. There were still cirl buntings breeding in Devon, which was the only place they could be found, then the RSPB took some birds from nests there, and released them in Cornwall.' The Armstrongs both smile. They obviously love telling this story. 'The location of the birds was a secret. Or supposed to be. The locals around here say there was some consternation when the bird experts returned to the sites and found the cirl buntings gone. But then they heard of sightings in some of the gardens in the area. The little birds were feeding on bird tables all around the coast of Cornwall.'

Because the birds are still uncommon, those whose gardens the birds visit have been sworn to secrecy, and in fact, some receive hefty sums of money to reimburse them for the time, care, and food they expend keeping an eye on the birds. Mr Armstrong says now, 'Do you know that the bird is breeding again in Cornwall? But we must be vigilant. The bird was nearly lost to us once and could be again if we're not careful.'

Mrs Armstrong is nodding her grey head up and down in

agreement, 'This summer is proving to be the best breeding year so far. Isn't it wonderful?'

I agree that it is, and we have a delightful chat about bird life before I finally tear myself away and carry on delivering the post.

CHAPTER TWELVE

All in a Day's Work

The balmy weather holds all week, and it's another perfect day as we wait for our house tenants so we can take off for St Petroc. They arrive early morning, having left before the sun came up, a sensible thing to do. 'Even so, the traffic was heavy,' murmurs Theresa. Bernard, her husband, agrees, but adds, 'It would have been worse if we left later. It's madness on the A30 from Exeter onwards. And it's only Friday! Think what'll it will be like tomorrow.'

A number of hotels and rental cottages are offering Friday to Friday now, to ease the pressure of that frantic holiday run to Cornwall on Saturday mornings, but unfortunately that seems to mean Fridays are getting just as bad.

We're standing outside the kitchen door. 'Where are the children?' I ask.

'Just coming. With Tiny and Topsy.'

'Who?'

'Our dogs.'

'Dogs?'

'Um, yes. We did ask if pets were allowed.'

Ben looks at me questioningly. 'I guess I did agree they were,' I say. I don't add that I was so thrilled at having tenants who didn't want everything to be perfect that I'd have agreed to space aliens if that clinched the deal. Though I have to admit, I don't like the idea of other people's dogs in our house. I'm fond of dogs, obviously, but because we've got Jake, we know how much sand a dog can carry into the house, and how much mud, wet grass, and soggy dog hairs after a dip in the sea. Also we don't allow Jake upstairs – will the tenants be as thoughtful?

But the die is cast; the place is rented. At least our tenants' dogs must be little ones, with daft names like Tiny and Topsy. As I think this, their two noisy boys charge up to us, with a couple of monster Great Danes in tow. Theresa says, 'Sorry about their names. The boys' choice. They were so cute when they were little pups.'

Little? They must have been the size of a grown fox. These two are like ponies. Not the little Dartmoor ones, either.

The minute we pile into our old car, I forget about our house. Theresa and Bernard are nice people, friends of Annie's, and so excited and happy about staying in our place that I can't begrudge them their monster dogs. And she did understand about not allowing them upstairs, thank goodness. Unfortunately our own dog, Jake, isn't with us; no pets are allowed in The Blue Seashell and though I'm sure the owners would have made an exception for us, we were worried he'd be too much of a hassle in a crowded seaside town with us too busy to do much with him. So when Daphne and Joe offered to look after him for the week, we were relieved.

When we arrive, the fishing village of St Petroc is positively glowing in the sunlight. It juts out on a kind of stubby peninsula, so it is surrounded on three sides by the sea. This gives it a stunning light, magical and elusive, as the many artists who have tried to paint here can testify. We follow the traffic through the main street, along the harbour, and into one of the car parks, where the owners of The Blue Seashell have a resident's permit. That's a relief, for the place is heaving, and every car park seems to be filled.

It's a short walk along a narrow cobbled lane to the B&B. It's a delightful place, tucked into this tiny lane, with pots of geraniums blooming outside. Ben came down for a day when we first agreed to fill in for the week, and at least knows some of the basics, like where the linen is kept, what's offered for breakfast, which are laundry days, and a host of other vital details. The rest we'll find out for ourselves as we go along.

The tide is out, and the beach we pass is crowded with umbrellas, wind breakers, and hordes of sunbathers. The surfers and body boarders are out in the sea, though the only waves out there are slow lazy ones, like this day which is hot, languid, and airless, with a thin white haze out on the horizon. Passing the harbour, we stop to look at the fishing boats moored in the sand; there's no water here at all now. Children and sea birds potter around the thin rivulets of seawater running in places between the beached boats. Watching them from above are scantily dressed holiday makers seated on benches, eating pasties, ice creams, and fish and chips, eyed all the while by the gulls. The pub at the harbour is bursting, the tables outside filled with mostly young people drinking cold lager and cider.

The quiet of The Blue Seagull is refreshing after the hubbub of the town. Dominic's dad left about an hour before we set out, off to Heathrow with his sister to catch the plane to Canada. His wife is in the care of a close relative who will take her to hospital for the operation and look after her until her husband returns, and Dominic will be taking a day or two off work to see his mum, to make sure she's all right. Everyone was effusive with gratitude that we've taken over at the last minute like this. We replied truthfully that it's us who are grateful; it's saved us from a week of camping out and given us a tidy bonus as well.

We have the keys and a list of the guests who are arriving later, from three o'clock onwards. Last night's guests have gone and it's a complete new batch coming tonight. There are eight bedrooms, which may not sound many but will be quite enough, we have been told, for the two of us. 'More than enough,' was the gloomy prediction of one of my customers, an ex-farmer driven by financial worries to run a B&B. ''Twill be a hard job, maid,' he warned. I deliver to quite a few farms and homes now turned into guest accommodation, and the owners all sounded quite discouraging when they heard what I was doing. I was regaled for hours with dire horror stories of unspeakable guests, but most admitted these were a minority. So I force myself to forget about the warnings and determine to enjoy the week at The Blue Seagull.

While Ben takes Will and Amy out to look at the beaches, I go up to talk to the cleaner who is at work in the bedrooms. Did I say talk? I find her in one of the rooms, Hoovering under the bed. The only problem is that she's Eastern European and I assume she's newly arrived as she doesn't seem to speak a word of English.

'Uh, Polish?' I say.

She shakes her head and says something I don't understand.

I resort to sign language and Tarzan-like communication, pointing to myself and saying, 'Tessa.'

She does the same, 'Oksana.'

'Glad to meet you,' I say, relieved that we're communicating.

She says nothing, just bobs her head a few times in a friendly manner. She looks young, no more than eighteen or so, blond and fresh faced and very pretty. She must be a hard worker, too, for this room looks spotless and she's still working on it.

I leave her to it and start checking the other rooms, making sure there are plenty of sachets of tea and coffee, a kettle that works, longlife milk cartons, as well as a few biscuits. Tiny shampoo bottles in the bathrooms, check; soap, check, clean towels folded neatly on the beds, check. Oh, everything is in order, what a doddle this B&B is going to be, I smile to myself. There's really nothing to do until 3 p.m. when we have to be here for a couple of hours to welcome the new guests.

There's a buzzing at the front door. I assume it's Ben and the children. It's now one o'clock so hopefully they've come back with the fish and chips we promised ourselves for the first day. I open the door and find myself face to face with two formidable-looking women wearing track suits and hiking boots. 'We're booked in for five days,' the tallest one announces. They look alike, with greying hair pulled back in careless pony-tails, and angular bodies and faces. They must be the two sisters from East Anglia that we're expecting later, staying in one of the twin rooms. 'I am Bertha and this is Martha,' the shorter one, who is about 5 foot 10 inches, announces.

They pick up their huge rucksacks and stride past me, as I'm saying, with what I hope is a welcoming smile, 'Actually, check-in time isn't until 3 p.m. The rooms aren't quite ready yet, but you're welcome to leave your belongings here until then.' I could have saved my breath, for they are already inside, their rucksacks cluttering up the entire passageway.

Martha says, 'Nonsense. We've had to take two trains, a couple of buses and a taxi, and we're exhausted. If you could show us to our room and bring a pot of Earl Grey, please?'

I'm a bit taken aback by her imperious manner but I say, 'I'll have to check if your room is ready. But if not, you're welcome to wait in our lounge. It's quite comfortable and I can bring you tea there.'

'That won't do at all, I'm afraid,' says Martha or Bertha, both of whom are shaking their heads. 'We really do need a nap.'

I scurry upstairs, find Oksana halfway through cleaning Room 5, the bedroom designated for the sisters.

Downstairs I run. 'It won't be long,' I tell the sisters who have not gone into the lounge but are standing firmly by their rucksacks.

Martha says, 'We'll have another room then. One that is ready now. I'm sure you have another twin bedroom.'

'We do, Room 3, but that's reserved for someone else. Every room in the house is booked.'

They are already hoisting up their rucksacks and climbing the stairs at the end of the hallway. Bertha says, 'No problem, then. We'll take that one and the others can have our room. Ah, Martha, this is it, Room 3.' I hear the door opening.

'Don't forget the tea, please,' Martha calls down. 'And you can bring our keys up then.'

I shout up, as sweetly and politely as I can, 'There's tea in the room, Earl Grey as well as English Breakfast, and everything else you might need.'

A silence descends from the stairs. Then, frostily, 'That will have to do, then. But please can you bring us some fresh milk. We loathe that longlife stuff.'

Milk! The four-pinter that was in the fridge when we arrived smelled slightly off, so I threw it out. Ben is bringing fresh milk, and later we'll stock up for breakfast tomorrow, but where is he? If he and the children are having fun on the beach, they won't hurry back; there is no need. The first guests are not due to arrive until three at the earliest and I told them there was no hurry for the fish and chips.

Oksana saves the day. She's trotting down the stairs carrying the Hoover, tidying it away in the cupboard, taking off the cute apron with little birds on it she'd been wearing, indicating that her work was finished. I rush to her and an elaborate display of sign language begins. I pull her to the kitchen, show her the empty space where milk should be, go to the recycling bin for plastics and take out the empty milk carton, sniff it, make a face. She looks perplexed then smiles sweetly, points to herself and says something that I'm sure is, me too. My face drops. She thinks I don't like milk and is agreeing with me. I try again. I'm doing an elaborate pantomime of taking a carton of milk from the fridge, opening it, smelling it, and making an even more distasteful face as I pour it down the sink. .

Then I look out past Oksana and there is Bertha – or is it Martha? – staring at me. I put on my cheery B&B owner smile and say, 'Oksana is from Eastern Europe and I'm afraid I don't speak her language.' I don't say that I still haven't a clue what her language is. I plunge on, 'I'm trying to ask her to go to buy some fresh milk. I'm afraid we're out.' My mouth turns downwards, hoping to convey to Martha – or Bertha – how sorry I am for this oversight. It's amazing how in the wrong

I feel, for they're the ones who arrived too early, who refuse to drink the perfectly adequate longlife milk we provide in all the bedrooms, and who took over another room without so much as enquiring whether it was all right with me.

The woman – either Martha or Bertha – walks briskly up to me, snatches the empty milk carton from my hand, shows it to Oksana, and says something to her which I don't quite catch. Oksana smiles and replies, a look of relief on her face. They exchange quite a few words before my formidable guest turns to me and says, 'The girl is from Ukraine. I don't know the language but I do know a bit of Polish, which I tried on her. Luckily she lives in Western Ukraine near the Polish border and speaks that language, too. She'll be happy to pick up some milk for you and wants to know if there is anything else she can get while she's at the shop. I'd suggest giving her some cash to purchase the milk.'

Meekly, I do as she says, and Oksana, radiant at finding someone who she can converse with, skips out of the door. Martha/Bertha and I regard each other. Her eyes narrow as she says, 'Have you ever considered a career in theatre? You'd be excellent in pantomime.'

Before I can react or think of what to say, she turns to go. But not before I see a twinkle in her eye, a twitch of her lips. She's trying hard not to laugh. Breaking into a relieved grin myself, I call out to her retreating back, 'I'll bring the milk up when it arrives.'

She calls back, 'Oh, didn't I say? I came down to tell you that it won't be necessary. Bertha and I are going out to explore the town.'

The rest of the day passes in a blur of confusion and activity. The guests arrive and are shown to their rooms. Most are satisfied, but one couple complain. 'This doesn't look like the room I saw on your website,' the man says. 'It looks far smaller.'

I smile that landlady smile I've got down pat now. 'It's hard to show sizes on a web photo, I'm afraid.' I don't know what he's on about; it's a beautiful double room.

'Haven't you got anything else?'

'I'm sorry, but we're fully booked.'

He still looks disgruntled. The woman hasn't said a word. She doesn't seem to have an opinion at all. They are both standing in the doorway, refusing to go into the room. The man says again, 'I'm sure this isn't the same room we booked on the net.'

My smile is wearing thin. 'I'm really sorry you're not happy with it, but I assure you that it's the same room.' And a bloody lovely one, I want to add, which it is. None of the rooms are tiny, all are spacious enough for two people, and tastefully furnished.

He murmurs, 'Well, I don't know. I'm really not happy.'

The doorbell is ringing again and I know Ben is upstairs showing another couple to their room. Why does everyone arrive at once? I say as sweetly as I can, 'Look, if you don't want to stay, that's your option. Why don't you go inside and have a look around before deciding what to do.' Then on an impulse I add, 'We won't charge you if you decide to go.'

I don't know if that's what the owners would do; theoretically I suppose we'd be within our rights to charge them for cancelling at the last minute. But it's a summer weekend and I know that if I change the No Vacancy sign to Vacancy, we'd have someone ringing the bell within minutes. And, quite honestly, I want this couple to leave. I feel very protective of this attractive house, the thoughtful care that's been given to make it truly comfortable. I don't want anyone here who cannot appreciate the place.

I leave them inside the room while I rush down to greet others. I hear the door close behind me and the loud voices of the couple arguing, then I forget them while we spend the next couple of hours greeting new guests, answering questions, telling people about breakfast times, and so on. What I hadn't anticipated was how some people like to chat when they arrive, asking about the town, the sea, the local attractions. To make it even harder, Ben has had to run to the pharmacy to get some medication for an elderly couple who forgot to bring some from home. They were exhausted after their journey, hardly able to walk they were so stiff, so Ben volunteered to collect the medication. I'm happy he did, but it's even crazier with me here on my own.

Except for the couple that I hope will leave, luckily everyone is very friendly, which makes the afternoon pleasant, if chaotic. One man insists on following me around asking about various pubs in the region; another young couple have spread out maps in the lounge and are calling to me to point out various places on the coastal path. It's not easy juggling all this while answering doorbells. And then there are the polite requests for extra pillows or a spare blanket. But the pandemonium only lasts a few hours until everything grows quiet. Amy and Will are out again, enjoying this warm sunny evening, and Ben and I slump down in our private quarters at the back with a bottle of chilled white wine. 'Phew, first hurdle over,' I say as we chink glasses and take that first relaxing sip. 'We deserve this.'

Suddenly I jump up. 'I nearly forgot in all the confusion. That couple in Room 8, up at the top? I haven't had a chance to tell you about them, how the man complained, didn't like the room. I told them politely that they could leave if they weren't happy here. Have they decided to stay? Or did they leave? I hope so. I can put out the Vacancy sign right now if they're gone.'

'Oh, I wondered what that was about. I saw them leave about a half hour ago, when you were busy with that young couple. The man said, rather rudely I thought, that they weren't staying and you knew all about it.'

I stare at him. 'They've only just gone? Half an hour ago? But they got here nearly three hours ago. What's going on?'

We rush up to Room 8, to find it a complete shambles. The couple had used the bed, the shower with all the soaps and shampoos, and every single one of the towels which are now strewn all over the floor. 'What a nerve,' Ben says. 'Well, we've got their address, we'll charge them for one night anyway.'

'We can't,' I say miserably. 'I told them they didn't have to pay if they didn't stay, said to go inside, have a look around, and make up their minds. I can't believe they've done this.'

Ben shakes his head. 'I've tried to anticipate all the things that could happen while running a B&B, but certainly not this.'

The worse thing is that it's too late to rent the room out for tonight; it'll take ages to get it right again. 'Oh Ben,' I sigh, 'my first day as landlady of a B&B and I've already blown one night's profits.'

He puts an arm around me. 'Only the price of one room, Tessa. Dominic's parents would have lost seven nights' profits for all the rooms if they had to close the place for a week. Think of it as a learning curve. I'm sure it's not the last mistake we'll make, anyway.'

It certainly isn't. That night at 10 p.m. we're searching for a supermarket that is still open, to buy organic bacon. The

Blue Seashell is an upmarket establishment which offers organic produce for breakfast, and a thorough search of the supplies the owners left has not revealed any bacon anywhere. Fair enough, the brother and sister were in a state about their ill father and I don't blame them for not remembering everything. We should have checked breakfast supplies earlier in the evening.

Resisting the temptation to buy ordinary bacon from the all-night Tesco on the outskirts of St Petroc, and hide the label, we phone the B&B's usual suppliers, a small butcher's in the neighbouring town, and luckily they're awake and willing to open up shop. 'All in a day's work,' the butcher says over the phone when I thank him profusely. But it turns out it was their fault in the first place, the butcher and his wife tell Ben cheerily when he goes to pick up the bacon; it should have been delivered that morning. They say they'll knock something off the bill for their error, but that doesn't help us get to sleep any earlier, nor get over the panic of not having bacon for breakfast.

The next morning Ben and I are up at six, preparing fresh fruit salad for breakfast which is between seven-thirty and nine-thirty. No one shows up until eight-thirty, and then it seems to be nearly everyone at once. Ben is behind the scenes, doing the cooking, while I'm front of house with a cheery good morning and would you like tea or coffee to start with? I'm bringing the hot drinks while Ben cooks full English breakfasts, scrambled eggs and smoked salmon, defrosts the Deli France frozen fresh croissants, and in general does a thousand things at once. Luckily he's a great cook and at ease in any kitchen. Will and Amy have offered to help but we tell them it's best they stay out of the way. I smile and smile, and take orders, but once again the customers, all very pleasant, stop me to chat, to plan their day with maps and guide books, to ask questions. It's a hard balancing act between being friendly and polite, and needing to get on bringing out more coffee and tea, asking people if they'd like scrambled, poached or fried eggs, brown or white toast, or hot rolls. Then there are more requests, some very strange ones. One woman is allergic to the posh Neal's Yard organic shower gel we have in the bathroom and could we please put another kind in the room. I'm perplexed; the Neal's Yard stuff is totally pure, a wonderful product, expensive, too. I ask her what kind she'd like and she shrugs, 'Oh, any old kind. Just none of that blue organic stuff.'

I'm learning fast how odd people can be. Then Martha and Bertha appear, and together I can tell them apart, which pleases me. I just have to remember that Martha is over six feet tall and her sister is shorter by about two or three inches. They look ruddy and fit, and order, 'Two full English, two large pots of Earl Grey, and we'll try some of that fruit salad after muesli, if you please. Oh, and a plateful of brown toast, lightly done.'

They eat and eat. Long after the other guests have left, Martha and Bertha order more tea, more toast. 'We're off for another long walk today,' Martha says as I'm clearing the table. Bertha beams then burps quietly into her napkin. 'We had a stunning walk yesterday afternoon.'

I'm dying for them to go as I'm exhausted, longing to sit down with Ben over a good strong cup of tea before we get on with the day. But Martha and Bertha, softened now and not so formidable after their huge breakfast, want to talk. 'Yes, a wonderful walk,' Bertha goes on. 'We sat on that rock formation about two miles from St Petroc, a kind of peninsula that goes out to sea. We'd bought sandwiches and ate them on the rocks on the cliff. And you won't believe what happened.'

Martha takes up the story, 'It was magical.' Her serious, stern face relaxes into wonder. 'We heard the seals singing. I've never heard anything like it before.'

I'm totally drawn in now. I have read about the seals' song, heard the stories of the mermaid legends that came about centuries ago when sailors heard the music of the seals. But not I nor anyone I have met before has ever heard it – we have all heard seals barking, of course, but never that mystical song. 'What did it sound like?'

The two sisters look at each other. They are at a loss as to how to describe it. Finally Martha says, 'Like a beautiful girls' choir – or perhaps a women's choir, coming from so far away you can't quite hear the words. It was like music from heaven.'

They look out over my head, through the window onto the cobbled street outside, but they're back on that cliff top, listening to the song of the seals. I leave them to their reverie, glad that I heard their story. When they leave for the day they give me a big smile, and I know I'm lucky that they chose to share their magical tale with me.

Because all the guests are staying at least one more day, no new ones are arriving, so Ben and I have time to go out at midday and join the holiday crowds. Oksana has been in to make the beds, tidy the rooms, and Ben and I have stacked the dishwasher and cleaned up in the kitchen. We've also checked that there is clean linen for the next batch of guests tomorrow, and phoned the laundry to make sure they remember to collect the used sheets and towels on Monday as scheduled.

It's another warm clear day. The tide is halfway in and the beaches are, as usual, totally crammed. Amy and Will have found friends from school who are staying with relatives in St Petroc for a few days. We know the aunt and uncle, who invite the children to spend the day with them on the beach. Relieved that Amy and Will seem to be set for a great holiday, Ben and I walk out onto the pier. The seaside smells of fish, salt, and spray assail us as we walk to the end. There are fishing boats out at sea, as well as the sightseeing boats and small motorised craft rented by visitors. I glance back at the village; St Petroc looks like a backdrop to some idyllic film, with the wonky fishermen's cottages crammed together along the harbour and up the hillside. The sea swells and dazzles with reflected sunlight.

'This is bliss,' I say, holding Ben's hand as we amble along.

'Yes,' he agrees then adds, 'but a brief bliss. We'd better get back. We need to buy more provisions for breakfast, check that Oksana has replaced all the soap and shampoos . . .'

'Oh, and buy replacements for that woman who can't use the organic bath products.' We start to turn back. 'Still,' I go on, 'that's not much to do. No one is checking out or in till tomorrow; we can come out again later, join Amy, Will, and the others on the beach, swim in the sea ourselves.'

But it doesn't happen like that. Back at the B&B, we expect the place to be empty, with everyone outside on this lovely day. But the minute we walk in, one of the guests pounces on us. His wife is ill with stomach pains, vomiting and diarrhoea, and he's blaming it on food poisoning, saying it must have been the smoked salmon and scrambled eggs she had for breakfast. Several guests ate the same thing so I'm envisaging the The Blue Seashell closed and ruined, the tabloids screaming headlines about a B&B in Cornwall poisoning its customers. But Ben manages to find an emergency doctor to come out

– the guest is too weak to move – and to our relief the doctor says it's not food poisoning but a stomach bug. He gives her an injection to stop the vomiting and a prescription to stop her dehydrating, says she should be fine in forty-eight hours.

Our relief turns to concern as now we wonder if the other guests will catch the stomach bug. How unpleasant for them if they do. And us – we simply cannot get ill, whatever happens.

The next day everyone but the sick woman is down to breakfast, a good sign. Her husband says she is much better. Check-out on Sunday morning for the weekend guests is as chaotic as the check-in on Friday, only worse with bills to settle, debit cards which don't work in the machine, and a thousand other time-consuming irritations. To top it all off, an Italian couple in their thirties who arrived last night, taking the trashed room which had been cleaned and made ready to occupy, appear looking for breakfast a half hour late. They are so crestfallen, so charming, as well as so totally gorgeous, that Ben, who has just come back from the organic veg shop before it closes, takes pity on them and cooks them the big English breakfast they say they adore, while I help Oksana start to make beds and clean the rooms, for there is far too much to do today for one person on her own.

And so the week goes on. I never realised how much work a B&B is. There are things like the rubbish to be recycled and put out for an early pick-up, and the used linen to be loaded in special laundry sacks to be collected by the laundry service. There's the constant shopping and replenishing supplies. And all the time there are phone calls, and emails, requests for bookings which have to be taken. Ben and I spend hours checking and rechecking that we haven't double-booked anyone in the weeks to come.

Our favourite time is the walk before bed, when all the work is done. We either walk along the beaches if the tide is out, or along the harbour and down the pier. When the tide is full in the fishing boats bob like bath toys in the safety of the harbour, and the lights of St Petroc shine across the water like stars.

'It's not exactly a doddle, is it,' Ben says on one of these walks, 'this B&B lark.'

'No,' I agree, 'but it's sort of satisfying, isn't it? Times like now, when we've finished the day's work, and all is well, at least for the moment.'

He agrees that it is, and we go back, have an early night, ready to be bright and cheerful again at breakfast time tomorrow.

CHAPTER THIRTEEN

Letting Go

'Well, that wasn't so bad, was it?' I say as we leave St Petroc and head for home.

'It was great!' chorus the children from the back seat.

'We did it, anyway,' Ben says. 'Without too many mishaps.'

'One or two tricky times,' I giggle, remembering the Italians (they never got to breakfast on time, and we never had the heart to refuse them their full English), and Martha and Bertha (whom we grew quite fond of in the end but who gave us a hard time the last couple of days, insisting on staying two extra nights despite the fact we were fully booked. We had to send the new arrivals to a different B&B because the sisters refused to vacate their room).

'There was that time with the laundry,' Ben remembers.

The laundry company had sent us the wrong clean and ironed bedding. Oksana opened the packages to find hideous flowered polyester duvet covers and sheets, and not a sign of our white Egyptian cotton ones. After frantic phone calls and tracking down the right sets at another B&B on the other side of the town, we hadn't finished making the beds when the new guests arrived, despite Ben, Oksana, and I working flat out. I took the guests into the dining room, apologised profusely and plied them with tea and luscious cakes I'd picked up at the bakery. Luckily they were a jolly, easy-going group, and took it all in their stride.

'It's not a doddle, though,' I say as we drive into Treverny. 'I'd rather be a postie any day.'

I do wonder about that remark, though, as I leave for my first delivery after my week's working holiday at St Petroc. The weather has changed and August has roared in with high winds, torrential rain, and a severe drop in temperature. It's been pouring all night and some of the roads I drive down are flooded already. One tarmacked lane leading up to several farmhouses has been totally cut off by a rushing torrent of water pouring from what was a lilting, bubbling brook. I stop, wondering what to do. There's no way I'm going to risk driving through that, the van will be swept away. I know another route to the cluster of houses but it's several miles out of the way, up and over the hill.

I'm forced to detour several times because of flooded lanes or roads, and it's quite late by the time I get the van back to St Geraint. As I park at the boat yard I run into Susie, another postwoman, a feisty and fun Cornishwoman who was a huge help to me when I started out. Susie's still a good mate and, since we've both finished our rounds for the day, we decide to dry out and warm up with a coffee at The Sunflower Café where Ben sometimes works.

The place is heaving with wet, steaming holiday makers, looking quite shocked at the sudden turn in the weather. Susie and I manage to find a table by the window overlooking the sea which is raging, white and churning with foam. The spray is hitting the footpath and road, drenching cars and people.

We order coffee, sit back for a gossip and a catch-up. I tell her about our B&B experiences and she tells me all the news from my round, which she took over while I was away. 'I spent ages in Poldowe,' she says, rolling her eyes. 'First there was that funny maid, Clara, the one with the cats.'

'I like her.'

'Oh, so do I, but she used to talk me ear off about those mangy cats she brought in from all over, trying to find 'em homes.'

'She does love her cats.'

'Yeah, but y'know something? She didn't talk cats once this time. I was that relieved, thought I'd get away quick, but she went on and on about her fella, Guy. Can't believe those two got it together,' Susie shakes her head in wonder. 'I thought that maid and that bloke would wander this world single the rest of their lives. Just shows, don't it?'

She's silent for some time, contemplating the strange way of love in this funny world, before she goes on, 'After a good quarter hour listening to love's bright young song – only them two are not so young, are they! – I had some post for Delia.' The grin on her face as she was talking about Guy and Clara suddenly vanishes. 'Tessa, maid, I be right worried 'bout that woman. She's gone funny.'

'I know. I've been worried about her myself. But she's got Clara, and her friend Ginger looking after her, and Melanie from the shop, and apparently some of the other villagers as well. She's not neglected.'

Susie takes a sip of coffee, adds more sugar, deep in thought.

Finally she says, 'I hate like hell interfering, but they can't cope any more. I know that lot, they be right loyal and they do loads, but Delia needs twenty-four-hour care, now. Last week she nearly set fire to the place, God knows how, or what she was up to. Clara found a burned tea towel on the kitchen floor.'

'Have you told them this?'

'Yeah, but they be stubborn. Think they're giving up on Delia if they call the social. But someone got to do it. She got no family.'

Susie looks me straight in the eye. Poldowe is my patch, and I know Susie well enough to know what she's saying. If it were her patch, her customers, she'd be in there, doing what she thought right. Now she says, 'Listen, Clara and Ginger, and the others, will carry on until Delia does something truly harmful, to herself or someone else. It's not good enough.'

Susie's warning stays with me until the next day, when I see Delia again. And I know Susie's right – the older woman needs more help than her neighbours can give her, no matter how willing. By the time I get there, someone has already been in to give her breakfast, make sure she ate something, and obviously washed her and got her dressed. But although that couldn't have been more than an hour or two earlier, Delia is already in a bad way. The front of her cardigan is soaking. She's standing in the kitchen holding an empty cup to her chest which, as I strip off the light summer cardigan she's wearing, is still soggy with hot tea.

Delia makes no response when I try to ask what happened, only looks at me with frightened eyes, not recognising me at all. Even though she doesn't seem in any pain, I see that a bright red patch has appeared on her upper chest. She must have dropped the near-boiling tea all over herself, and not that long ago either.

She winces as I gently unfasten the top buttons of her blouse; the pain is there although she still hasn't spoken. It looks as if it might be a nasty burn. I don't hesitate but get out my mobile phone to call the local doctor. I happen to know that he has a surgery once a week in Poldowe, just at this moment and only down the road.

He's with us in moments. Right behind him is Clara bringing over Delia's sheets which she has washed and dried. While the doctor is with the injured woman, tending her burn, making her comfortable – she's started to moan with pain – I have a chance to talk to Clara. 'This can't go on,' I say.

She stares at me, defiantly at first, but then another long, drawn-out, pitiable moan from Delia pierces us both. Clara's eyes fill with tears. She looks defeated. 'No,' she says finally, quietly. 'No, it can't.'

When the doctor has made Delia as comfortable as possible, he says he's calling an ambulance, taking her to hospital for tests.

Clara's tears spill over and she's weeping in earnest. 'That's the end, then,' she gulps between sobs, confronting him. 'You know they won't let her back home, ever.'

The doctor is a good man; he has been treating these villagers a long time, and knows Clara, Ginger, and all the other villagers, knows how diligent they've been caring for Delia. He takes the weeping Clara by the shoulder, gives her a paternal hug, and says, 'It's time to let go, Clara. All of you.'

She blows her nose, pulls herself together. 'I feel we're abandoning her. She does so love her home. Me and Ginger, and Melanie, wanted to keep her here in it. She's such a sweet old lady, always so kind to us when we were kids.'

Ginger arrives, and starts talking to the doctor, like Clara upset, but agreeing with him that there is nothing more anyone in the village can do. Delia is lying on the sofa, eyes closed, tranquil, at least for the moment. I hear the doctor say to Ginger, 'I'll keep an eye on her, make sure she gets good care, gets sent to the best nursing home there is around here. She'll be safe.'

I lean down, put my hand gently on Delia's shoulder, wanting to say something comforting but she's oblivious now to everyone around her. I, like the others, will visit her wherever she ends up, but it still is goodbye. I've always been fond of Delia, and knowing she's not going to get better saddens us all. But I take heart in what the doctor says: she'll be safe.

I see Susie again in the little post office in St Geraint. The attached shop is filled with wet customers all talking about the latest flooding of roads, lanes, and unfortunately some low-lying homes near rivers and streams. We manage to exchange a few words in private. My concern and sorrow over Delia must show through, for she puts her hand on my shoulder, saying, 'It's worked out for the best. You had no choice, you had to phone the doctor; hot tea on her thin old skin could have been nasty.'

'I know. But maybe it wasn't that bad? I know some first aid, I could have dealt with it. And the doctor was more concerned with her mental state than the burn.'

'So he should have been.'

'But don't you see, Susie? She'll never go back home now. I feel so responsible for that.'

'Thank heavens you be a responsible sort! Them others in

the village, good souls, all them women, wanting to look after her. But they didn't know when to let go. Thank the good Lord you did before Delia did much worse than burning herself with hot tea.'

Her words reassure me. Susie says she'll check up on Delia, talk to the doctor, find out what nursing home she'll be in, and let me know. 'Don't you be worrying, maid,' she tells me kindly as we part. 'Not easy, sometimes, doing the right thing. Bloody necessary, though.'

After the crisis on my postal round, I come home to find another in the village. As I pull up to the house, I see someone with waterproof and hood hurrying along our path, head down against the still-pouring rain. 'Oh Daphne, I didn't recognise you,' I say as we meet. 'Come on inside.'

She follows me into the kitchen where we pull off our soaking coats, shake the water from our hair. We talk about the continuing rain, as everyone is, and Daphne tells me about her flooded farmyard. After I've commiserated, she says, nodding her head to an offer of a cup of hot tea, 'There's something I want to talk to you about. I'd have mentioned it sooner, but you were so excited to be off on your B&B adventure – which I want to hear all about, by the way – that I didn't want to trouble you.'

'What is it? Nothing wrong with you or Joe, or the children, is there?'

'It's your neighbours again. The Wintersons. Tessa, I don't know why the bloody hell they're living here. They don't seem to like a single thing about Treverny, or about Cornwall for that matter.'

I've never heard Daphne this cross. I find myself back in

my old position again, defending Kate and Leon, trying to explain away their city ways to my friends in the village. 'I've not had a chance to see them since we've been back, so I don't know what the problem is this time, but whatever it is I'm sure it must be a misunderstanding. It'll take time, but I'm sure they'll settle.'

Even as I say this, I realise that I'm having doubts. Kate and Leon had us over for drinks and nibbles a few nights before we left for St Petroc, 'To wish you good luck,' they'd said. As usual we had a lively evening, enjoying their company, but this time, as has been happening increasingly, it was marred by a disagreement over village affairs. Poor Emmanuel the peacock was cited again, and also the ongoing annoyance the couple have felt for most of the summer over the smell of dung-spreading all around the village.

Daphne is shaking her head, 'You can go on defending them, Tessa, but they'll never fit in here. You haven't heard the latest, either. You know that Joe's a bell ringer at the church, and that they practise on Monday nights.'

I have a sinking feeling that I know what's coming. 'Um, yes?'

'Those two neighbours of yours have complained about it. Loudly. To Joe, to every one of the bell ringers, and to the vicar himself. Kate and Leon actually wrote him a letter, saying that the noise of the practice every Monday night was disturbing the whole village.' She takes a deep breath, to calm herself. 'Which is a load of rubbish. They've been practising once a week for years and no one's ever complained.'

For once I can't defend the couple. They chose a house right opposite the church, for goodness' sake, they weren't forced to buy it. 'So – what's the vicar said? Anything?'

'He came around to see Joe and the other bell ringers, most apologetic. He doesn't know quite what to do. He hates conflict. He did hesitatingly suggest that perhaps they practise once a fortnight, but as Joe and the others pointed out, that's not nearly enough practice for them. Also, how does he know that'll satisfy the Wintersons? They want it stopped altogether.'

'That's ridiculous.'

'Hah. Finally. You're not sticking up for them! You're on our side at last.'

I sigh. I'm just about to say I'm not on anyone's side – there shouldn't be any sides as we're all a community, all part of one village. Then I realise that unfortunately there is conflict, and although I've not exactly sat on the fence, neither have I admitted loudly and clearly that my sympathies are all with the villagers. I *am* one, and on all the issues that have come up since the Wintersons' arrival, the truth is that I have been solidly on the side of the locals. Kate and Leon have not adapted to life here, and now I have to admit that they are not even trying. All they've done is to bring their city ways, their style and manners, and yes, their prejudices, into our little Cornish village, and not met anyone in the community halfway.

Daphne is watching me, waiting to see what I'll say next. I sigh, 'OK, I see what you're getting at. You're right. Kate and Leon have not been able to adapt. And like you, I'm now beginning to wonder if they ever will.'

Daphne smiles and her shoulders sag in relief. I realise now how tense she's been. I suppose she was expecting me to argue with her, tell her yet again that she and the others should be more patient with the Wintersons, or worse, blame the locals for Kate and Leon's discontent. The fact that I haven't seems to please her enormously. 'I'm so glad to hear you say that,

Tessa. Although you never signed any of their ridiculous petitions, or agreed with some of the things they did, I was still a bit worried that you saw their point of view more than you did ours – being a Londoner and all that yourself.'

I lean across the kitchen table and give her a hug. 'Daphne, I'm not a Londoner, not any more. You ought to know that. I'm just me, happy to be here, loving it here.'

She hugs me back and we break apart, grin, chink our teacups. 'To Treverny,' she says. 'Home sweet home, for better or for worse.'

'To Treverny,' I echo, and we both relax, relieved that the air had been cleared between us. I realise how fond I am of Daphne, what a good friend she is, and Joe, too. Outside, the wind gusts and howls, and the rain beats on over the rooftops, but I'm cosy and happy, and wouldn't be anywhere else for all the clotted cream in Cornwall.

Just before our second rental begins, and we take the next week of our holiday up on Dartmoor with Annie and Pete, Kate calls to see me. I've not seen her other than to wave hello since we returned from St Petroc, which has been a relief because I wasn't relishing hearing her go on about bell ringing. I was planning to talk to her, to tell her in the nicest possible way, what the villagers were saying. Perhaps if they knew just how they were antagonising everyone, they'd take a good hard look at themselves before it became down and out warfare. I hadn't a clue how I'd go about it, but I knew I couldn't go on without saying something.

But Kate surprises me. Once more we are in our kitchen but unlike Daphne, she refuses coffee or tea. 'I'm in a bit of a rush, Tessa, off to Truro. I have a hair appointment. I wanted to have it done in London when we were there last week but my stylist couldn't fit me in. I'm not sure of this Truro salon.'

'Kate, they're supposed to be quite good. A number of second homers I know actually choose to go there when they're down here.'

She hardly listens. She'll never believe anything is as good, let alone better, here in Cornwall than it is in London. I'm about to say something to this effect when she speaks first. 'I've got to dash, but I wanted you and Ben to know first. Leon and I have seen an estate agent; we're putting the house on the market today. We're moving back to London.'

I can't think of a thing to say. I'm conscious, however, of feeling a great sense of relief. Luckily she doesn't notice my hesitation; she's so caught up in her own thoughts and plans. 'Cornwall's not the place we thought it would be,' she muses, more to herself than to me. 'It's been a huge disappointment. It's best if we cut our losses and go back now.'

I mutter something or other that seems to satisfy her and off she goes, worried now about this new stylist who will be messing about with her London haircut. I go to the door to see her off and step outside. The stormy days have cleared and settled into a cooler August that's full of light. The trees are heavy with dark green leaves that sparkle as the sunbeams weave in and out of the laden branches. The air smells fresh and clean. Above me, a couple of seagulls swoop and cry, reminding me that we're less than a mile from the sea. Though it's holiday time and the coast, the beaches, will be packed, here in Treverny, our little pocket of Cornwall, it's as still and peaceful as it has been for centuries. I think about Kate, wanting to tell her that it's not Cornwall that disappoints, but whatever it is in her and Leon that can't relate to it, can't appreciate the unique character of the place. But then that's fine. We all come from different places, need different things, different backgrounds to live our lives fully.

With Jake bounding along after me, I walk across to our ancient stone church, wander around the churchyard for a few moments, then continue down the lane and across to the village green with its pond, admiring the dense August foliage everywhere, the weeping willow gracefully skimming its heavy branches over the water. I walk slowly back, relishing the way time slows as I slow, not rushing, just walking for the sake of walking, rather than getting somewhere fast.

I'm nearly home when I hear it. A horrendous screech, grating and loud. It's Emmanuel, of course, reminding me and everyone in Treverny that life isn't perfect wherever you go, that there is disharmony always lurking somewhere in the background and it's up to us to learn to live with it.

In the end, I suppose that's what drove Kate and Leon away, expecting some earthly paradise and not finding it. They obviously hadn't found it in London, either, otherwise why would they have moved in the first place? But maybe now, when they go back, they'll appreciate life there, having endured living away from their beloved city. I hope so. I wish them well.

Emmanuel shrieks again. One of the locals passes by, rolls his eyes at me as the peacock cries. 'That bugger be a bit of a pain, my handsome, don't-ee make a row!' He shakes his head ruefully, then grins, shrugs his shoulders in an easy, resigned kind of way. And that's the difference, between the villagers of Treverny and the Wintersons. The locals may not all like the peacock, they may be just as bothered by the cries, but they'll live with it, let it wash over them. The Humphreys, Edna and Hector, are part of the village, too, and if they need a peacock around them in their twilight years, so be it. The village has a big enough heart to accommodate the occasional screeching.

Before we vacate our house again to the second lot of tenants, I give it a good clean, checking everything is in place. The last people had left it perfectly, even Hoovering up the many dog hairs that must have accumulated during their stay. The next couple have no pets but have a three-year-old boy and twin girls of a year and a half. We've had to go out and buy a cot, which we'll need when we rent next summer anyway, and borrow a nearly-new second one from some friends. The same with high chairs. Ben even fitted a stair guard on the top and bottom stairs. All this has added to the expense of doing up the house, but at least it will be paid for by the money we'll earn for the week.

Susie and I meet up again before I leave for my second week's holiday. She'll be taking over my round, so I want to fill her in on some of the little peculiarities of my customers that she doesn't know about, like the new couple from Up Country in Creek who have a nasty dog that hates postwomen. This time we're sitting outside on the harbour, at the tiny café /bakery there. We'd never have got a table – St Geraint is heaving – but we both know the owners who brought us out a rickety little folding table and two chairs where we are sitting now, sharing a large pot of tea and great hunks of chocolate cake.

We eat heartily, not talking but contentedly enjoying every mouthful. Some of the people we know from the town stop by for a few moments for a chat. One of them, Harry, pulls up a chair for a time before going on his way. Like me, Harry is a Londoner now happily settled in Cornwall, living with his partner Charlie, the son of a Cornish fisherman and a successful artist. I've not seen much of Harry lately – we were quite close when I first moved down, sharing our experiences as we adjusted to our new lives. But friendship is relaxed and easy here; we know our mates are well and happy; they know we are; we all know we'll get together by and by, catch up. No stress, no angst – it'll happen.

I do have a little chuckle to myself when Harry says, as he gets up to go, 'I'm off to see that nice woman who knits those fantastic gloves; she's called Angela, isn't she? I saw some at the post office, and they'll be great for our new gallery/shop, the one Charlie is opening here in St Geraint. We want to stock a wide variety of things made by local craftspeople, and those gloves would go down a treat.'

When he's gone, Susie and I settle back in the precarious wooden chairs to watch the gulls following a fishing boat out at sea, hoping to snatch some treats. Quite a few yachts are on the water on this slightly hazy day. The pier is crammed with holiday makers exclaiming loudly about the boats, the seabirds, the beautiful day. ''Tis noisier than Piccadilly Circus,' Susie mutters, then laughs. 'Not that I got a clue 'bout that. It's me auntie, she used to say that. She went up to London once, hated it, said 'twas smelly and dirty. But the worst was the noise. 'Twas awful, she said.'

Before we part, we talk about Delia. Susie tells me she's in a nursing home not far away from Poldowe, where Ginger, Clara, and the other villagers can visit. ''Tis not a bad place,' Susie says. 'I had one or two of my customers go there. 'Tis the best place for her, Tessa.'

'Her house is up for sale,' Susie looks at me, rolls her eyes.

'That's another local gone, another second homer in Poldowe. 'Twill be another ghost town in winter soon, like t'others.'

There's not much I can say to this. Susie is right. And I think some of Clara and Ginger's determination to keep Delia in her home as long as possible was in part their fight against this, their battle to keep their village alive all year around.

Susie wishes me a good holiday, says she'll keep an eye on my customers, and off I go, home to pack and make sure everything is in tip-top shape for the week's rental. Thinking about seeing Annie and Pete at last, and for a whole week, makes me take a tiny, leaping skip as I go up our still uneven path (that's a job for next spring). A voice calls up to me from the lane, 'Steady on, maid, you be falling on your face if you be carrying on like that.'

'Oh hi, Doug, thanks for the warning,' I call out merrily to him.

He wants to talk; he's already halfway up the path. 'Listen, my handsome, get a load'a that,' he says in a loud whisper. Not that there is anyone around to hear. Doug grabs my elbow, points at the Wintersons' house. There, outside the gate, is a For Sale sign.

I don't spoil Doug's delight in being the bearer of grim news – he's convinced Ben and I are soulmates with Leon and Kate because we all come from London – so I pretend surprise. 'Oh my! Well, fancy that!'

'You'll be missing them two, now won't you, maid. Your sort of people.'

At that moment, Kate drives up, gets out of her car, gives us a quick wave and smile. She's dressed in gorgeous designer casuals; I recognise the cut of those culottes, those sandals to die for. Her hair is swept up in a new sophisticated style and

I get a quiet satisfaction at seeing what a great job the Truro hairdresser has done.

Doug and I watch her then turn back to each other. I start to grin. 'Now Doug, tell me honestly, do you really think that Kate is anything like me?' I throw open my arms, indicating my faded red shorts, my muddy knees (I was helping Jake find a ball earlier at the edge of a creek), my ancient baggy T-shirt. My hair is in desperate need of a cut, not to mention a good brush; it's totally unmanageable these summer days but I don't mind. Right now I've put it up in a rough ponytail but it's sticking out all over the place.

Doug tries to keep solemn, but then can't help smiling back. He's actually chuckling when he finally says, 'No, maid, I gotta admit, you and her, like chalk and cheese.' I get the giggles, too, and we're both laughing our heads off when Kate comes out again. She glances at us as if we're both totally crazy and rushes off in her car with only the slightest of waves in acknowledgement of our presence.

When Doug and I finally calm down, he says, 'Y'know, maid, if anything, I'd say you be looking more like one of us, instead of her.'

It's the sweetest thing he's ever said to me.

The shop at Morranport is heaving as I fight my way in to pick up the post. Holly is serving holiday makers who are mostly buying beach equipment and postcards, and Nell is behind the counter weighing a large package one of the locals is posting, an elderly man who lives in the village. The transaction with the package is finished, but Nell and the man are still laughing and chatting.

Holly, having finished with the customers – the shop is

thinning out now – says to me, 'Look at Nell. At her age, can't stop flirting with every man that comes in.'

I look at Holly in surprise, for she sounds upset about this. I say, 'But that's just Nell, you know that. She's always the same. I think it's great, the men love it, it keeps Nell young, and it's not harming anyone.'

Holly sighs. She's so young and fresh-looking, her baubles and beads so bright and colourful, yet she looks mournful and troubled. 'Holly, what's up?'

'Oh, I shouldn't blame Nell. I know the flirting is all in fun and she doesn't mean anything by it. I just hate to see Sydney hurt.'

'Why should he be? Nell seems to have taken quite a fancy to him.'

Holly looks around to make sure Nell is out of earshot. 'Not any more. She's dumped him.'

'Really? I didn't know that. Last I heard, they were still seeing loads of each other.'

'That was the trouble, according to Nell. Sydney wanted to be with her all the time. She told him yesterday he was crowding her and she needed a break. The poor man is devastated.'

More customers come in and Holly goes off to deal with them. I go behind the post office counter to the tiny cubbyhole that is the office. Nell, her gentleman friend gone, says without preamble, 'So you be talking to Holly, I see. And I suppose you be thinking that Nell is a hard old biddy, breaking off with poor dear Sydney.'

'I wasn't thinking anything of the sort, Nell. But I have to admit I was wondering what went wrong. You seemed to be quite a couple, you two.'

'Hah.' Nell plonks down on one of the two folding chairs

squeezed into the small space and motions me to sit on the other, first making sure that Holly is coping all right with the customers. 'That be the problem, maid. Everyone thought the same. All me old mates stopped having me around on me own. "Bring Sydney," they all said. Well, me handsome, I didn't always want to bring Sydney, and now I suppose you be saying I be a selfish old cow?'

She's glaring at me as if I've already said it, but I know Nell well enough to ignore her glaring and much of what she says. I say truthfully, 'You know I think you're as soft as a pussy cat, Nell. You don't have a selfish bone in your body. You're all talk, and I and everyone else knows it.'

She snorts. Despite the frown on her face she's looking good, healthy and tanned, a red cotton T-shirt on over jeans, her great bosom heaving with indignation as she says, 'Folk don't think that now, maid. They be saying I gave old Sydney the heave-ho and broke his old heart.'

'Well, you did. But it can't be helped. I'm sure you had your reasons.'

The frown is replaced by a sudden look of sadness. 'Y'know something, maid, I be a widow over twenty years. Before that I lived with me mum and dad, so I never did have a home, a life, of me own. I loved m'husband, we was close, never having no kids. So when he passed over, I didn't want nobody else. Still don't, not all the time. Sydney, he does. He won't settle for seeing me now and again. And me, I be needing my space. So 'tis best we don't see each other at all.'

Nell gets up abruptly, signally the conversation is over. 'Now me handsome, I reckon you be saying that Nell be getting lazy in her old age, sitting round when there's work to be done, am I right?'

She doesn't expect an answer but goes out to the next

customer. As I leave the post office, Holly says, in a whisper, 'Can you have a talk with Sydney if you see him today? He's taking this very badly.'

I deliver some post to Woody at the caravan first, who asks me straight away if I've heard how Nell has broken his grandfather's heart. Oh dear, surely it can't be that bad? At this rate Nell really will be made out to be a cruel, hard woman, but I can totally sympathise with her. I've seen the way Sydney has followed her around, seen the way Nell has begun to pull back over the last few weeks.

'Woody, I think it's for the best. Nell doesn't want a full-on relationship.'

'How full-on can you be at eighty-something?' Woody rolls his eyes.

'That's not for us to decide. It's up to them.'

He sighs, 'I know. Talk to the old man, would'ya?'

Sure enough, Sydney is waiting for me. He's pretending to be stroking one of the cats sunning itself on the garden bench, but as soon as my van drives up he's coming up the path to meet me.

We talk awkwardly about the cats, the fine weather, Woody and Holly, everything but what is on his mind. He looks and sounds ten years older, and hasn't smiled once. Several times I can tell he wants to bring up Nell but doesn't know how, so I finally decide to help. Bluntness is called for here. 'Sydney, I hear you and Nell have split up.'

For a moment, as I listen to my words, I think how ludicrous this is. These are two octogenarians who should be able to sort out their own lives, without the grandchildren and the local postie giving advice and doling out therapy. They're not teenagers, for goodness' sake.

Then I see Sydney's face. It's the saddest, loneliest face I've ever seen. And I remember that if they were teenagers, they'd have so many more years of looking for, and finding, someone to share their hearts and their homes and their lives with. For Sydney, Nell was probably his last chance, his last hope.

As if reading my thoughts, Sydney's eyes fill with tears. He tries to hide them and I give him his dignity, let him take out a handkerchief, pretend he has something in his eyes. When he's got himself under control he says, 'She's a wonderful woman, Nell. I'll miss her.'

'And you're a wonderful man. I'm sure she'll miss you, too. But maybe you can still be friends? See each other now and again? I'm sure Nell would like that very much.'

He shakes his head, blinking back tears again. 'I couldn't. The thing is, I want too much. More than she does. Won't do, won't do at all. Best we don't see each other.'

I tell him I'm sure he knows what's best and we leave it there, talk again about the cats. As I leave he's stroking the one on the bench, while the other appears from behind a bush and walks me towards my van. 'Look after him,' I whisper. 'He'll need it.' When I drive off I see that Sydney is sitting on the garden bench with both cats curled next to him.

CHAPTER FOURTEEN

Farming Life

The drive Up Country to Dartmoor is bizarre. It's Friday afternoon and we seem to be swimming against the tide – all the traffic is streaming down the A30 into Cornwall, not out of it.

We waited for the new tenants to arrive so that we could welcome them, show them where everything is. Like the others, they seemed very nice, very thrilled to be living in our home for a week. It's great to have people staying who have been vetted by good friends, though I know it won't be like that when we're with the rental agency. But this is a perfect way to ease into this letting business.

We leave the A30 at Okehampton, stop at the Waitrose there to buy treats for Annie and Pete. It's totally heaving, mostly with visitors. I can almost pick out the locals, looking resigned at this annual taking-over of their town. It's the same look I see on the faces of the locals at St Geraint and Morranport. We grab some bits and pieces and leave quickly.

Once on Dartmoor, we get hopelessly lost. The tiny lanes are signposted to villages that aren't there, or if they are, we can't find them. To make things more difficult, a fine summer's mist has come down, damp and clingy. Every time the road turns sharply we seem to find ourselves on open moorland and we can't see a thing, the visibility is so bad.

I try to phone Annie when it looks as if we're going around in circles, but there's no phone signal where we are. Finally Ben pulls over in an empty layby next to some gorse bushes where we get out, let Jake run about, try to get our bearings. The moor is eerie in this drifting mist, but beautiful. The gorse is bright yellow, like stars peeping out in a foggy sky, and I can see heather, too, already turning purple and blue. The great granite slabs of Dartmoor loom out like giants in the white wispy film of mist, adding to the air of mystery and magic.

As we get back into the car Ben says, 'I can't imagine Annie living in a place like this.'

'Nor can I. But then I couldn't imagine her living in Cornwall, either. Until she met Pete.'

And then suddenly we're there. An ancient wooden sign tacked onto a beech tree states: Coombedown Farm. God knows how, but we've found it. As soon as we pull up, Annie is there, whooping with greetings, laughter and hugs. 'At last! I've been so excited. Oh, I can't believe you're here, really here! Let me look at you, all of you. Goodness, how grown up you two look, let me hug you again. And you, Tessa, and Ben, you look terrific. Yes, Jake, I see you, too! Now come in, all of you. Pete's down in the field with the cattle, I'll give him a shout.'

She herds us into the farmhouse, once a Victorian rectory. It's dilapidated and scruffy, but wonderfully homey and delightful. The kitchen is massive, and filled with an assortment of flowers Annie has picked – big white daisies, various kinds of orange marigolds, some blowsy red roses. Everything looks old, slightly shabby, but clean and comfortable, from the old-fashioned sink and stove, to the open homemade shelves, filled with herbs, spices, cooking oils, and all kinds of kitchen necessities. In the middle is an ancient butcher's table, scrubbed clean and filled now with mugs for tea, a pile of delicious-looking sandwiches, buns, and cakes. 'We'll have a proper dinner tonight, so just dig into those, all of you. Where's Pete?' She goes to the door, gives a shout. 'Pete, they're here!' I've never heard my elegant city friend bellow like that.

She looks amazingly well, her face tanned, her cheeks rosy with health. She's in a scruffy pair of jeans, but ones I recognise as being a very posh brand that she used to wear when she visited us in Cornwall from London. They're muddy now and frayed at the bottom, as is the loose shirt she's wearing that looks like an old one of Pete's. Her hair is much longer than I've ever seen it and it suits her. She laughs when I comment. 'It's only because I haven't had time to get it cut; it's not some new style I'm trying out.'

Then Pete comes in and there are more hugs and kisses all around, and more food brought out, and then a whirl of activity as we finally get up from the kitchen table. Annie shows us our rooms – plain furniture, simple wooden floors, old and quietly pleasant. Everywhere seems light and airy despite the mist; and the view from every window is of the ancient landscape of the moor with its hills, trees, and rocky tors. 'Wonderful,' I enthuse, and it really is. 'I'm so happy to be here,' I tell Annie.

Later, we have a look around the farm. We see Timothy, the famous pet sheep with arthritis. Will and Amy have a quarter of a banana each to give him. Annie remembers their own pet lamb and asks how Patch is getting on at the farm in Treverny. I listen to the three of them talking, equally animated, and think that's one of the things I love about Annie, her keen interest in everyone and everything around her.

Like her enthusiasm for her new adventure up here on Dartmoor. After we've all taken a look around, Ben goes off with Pete to fill the cattle troughs with water, and Amy and Will run off to collect the eggs. Annie and I are on our own. 'Are you really happy here?' I ask. I know I've asked her this on the phone, but I want to look at her, be with her, as I ask it again.

'Oh yes,' she turns to me, glowing with contentment, and amusement, too. 'It's so weird, isn't it? Who'd have thought it? I don't miss London, my old life for a second.' She stops, squeezes my hand. 'You won't get upset if I tell you I don't miss Cornwall either? I miss you, and Ben, and the children, but I'm growing to love the farm and the animals. And Dartmoor is fantastic.'

We wander around the farm together and I can't get over how knowledgeable Annie is about it. 'We've got about one hundred and fifty acres, but we've also got moorland rights for the sheep and cattle. It helps financially, too; we get subsidies for that. It's a struggle – Pete's uncle went organic about ten years ago so he's pretty established, but it's still tough. We've got about twenty cattle, mostly the black and white Galloways as they're slow growing and survive well on the moor. And a few Aberdeen Angus. They're small but hardy, good beef stock and good on Dartmoor as well.'

Is this Annie I'm listening to? After we've had a look at the cattle and then the fifty-odd ewes, with Annie telling me how they sell the lambs both for meat and to organic breeders, I say, 'Annie, can you hear yourself talk? Are you really you, my London friend, or have you turned into her twin country sister that I never knew existed.'

She turns to me, eyes shining, 'I know, I know, it's crazy, isn't it? I guess I never had a chance, before, to let this side of me out.' She tugs at my arm. 'C'mon, let's go see the pigs.'

We tease and chatter all the way to the pig house. 'We've got ten sows,' Annie says proudly. 'And like the sheep, we sell to both organic meat suppliers and to breeders.' The black and white sows look up at us as we pass the field where they're rooting around in the grass and mud. Annie talks to them, coos to them, as if they were her children. Then she takes me around to another pig house on the other side where there is a sleeping sow and at least a dozen three-day-old piglets running about. 'Aren't they adorable?' Annie cries.

We watch them for quite some time as they jump about, play, squeal and nudge their mother to get up so they can have another feed. The sow ignores them, lying firm on her belly, getting some well-earned peace. Her brood certainly seem healthy and plump, not that I know much about piglets.

'This one's a good mother,' Annie tells me, 'but we have another one who isn't. When she farrowed, gave birth that is, I had to be on call as Pete was out with an ailing ewe for quite some time. Every time the sow gave birth, I had to rush into the pen, grab the little one and gently toss it out of the mother's way. She would have savaged it, would you believe.' Annie looks grim at this deviation from her idea of piggy maternal love. 'I had to make sure I kept well out of the sow's way, too; she goes quite crazy and vicious when she's giving birth. She would have had me, too.'

I stare at her. 'You did all that? You weren't frightened yourself?'

'Of course I was, the first time. I was terrified. But you get used to it. It was sort of exhilarating, you know?'

I'm not sure I do know but Annie goes on, trying to explain, 'It's probably a bit like you were, that first day you were a postwoman. After living the high life of a career girl in London, there you were in Cornwall, in the sorting office at Truro for the first time. I remember you telling me all about it. You lost your van, you were terrified you'd never get the post sorted, or find your way about. But in the end, you were over the moon. You'd done it!' She turns to me, looking earnest. 'That's how I felt.'

I acknowledge the similarity, but add, 'At least the other posties didn't eat their young, like your scary sow.'

I remain in awe of Annie's bravery in the face of challenging pigs as we continue our wander around the farm.

The week passes quickly. We're all given chores on the farm – we've insisted on this – and we have a marvellous time as well as feeling we're helping out. Pete gets Ben to help with a lot of fencing which is a job for two men. The children collect the eggs, feed the pigs, help fetch and carry water when needed as well as other odd jobs. Feeding Timothy his half banana is one of their favourite tasks, keeping them occupied for much of each morning. Annie and I gather masses of sloes; the trees are laden this year. 'I read somewhere they should be touched with frost before they're picked,' she says, 'but one of the local wives told me she picks them now, before the birds get to them, and sticks them in the freezer.' She sighs contentedly.

'I'm going to try to make sloe gin, for Christmas presents this year.'

'Good heavens, Annie. How did you learn to do that?'

'I haven't yet. But I will. There are lots of friendly neighbours around to ask advice.'

'Where? You're totally isolated here.'

She looks sheepish. 'OK, well, the nearest is two or three miles away, but they're still neighbours. Besides, there's always Google. Loads of ideas there about sloes and every other thing.'

'I'm surprised you have Internet access here.'

She laughs, grabs me around the waist and whirls me round. 'Oh Tessa, haven't we been turned about! A few years ago, that's the kind of remark I'd say to you, about living in Cornwall. Remember?'

'I remember. Well, Treverny seems the height of sophisticated city life compared with Coombedown Farm.'

After a couple of drizzly days, the weather brightens and we have some great walks on the moor. There's a fine stone circle not far from the farm and we take a picnic there one day, munching our sandwiches in the circle and feeling far away from civilisation. This Bronze Age site is quite a distance from the nearest public road, so we're lucky, there's not another person in sight on this part of Dartmoor.

After we've eaten, drunk some great organic cider Pete brought along in a cool bag, with some homemade pressed apple juice for Will and Amy, the two men take the children off for a walk while Annie and I opt to be lazy, and lie against the stones soaking up the warm sunlight. I'm about to doze off, thinking that Annie is, too, for she's been exceptionally quiet during lunch. But as soon as everyone is gone, she's sitting up, alert, looking at me with barely-contained excitement. 'I told Pete to take the others on a walk; I've got to have you alone for a few minutes, tell you myself first. Tessa, I'm pregnant.'

I should have known. So that explains the glow, the radiance, the joy that's been written all over her face the last few days. After we've hugged, and shed a couple of happy tears, she says, 'I didn't tell you when you first arrived as I wasn't sure. I've had a couple of false alarms before, and I thought maybe I was too old to start a family. But I got Pete to pick up a pregnancy testing kit yesterday when he went to town, and did it this morning. It's positive, Tessa. We're going to have a baby.'

There are more congratulations all round when the men and the children come back, and a toast is raised with more apple juice and cider. Annie says, 'I'm surprised you didn't notice that I kept off the cider at lunchtime and stuck to juice. I thought that would be a giveaway.' I tell her truthfully I never even noticed.

That night we four adults stay up late, talking well into the night. Old times in London, new times in Cornwall, and now in Devon. Pete listens contentedly to our reminiscences, offers some of his own about growing up in Cornwall. He, like Annie, looks aglow with happiness. Not only has his dream about running a farm come true, but he's also married to the woman he loves and is now about to be a father. He a lucky man, and fortunate enough to know and appreciate this.

On the day we leave there's a nip in the air, a reminder that summer will soon be over. Already the days are growing shorter. 'Won't you be lonely here, come winter?' I ask Annie.

'With Pete?' she says. 'With piles of wood for the wood burner stacked up in the shed? Thanks to Ben's help, by the way, for that. I can't wait for winter. And then in spring . . .'

She breaks off, too overwhelmed to speak for a few moments, then finally goes on, 'All being well, God willing, in spring there will be our baby.'

As we say goodbye tearfully – this has been quite an emotional reunion – I say, 'Hey, Annie, you aren't going to learn how to knit, are you? Sitting by the fire those long winter nights knitting little jackets for the babe?'

She makes a face. 'No way am I going to take up knitting at my age, thank you very much; I've already taken on enough new things. But hey, I'll make stacks of blackberry jam. You should see the bramble bushes, full of berries this year. The cold winter, you know. Can't wait till they ripen, won't be long now.'

Good old Annie, now into making jam. My head is whirling with all these changes in her as we cross the Tamar, leaving Up Country for Cornwall and home.

CHAPTER FIFTEEN

Harvest Moon

Suddenly it is early autumn, and all the talk is of the coming winter even though the air and sea are warm, the land glowing with abundance, the trees slightly burnished, though still mostly dark green and full.

It's not as if anyone wants to hurry the seasons along, but we've all realised, after the severe early frosts of last year, the snows and blizzards throughout the winter, that it's never too soon to prepare. In the village shop the talk is centred again on wood: what kind is best to quickly warm a cold house, which is best to slow-burn throughout the night if necessary, and where to find good quality firewood at the lowest possible price. As most of the people around here have wood burning stoves, this is a hot topic, no pun intended.

Woody, the tree surgeon, has become a woodsman during this autumn. He has access to a small forest that he maintains for the owner, and in return gets to take out some of the wood to sell. He's busy cutting down rotting or dead trees for next year while chain sawing last year's wood into manageable pieces before delivering it. Holly helps him by loading and stacking when she's not at the shop, for Nell has kept her on part-time until after New Year when the second homers, having spent Christmas at their first homes with family, rush down to Cornwall with friends to relax after the stress of the holiday. 'Don't see as how being with family be so stressful for folk,' Nell grumbles every year. 'All that holiday time, all them loved ones milling around, enough cash to pay for it all, obviously, since they can afford a second house – can't see what there be to complain about, if you're asking me.'

No one is, but she tells us anyway, and because it's dear Nell, we listen and agree. She does have a point after all. There's a good deal of moaning about the stresses of life from the second homers, and Nell hears it all in her shop. 'I do believe that lot expect me to feel sorry for them,' she snarls at me, as if daring me or anyone else to disagree.

Nell and I both got a shock a few days ago when Holly came into the shop with a shaven head. Nell said, when she got over her surprise, 'So that be the latest hair style in Morranport, be it?'

Holly, instead of bantering back with Nell as she always does, said seriously, 'No. I'm raising money for charity. One of my friends got ovarian cancer, is having chemotherapy. She's starting to lose her hair, like, so me and me mates, well, we want to, make her feel less self-conscious. And raise some dosh for a good cause, too.'

Nell went to her, and to both Holly's surprise and mine, gave her a huge hug. This was so unlike Nell – she's not a touchy kind of person, far too feisty for that sort of display – that Holly couldn't say a word. Finally, when she let Holly go, Nell said gruffly, 'There now, maid, I got work to do, and so have you. But I got to say, what you be doing touches me old heart, d'ya hear? I've a good mind to do it meself.' She chuckles. 'Except that I'd be scaring the bejesus out of the customers! One of us in the shop be plenty, and you be the pretty one.'

There's a sense of ending all around this time of year, even though there should be a few weeks more of decent weather. It's not just nature, the trees and leaves, it's also the manmade things. Houses are being closed up, boats cleaned and put away. It starts happening slowly, a few at first, then, with the first real cold snap, usually after October half term, everything begins to shut down. Cafés in the seaside towns and villages close, except for the few catering mainly for locals which stay open all winter. But there are few of these, and fewer every year as the financial situation worsens. Pubs will struggle to keep going, but they are laying off staff, and closing rooms, keeping only one warm and ready for the odd visitor or local. In summer, it was easier to forget these tightened times, but now with the onset of winter, it seems everyone is reminded. There's a feeling of hunkering down amongst us all, not just against the coming wintry weather, but also against the economic crisis that everyone predicts will hit soon, if not already upon us.

In this hunkering down, there is also a congenial feeling of solidarity, of community. Customers give me sacks of blackberries they've picked and spare apples from their gardens, and in turn, I promise to supply them with blackberry and apples pies. I go blackberrying with the family and give the extra to Daphne who makes the best jam in the village. We trade and barter, and while we do this, we look at the sky, at the masses of berries on the holly tree, the mountain ash, and try to predict the coming winter's weather. All the signs are that'll it will be another cold one, but the signs can be misinterpreted. In the meantime, people who have a stretch of woodland trade firewood for an afternoon's cutting and bringing it in. We're all like squirrels, gathering our nuts and preparing for the months ahead.

And now it's early November. Great swirls, or murmurations, of starlings darken the afternoon sky as they sweep gracefully over the yellow and red leaves of the autumn trees. Chrysanthemums of all shapes, sizes, and colours take over the gardens, and the Virginia creepers on some of the houses have turned a wonderful scarlet.

Tonight in the village there is a Guy Fawkes bonfire and firework display. Ben and I will be on hand to help, selling hot cups of soup, while others are in charge of the fireworks. A lot of work goes into the evening, making sure everything is safely run, that nothing goes wrong. Yet despite all the many health and safety rules and regulations that the villagers say they've had to contend with over the past few years, it's still basically the same simple format – a half hour of excited children milling about with sparklers, adults drinking cups of soup to keep warm, then the firework display, followed by the burning of the Guy – as it's been since the old-timers were little ones themselves.

But that will be tonight, and right now it is late afternoon and I'm at Poet's Tenement, standing outside looking at the ailing holm oak and the rooks cawing around it, flying home in droves to their rookery. The clear sky, now golden in the twilight, seems filled with their black shapes, resounds with their raucous cries. It's going to be a good night for the bonfire, and a full moon is already rising bright orange over the horizon. 'Look, a harvest moon,' Hector murmurs, to no one in particular.

He and Edna, and Woody and Holly, have been standing here for some time, discussing the tree. I'm here to give the Humphreys an apple pie I baked from the windfalls I salvaged from their neglected old orchard. Woody has roped me in on the discussion, muttering in a low voice, 'You've got to talk sense into them, Tessa. I can't, and neither can Holly. She's worried about them, too. So is Sydney.'

'Sydney?' Edna must have heard that last bit. She's muffled up against the sudden cold spell today with a woolly hat, a long velvet cape, and some very ancient sheepskin boots. 'How is your dear grandfather, Woody?'

'Oh, fine,' Woody says. 'Though worried about you, as I said already. This tree . . .'

Edna politely but firmly cuts him off. 'Do give him my love. And tell him I'm sorry it didn't work out with little Nell.'

Little Nell? Well, I suppose she's about ten years younger than Edna, maybe more. I keep forgetting that they all grew up together in the area, and knew each other well. And no doubt still keep tabs on each other, through the Cornish grapevine that winds from village to village, from coast to coast.

Hector, also woolly-hatted and wearing an ankle-length black overcoat topped with a rather holey crimson scarf, says benignly, 'Ah, Sydney and little Nell – yes, it's a pity it didn't work out.' He turns to his wife. 'She would be much more suitable for him than you'd ever have been, my dear. Aren't you glad I came along just as I did, that time in St Petroc when we were so young, and hanging about with all those strange artists?'

Woody, Holly, and I have all turned to stare at them, waiting for them to go on. The young couple look almost bewildered, as if they can't imagine all these ancient folk ever being as young as they are. But of course Hector and Edna don't say another word. They never do, and we're always left wondering, tantalised.

Edna brings us back to the present, 'How lovely that moon is.'

'And the rooks, settling down, getting ready for the night,' adds Hector.

Woody says, with desperation in his voice, 'Please. We've got to come to some decision about this tree. It's got to come down. Winter's nearly here and there's a real risk a strong wind could blow it right over.'

'It survived that terrible summer storm. It must be sturdier than we give it credit for.'

'But there'll be more storms. The ground will be wetter in winter, the roots could weaken even more. The oak really should come down, for your own safety.'

Edna says kindly, 'You've already told us that, dear. Quite a few times.'

'He's right,' Holly cries. 'We'd never forgive ourselves if anything happened to you, because of that bloody tree.' She stamps her foot in frustration. She's a wearing a woolly hat which covers her still-shaven head. Earlier, I saw the Humphreys contributing to her fund for charity. She and her mates have raised quite a sum already. Holly says they'll keep their heads shaven until their friend's chemo is over and her hair is growing back.

Woody echoes Holly's words, 'She's right. I'd sure as hell never forgive myself if that tree comes down on you.'

'Oh my dear children,' Hector says, 'you must never, ever say that.'

'Or feel any kind of guilt over us,' Edna adds.

Woody nudges me to say something. 'Well, I feel the same,' I murmur. 'We all feel terribly responsible. All your friends and neighbours do. Woody's the expert, and if he says the tree needs cutting down, it's the right thing to do.'

They both look at me with fondness in their eyes, yet firmness, too. Hector speaks first. 'Thank you, Tessa. And you, Woody, and you, Holly,' he adds, turning to us all in turn. 'But you're wrong. As long as that tree is in no danger of crashing down into the road, hurting others, then the right thing to do is what we feel in our hearts.'

'And that's to let it stay,' Edna says. 'For the rooks, yes, but also for us.' She looks around at each of us then up at the sky which is beginning to darken, a lone star shining. 'We've been here a long time. Hector even longer than me; he was born here. And this tree was here before that.'

'When I'm gone, it's up to others to decide what to do with it,' Hector says, after a pause. 'But I'm here now, and I say it stays where it is.' His smile as he looks around at us is warm and tender. 'And let's be optimistic, shall we? The tree might not blow down, or fall down. It might stay up for a few years more, isn't that right, Woody? No one can tell for sure.'

Woody nods, reluctantly, 'No, you can't say for sure I s'pose.'

Hector goes on, 'So we'll let it be. And what happens, happens. No good worrying about it now, is it? On such a still, clear night, with that incredible moon rising higher and higher, even as we speak.'

There's no more to be said. We stand for a few moments more, watching the moon, and then comes a burst of noise and light as someone, somewhere, lets off the first firework of this Guy Fawkes night. We say our goodbyes, head towards our own homes. And suddenly I'm no longer worrying about the Humphreys, about their rooks, or their tree, or about them. They are right, I feel; they've lived long enough to know what is best for themselves, what path to follow.

The heart's path, Hector had said. And with a sudden joyous lilt in mine, I start to run towards home, towards my family, and towards this cold, clear Cornish autumn night which is alive with the moon and stars, and the fiery crackle of distant fireworks somewhere by the dark, calm sea.